MW00979990

REDISCOVERING
ART DECO
U.S.A.

Barbara Capitman in front of the Cavalier Hotel, *1320 Ocean Drive, Miami Beach, Florida.* ARCHITECT: *Roy F. France, 1936. Barbara Capitman stood in front of the Cavalier Hotel for this, her most celebrated portrait. The Deco Doyenne posed here for a November 1988 feature in* Town & Country *magazine. Later,* The Wall Street Journal, *perhaps becoming aware of all the money that could be made in Barbara's burgeoning Art Deco District, ran its own piece on her with the same portrait. The Cavalier has an elegance and an intimate scale that add charm and flair to the picture. This is a major reason the District has become a mecca for fashion photography. (Photograph by Tom Hollyman, copyright © 1988. Used by permission.)*

REDISCOVERING ART DECO U.S.A.

BARBARA CAPITMAN

MICHAEL D. KINERK

DENNIS W. WILHELM

Photographs by
RANDY JUSTER

VIKING
STUDIO
BOOKS

DEDICATED TO: The Capitman family, which made this book possible through their love and encouragement: Margaret Doyle, Valerie Batts, John Capitman, and especially Andrew Capitman, who removed all obstacles when things seemed impossible, and of course to the late Barbara Capitman, who among other things was the mother of this book.

VIKING STUDIO BOOKS
Published by the Penguin Group
Penguin Books USA Inc., 375 Hudson Street, New York, New York, 10014, U.S.A.

Penguin Books Ltd, 27 Wrights Lane, London W8 5TZ, England

Penguin Books Australia Ltd, Ringwood, Victoria, Australia

Penguin Books Canada Ltd, 2801 John Street, Markham, Ontario, Canada L3R 1B4

Penguin Books (N.Z.) Ltd, 182-90 Wairau Road, Auckland 10, New Zealand

Penguin Books Ltd, Registered Offices: Harmondsworth, Middlesex, England

First published by Viking Studio Books, an imprint of Penguin Books USA Inc.

First printing, January, 1994
10 9 8 7 6 5 4 3 2 1

Library of Congress Catalog Card Number: 93-85067

Book designed by Kingsley Parker
Printed and bound by Dai Nippon Printing Co., Ltd., Tokyo, Japan

ISBN: 0-525-93442-1 (cloth); ISBN: 0-525-48604-6 (paperback)

CONTENTS

Berkeley High School and Auditorium, *2246 Milvia at Martin Luther King (formerly Grove Street), entrance via quadrangle courtyard, also near 1930 Allston Way, Berkeley.* ARCHITECT: *Gutterson & Corlett; Sculptor: Jacques Schnier, 1938. Schnier's design incorporated the name Berkeley High over the door. There are also many references to the arts and sciences in panels between the banks of windows.*

ACKNOWLEDGMENTS

VERY SPECIAL THANKS TO: Christine Giles for proofreading every page and suggesting numerous improvements; Richard Hoberman for helping us gather information and dropping everything to do it; and to Dr. Nedra Kinerk and Coman C. Leonard, III, for spending hours at the computer helping us type in data.

WITHOUT HELP FROM THE FOLLOWING PERSONS, THIS BOOK WOULD NOT HAVE BEEN POSSIBLE: Lynn Abbie, Lisa Ackerman, Fred Albert, Margo Ammidown, Joanne Arany, John Axelrod, Jean Claude Baker, Lillian Barber, Bob Barrett, Carol Becker, Les Beilinson, Bill Benedict, Carolyn Bennett, Lynn Bernstein, Mr. and Mrs. Irwin L. Bernstein, Tom B'hend, Marge Blewett, Daniel Bollman, Arn Bortz, Robert Breugmann, Nan Brewer, Steven Brooke, Annella Brown, M.D., Ralph Buchalter, Lilli Burns, Daniel Bollman, Diane Camber, Alma Carlisle, Gaylord Carter, Nick Chaparos, Chuck Cirgenski, Sam Cleland, Susie Clinard, Judith Singer Cohen, William S. Colburn, Philip Collins, Davis Cone, Sherry Cucchiella, Larry Cultrera, Denis Curley, LuEllen DeHaven, Chris T. Delaporte, Sharon Delee, J. F. Donnelly, Elisabeth Donovan, April S. Dougal, Mary Dreblow, Joseph R. DuciBella, Ann Duke, Don Elder, Brad Evans, Richard L. Farnan, AIA, Kenn Finkel, Yvonne Foote, Robert Four, Jonathan Fricker, Tony Fusco, Ronald H. Frantz, Jr., Denis Gallion, Carolina Garcia, Randy Garratt, David Gebhard, Charlene Gilbert, Lori Leigh Gieleghem, Raymond Girvigian, FAIA, Irvin Glazer, Dan Grant, Martin Greif, Annie Groer, Anita Gross, Marsha Hagen, Helen Hobbs-Halmay, Larry Herkel, Andrew Hirshl, D.D.S., Dwight and Sandra Holden, Stephen R. Hofer, Craig Holcomb, Edward Horvath, Kerry Hughes, Charlene Johnston, Glory June, Joan Kahr, Christine Knopf Kallenberger, Jay Kamm, Gersil Kay, Robert Kinerk, Steve and Aileen Kinerk, Cheryl Kinerk, Ruth and Bill Knack, Kirby Kooluris, Sharon Koskoff, Larry Kreisman, Martin Kreloff, Jud Kurlancheek, Rick Lambert, Orden Lantz, Lyn Larsen, Maxwell Levinson, Tom Lind, Peggy Loar, Edward Lyon, Jacqui May, Judy Malone, Philip S. Manning, Diane Mansfield, Dennis McClendon, Lawrence McKinney, Don McMasters, Janine Menlove, Bruce Michael, Peter Miller, Richard Miltner, Tony Minnino, Mitzi Mogul, Wendy Moonan, Daniel Morris, George Neary, Gay Nemeti, Lea Nickless, Gustavo Novoa, Tim Needler, Richard Neidich, Pat Northcutt, Tim Olsen, Kenneth D. Park, Dori Partsch, Frances Pen, Dr. Gale E. Peterson, Gib Petzke, Margaret Pickart, Robert Powers, Irma L. Popp, Richard Rauh, AIA, Richard Rickles, Anthony Ridder, Robert Ridgeway, Anthony W. Robins, Randall Robinson, Richard Rowan, David Ryan, Robin Salmon, Tim Samuelson, Anne Schnoebelen, Larry Schoonover, Ann Schrupp, Charles Senseman, Joe Sgromo, Belford and Betsy Shoumate, Robert Sideman, Jarrett Smith, Ronnie Spradlin, Jim Steely, Shifra Stein, Lawrence Steinecker, Joe Stephens, Steven Strom, Alden Stockebrand, Richard Striner, Walt Strony, Steven Strong, Margo Taylor, Rose Thiemann, Bernice Thomas, Amy Torres, Jeffrey Tucker, Karen Tupek, Clyde Treco, Sue Turner, William Weber, Gabriel Weisberg, Roger and Bevan Wilhelm, Marvin and Shirley Wilhelm, Richard Guy Wilson, William Whiting, Mitchell Wolfson, Jr., Alan Wood, Ty Woodward, Chuck and Kim Zuccarini.

ORGANIZATIONS:
Barbara Baer Capitman Archive, Bok Tower and Gardens, Brookgreen Gardens, Buffalo and Erie County Historical Society, Cheney Cole Museum, Chicago Landmarks Foundation, Cincinnati Historical Society, City of Miami Beach, City of Syracuse, Department of Veterans Affairs, Federal Trade Commission, Folger Shakespeare Library, Foundation for Historical Louisiana, Fountain County (Indiana) Historical Society, Indiana University Museum of Art, Kress Foundation, Miami Design Preservation League, Newark Historical Society, New York City Landmarks Commission, Onondaga (New York) Historical Society, Philbrook Museum, Philadelphia Savings Fund Society, Preservation Wayne, S.C. Johnson Foundation, Texaco Archive, Theatre Historical Society and Archives, San Diego Historical Society, Syracuse Tully Historical Society, Ward M. Canaday Center.

Thanks also for the patience and generosity of our employers The Miami Herald and The Wolfsonian Foundation. Many thanks to our faithful photographer Randy Juster, who contributed major portions of the research and tried to give us pictures of every building we asked for, even if he had to fly there to shoot it. And finally, thanks to our editor, Cyril I. Nelson, a great professional who has published several books on Art Deco, including the first one in 1968. He gave us all the time and encouragement we ever wished for in order that we might properly complete this book after Barbara Capitman's untimely death.

Michael D. Kinerk
Dennis W. Wilhelm

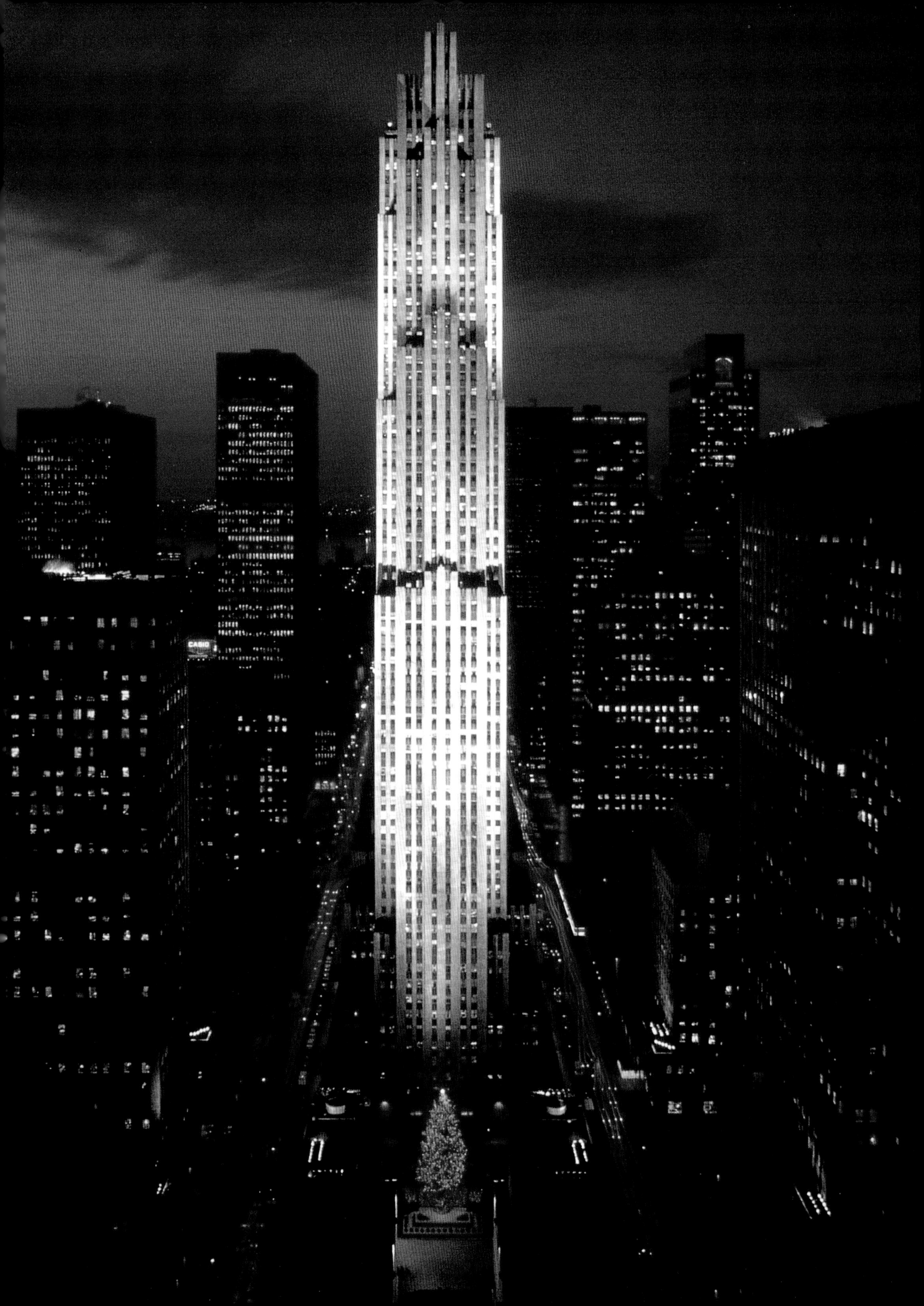
CASIO

ABOUT THE PRINCIPAL PHOTOGRAPHER

Randy Juster's best work from a lifetime of photographing all varieties of Art Deco buildings and artifacts was shown in an exhibition, "American Art Deco," that was mounted in 1987 at the Renwick Museum, Washington, D.C., and traveled to the Philbrook Museum, Tulsa, Oklahoma, and to the Minneapolis Institute of Arts.

PHOTOGRAPHER'S NOTE

What I like most about Art Deco buildings is that they always seem to be more than is strictly necessary. Details abound. Lighting is often dramatic. There may be any or all of the following: spectacular elevators, murals, elegant lighting fixtures, a stylized mailbox, inlaid floors, and so on. Modern tastes (and economics) prohibit this type of building today.

In 1975, I began a self-assigned project to document all of America's Art Deco buildings. Had I realized the size of this undertaking, I would never have started.

There had been a number of books on New York's Art Deco, but what of the rest of the U.S.A.? My first trip turned up some delightful surprises. There were fine Deco examples not only in Chicago and Los Angeles, but also in places like Detroit, Cincinnati, and Dallas. As the project progressed, I became a collector, seeking missing places to complete the set. Eventually, the road narrowed and led to places like Covington, Indiana, and Anaconda, Montana. At times, it seemed that every city in America had at least one Art Deco treasure.

Barbara Capitman realized this. She also knew that without intervention, much of America's Art Deco would be bulldozed before people came to appreciate it.

Those who built what we now call Art Deco strove to create a totally new architecture. With hindsight, we can see that Art Deco buildings were often innovative but rarely revolutionary. Yet, this in no way detracts from their extraordinary richness.

One of the magnificent sights that New York has to offer is the RCA Building (G.E. Building) gleaming at night in the superb floodlighting designed by Abe Feder, which transforms the great Art Deco tower into a gigantic piece of sculpture. (Photograph by Bo Parker courtesy Rockefeller Center. © The Rockefeller Group)

PHOTOGRAPHER'S ACKNOWLEDGMENTS

Although this book has been in production for about three years, some of the photographs date back more than fifteen years. The list of people who helped make these pictures possible is a long one, and I am certain to have forgotten some names. I thank all those who helped for their cooperation, encouragement, and kindness:

Lynn Abbie, Bob Barrett, Fred Beall, Marge Byers, Shirley Davy, Alastair Duncan, Allan Eyles, Ben Fernandez, Paul Ganz, George (the guard at the Chrysler building), Richard Gray, Ronnie Greico, Martin Hadden, Bronwen Howles, Tim Jennen, Fred Katz, Donald Leap, Glenn Loney, Henry Lussy, George Mazarakos, Allan Michaan, Randall Michelson, Michael Monroe, Anne Marie Murphy, David Naylor, Terri Niccum, Charles Nurnberg, Gale Peterson, Richard Rauh, Anthony Robbins, Melvin Rose, Anne Schnoebelen, Roxanne Elizabeth Smith, Marco Suarez, Hank Sykes, David Travis, Susan Tunick, Suzanne and Michael Wallis, C. Craig Washing, and William Weber.

For their input and encouragement, special acknowledgment goes to Martin Greif, Larry Grow, Mel Lerner, Bob Rose, and Larry Zim.

Finally, for his many, many hours of research and correspondence, my warmest thanks to Brother Andrew Fowler.

I dedicate my photographs in this book to my parents.

TECHNICAL NOTES

I began this project using 35mm for small details and 4x5 for everything else.

Initially, my intent was to produce a photo exhibit, so I shot black-and-white and color negatives in 4x5 and, usually, Kodachrome 35mm.

Later in the project, I purchased a Pentax 6x7 outfit. This camera, which produces images 2¼ x 2¾ inches, has almost, but not quite, supplanted the 4x5. I usually use Fujichrome 50 or 64T film in this camera.

On occasion, supplementary lighting was used, but in general, I prefer to work with existing light. For very large spaces and/or photographically undesirable lighting (mercury or sodium), I used color-negative film and made a color-corrected print.

In order to make this book as comprehensive as possible, several photos have been included that are the work of others. Where this occurs, the photographer's name appears alongside the photo.

Randy Juster

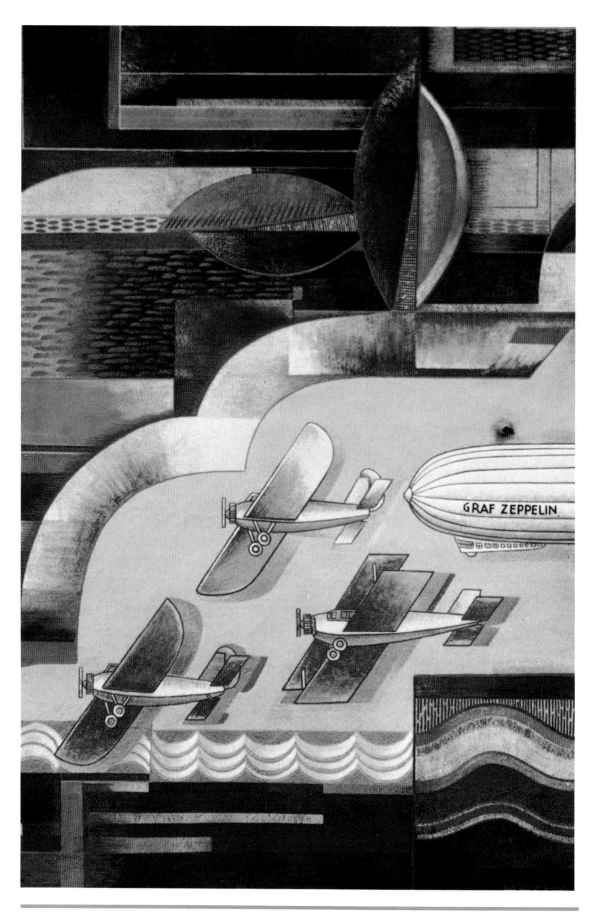

Detail taken from the ceiling fresco of the porte-cochère at the Bullocks Wilshire Department Store (I. Magnin), which was painted by Herman Sachs, 1928. The complete painting is illustrated on page 116.

FOREWORD

I found out from a friend last week that Barbara Baer Capitman had passed away.

I met, got to know, and worked with Barbara in the formative stages of her successful campaign to create the Miami Beach Art Deco Historic District. At the time, I was serving in the position of Director of the Heritage Conservation and Recreation Service, the agency within the U.S. Department of the Interior that ultimately had to rule on the adequacy of the district's nomination to the National Register of Historic Places.

Barbara's project attracted my attention because, on its merit (detail, scale, volume, and homogeneity), the potential district stood alone to be our nation's largest collection of Art Deco architecture and, with its nearly six hundred structures, represented a mammoth undertaking to properly record, document, and file as a district. Moreover, it was unique at the time, because it was to be the nation's first "modern" historic district. (It barely met the "fifty-year rule" for inclusion in the register.)

To make matters more interesting, of course, the development interests and some elected Miami Beach officials looked with great doubt on the wisdom of having a historic district in Miami Beach.

In short, this was a big, important job to do, but in a tough place to do it.

Enter, of course, Barbara Capitman. I remember vividly meeting her at the Miami Airport late one night, when I took a flight from Washington to see about her project. At other places in America, I was most often met by a delegation, usually some city officials, and was taken off to some city night spot for a group dinner. When I arrived in Miami, only Barbara was there. But was she ever there! She was there to tell me in her certain, special, and willful manner that hers was a job that had to be done and that she couldn't get the job done without the help of the Carter administration! She was there to tell me of her dream of a revival of south Miami Beach and of how making a historic district would help in that process!

On and on she went, taking me away in her little two-seat convertible, showing me drawings, and taking me for an immediate tour through the proposed district. That was the beginning of an almost two-and-a-half year intense relationship I had with Barbara Baer Capitman. Her leadership, willful personality, and vision caused me to recommend to Secretary of the Interior Cecil Andrus that we provide what resources we could to help Barbara get the job done. That we did. And of course, Barbara did her part, and as they say, the rest is history.

As people look back on Barbara's time in Miami Beach and the enormous commitment she made to it, I hope they will realize how special an American she was. She was engaged, full throttle, with what was her passion. Her passion is now becoming a city's greatest public legacy. Some day, I hope someone will write her story for all to read, because she showed what one person, with little money, full vision, and a total commitment can do to measurably affect a city, its resources, and its people.

Chris T. Delaporte
Baltimore, Maryland
April 24, 1990

INTRODUCTION

Art Deco is my whole life.

—Barbara Baer Capitman
Miami Beach, 1990

Good forms are but few; and they are eternal.

—Paul Frankl
Form and Re-Form, 1930

THIS IS A BOOK ABOUT THE GRASS-ROOTS MOVEment in America to preserve the architectural style of the 1920s and 1930s called Art Deco. It is a book Barbara Baer Capitman began researching in 1981 but was never to complete. Since Barbara's death in 1990, it has also become the story of her quest to preserve the recent past and to succeed in Rediscovering Art Deco U.S.A.

Barbara considered the 1920s and 1930s the richest architectural and design period of the twentieth century. Before 1970, few critics saw much that was worthwhile in the architecture or decorative arts of the period. Art Deco fine arts—painting and sculpture—were beginning to be esteemed, as was Art Deco jewelry, but not the buildings.

An influential few had earlier recognized the importance of Art Deco architecture. The term *Art Deco* was introduced into English by Bevis Hillier in his 1968 book of the same name. In French, the term *Art Déco* was first used in the title of a 1966 retrospective mounted at the Musée des Arts Décoratifs in Paris. The subject of this show was the legendary 1925 exposition. Of course, there, the term referred only to French works. Other terms used in the period to describe contemporaneous work were *Moderne, Streamline, Jazz Age,* and *Skyscraper.*

Terra-cotta façade decoration for the Norris Theater, Norristown, Pennsylvania. Now in the collection of The Wolfsonian Foundation, 1001 Washington Avenue at Barbara Capitman Way, Miami Beach, Florida. ARCHITECT: *William Harold Lee with Armand Carroll; terra-cotta manufacturer: Conkling Armstrong, 1929. This stunning "Frozen Fountain" motif is the epitome of theatrical Art Deco. The "Frozen Fountain" was one of the most popular Art Deco designs at the great 1925 Paris Exposition, and here it is rendered in brilliantly glazed terra-cotta. Once installed over the entrance and marquee of the Norris Theater, this decoration was rescued along with two three-panel art-glass windows when the theater was demolished in 1983. The "Frozen Fountain" was restored and made the centerpiece—as seen here—of the main-entrance atrium of The Wolfsonian Foundation, a museum and study center established by Mitchell Wolfson, Jr., a citizen of Miami Beach and a long-time friend of Barbara Capitman. (Photograph by Steven Brooke, copyright © 1992. Used by permission.)*

Hillier chose to use the French term. He analyzed many design influences from Art Nouveau to Bauhaus, from Egyptian to Aztec, from Josef Hoffmann to Charles Édouard Jenneret (aka Le Corbusier). His decision to go with *Deco* is testimony to the enduring impact on the world of the 1925 Paris *Exposition des Arts Décoratifs et Industriels Modernes.*

Herbert Hoover, then U.S. Secretary of Commerce, had decreed there would be no American entry in the 1925 Paris exposition because, in his view, nothing in the U.S.A. was *avant-garde* enough. Instead, he dispatched an army of industrial, academic, and design specialists to study everything. While Hoover's decision now seems very short-sighted, his nominations for the delegation were more astute: represented were the American Institute of Architects (AIA), the Architectural League of New York, the Association of National Advertisers, the American Society of Interior Designers (ASID), the New York Department of Education, the Silk Association of America, The Metropolitan Museum of Art, and, of course, *The New York Times.* They were to report back to Hoover on just how the United States could get on the Modernist bandwagon. What they and many more of their compatriots saw in Paris profoundly changed the course of art and design in this country.

But the Paris Exposition of 1925 was by no means the beginning, it was more like a debutante ball. In the words of Boston physician and Art Deco collector *par excellence* Annella Brown, "It was the only movement that ended before it began,"—at least in France.

But Art Deco elements may be found at the dawn of the twentieth century in the work of designers like Vienna's Josef Hoffmann and Otto Wagner. Similarly, in the U.S.A. its tenets had been set forth by visionaries like Louis Sullivan, Bertram Goodhue, Paul Philippe Cret, Frank Lloyd Wright, Irving Gill, and Walter Burley Griffin, all of whose work we shall visit in later chapters. Each wanted to turn away from the past and chart a new course. Each sought to explore new possibilities allowed by the Machine Age.

Most of these architects were searching for architectural "purity." This precept was refined and crafted at Walter Gropius's Bauhaus, the famed German applied-crafts academy. Here work emerged that arguably gave a "masculine" side to Art Deco.

The American brand of Art Deco was greatly influenced by seemingly conflicting elitist and populist forces. The modern movement turned away from ornament and decoration in a repudiation of earlier eras, while the products of Paris continued to stress an artistry and sophistication that was unmistakably French.

In America, it was easy to use the best of all worlds. Contradictory French and German ideas in design and architecture—products of a fierce cultural rivalry and economic competition in Europe—were simply blended together. At New York's Alvin Theatre, on November 21, 1934, Cole Porter summed it all up: "Anything Goes."

Borrowing from other cultures was intrinsically American. The Yanks took the best of European nationalistic styles and updated them, using new techniques and materials. For the first time, buildings contained aluminum, stainless steel, plate glass, tubular steel, Bakelite, Monel, Vitrolite, special glazes, and colors in terra-cotta—whatever technology had to offer.

This was a time when architecture needed to be uplifting. After 1929, the Depression gave most people a strong need for escapist entertainment or diversion.

During the 1930s, a trip to the cinema was the most frequent means of escape. The lure of Hollywood was in its invitation to all to dwell in another world. Charles Chaplin and Clara Bow were among the Art Deco era's earliest stars. Astaire and Rogers were its terpsichorean deities. Art Deco was popularized in a very democratic way at the movies. Hollywood was a vital part of the birth of Art Deco in the U.S.A. It gave us collective memories of the naughtiness of Prohibition, as well as the cruel burden of the succeeding Depression. Most Art Deco–styled films—with their dazzling interiors and exteriors—were created in an attempt to make us feel better.

A VACATION IN MIAMI BEACH

A vacation in Miami Beach was rather more expensive than going to the movies, but it was taken by thousands, nonetheless. The lingering grandeur of sand and sea and dressing for dinner had nearly faded into oblivion in 1976, when Barbara Capitman stumbled onto a fantastic concentration of hundreds of small buildings in south Miami Beach. Barbara saw that they must be saved. She found that the area, with its whimsical hotels and apartments, framed by lush palm fronds, sparked her interest but could sustain only the most oblique comparison with edifices like the Chrysler Building and the New York Daily News Building—the truly awesome towers of her Art Deco childhood. On closer examination, however, she saw the same collaborations of architects, sculptors, and muralists.

Until then, architectural historians had ignored most Art Deco work, possibly out of embarrassment at its impurity and failure to shed its un-Modern "decorative" wrappings. But in 1976, Barbara Capitman decided it must be preserved and treasured. She began trumpeting this decision to the world.

FROM THE CRADLE OF THE SKYSCRAPER

Barbara was born April 9, 1920, in Chicago, cradle of the skyscraper and home of the Prairie Style. While she was very young, Barbara's family left Chicago and moved to New York. At the age of nine, she made a memorable Atlantic crossing with her mother, Myrtle Bacharach Baer, an industrial designer, artist, and sculptor. They traveled on the *S.S. Bremen.* Designed by Fritz August Breuhaus de Groot, this ship was the ultimate German Moderne luxury liner and a design prototype for much Art Deco to come. Together, Barbara and her mother experienced London and Paris, where Barbara was exposed to Cubism, Futurism, Suprematism, and Dadaism—not to mention Bolshevikism and Nazism. She later chose to become a journalist, working for exciting New York magazines covering the design industry. In this capacity, she continued to be influenced by the greatest design professionals of the age. She encountered Raymond Loewy, Walter Dorwin Teague, Peter Muller-Monk, Gordon Lippincott, Buckminster Fuller, Gilbert Rohde, and Donald Deskey. In 1975, after the death of her husband, William, a marketing professor, she returned to her designer roots. During her last two decades, spent mostly in Miami Beach, she formed associations with movie-set and interior designer Edith Irma Siegel, critic Paul Goldberger, and architects Denise Scott Brown, Robert Venturi, and Stanley Tigerman.

In Miami Beach, she rediscovered the design styles she had encountered as a young girl. To Barbara, Art Deco was a continuation of the themes of Art Nouveau, in a new symmetrical fashion. Her Art Deco combined elements of Modernism, Expressionism, Classicism—all the *isms* she had once discovered in Europe, where each country had developed a distinct style. But these were all part of a worldwide movement away from overstuffed and lavishly embellished Victorian, Romanesque, and Nouveau idioms of the prior century. The new "isms" embraced function, symmetry, mathematics, technology, and innovative industrial materials. Never mind that there were often found in these *isms* the faint echoes of ancient styles from the Mesopotamian, African, Egyptian, Roman, Mayan, and Asian empires.

Thus was Barbara imbued with an all-encompassing vision of Art Deco. It embraced the decorative arts, the literary arts, the graphic arts, and the musical arts, but finally, it came back to architecture. Her view was often at odds with that of scholars and experts. A Miami author and lecturer, readying her own exhibit on Art Deco for a local museum, wrote a nasty note warning Barbara not to promote her, use her name, or imply any affiliation with her work, because Barbara's tireless proselytizing on behalf of Art Deco seemed bound to overwhelm and eclipse this woman's own work. Clearly, she was distressed by Barbara's Madison Avenue approach to popularizing Art Deco and historic preservation.

But this extensive background in marketing was precisely what enabled Barbara to generate interest in saving these buildings: a snappy catch phrase, something to bind the buildings together into an easily understood product. She needed a name—something like *Cellophane tape* or *Thermos jug*. Barbara was looking for—and certainly found—a generic American design ethic. The name *Art Deco* stuck.

She chose it because it is short, and it emphasizes ART! It represents the intrinsic artistic collaboration she found so irresistible. Barbara had noted the pioneering scholarship of Elayne Varian and Bevis Hillier. Following Hillier's cues, she declared Art Deco an American treasure. She toured the country, spending her last fourteen years in a struggle to save

and preserve it. Marshaling everything she liked under the banner of Art Deco, Barbara was quickly greeted by a rising public ovation.

Her quick and easy grasp of the strategy for the essential Art Deco promotion campaign came from an unusually thorough education. She had always been in tune with the great design theorists of the Art Deco period. The thinking of the day had been set forth by Le Corbusier in *Towards a New Architecture*, by Paul T. Frankl in *Form and Re-Form* and *New Dimensions*, by Sheldon Cheney in *Art and the Machine*, and by others, like Frank Lloyd Wright, Walter Gropius, and Ludwig Mies van der Rohe. They had all explored the new twentieth-century construction formula: a careful blending of art and industry. They espoused beauty combined with utility. They wrote and lectured to win converts.

So, in 1979, Barbara knew what to do: She founded the Miami Design Preservation League (MDPL). She began to identify and celebrate the products of early twentieth-century America. In her subsequent work, she expanded her project to involve Art Deco around the world.

She was amazingly successful. The popularity of Art Deco may be explained by the quality of its underlying classicism. Art Deco also has certain reassuring, rhythmic, recurring elements:

- The reduction of most designs to groups with three elements—the Art Deco "Rule of Threes."
- The cloaking of façades with balanced, streamlined bands.
- The use of smooth metal and machined surfaces.
- An interplay between light and dark.
- A partnership between art and engineering in each project.

Consistently, Barbara predicted that Art Deco would eventually be recognized for generations to come as the most vigorous and truly American of all the architectural, interior design, and graphic modes.

The rediscovery of Art Deco was all the more amazing coming, as it did, after just fifty years. It had most assuredly passed into obscurity, but it never really stopped happening. Art Deco buildings were built throughout the 1950s. Even in 1993, the Art Deco style is being used in Los Angeles, New York, Miami Beach, and Chicago.

Because of Barbara's high-profile Art Deco publicity campaign, Ocean Drive in south Miami Beach captured the public's imagination. Visitors began coming. Barbara asked for help—and money—from every government agency from Miami to Washington, D.C.

Soon she had a grant from a brand-new government program, a 1970s replay of the 1930s alphabet-soup program-name amalgam. Barbara had long known about 1930s New Deal agencies like the WPA, the PWA, and the NRA. Now she learned a new one: CETA—the Comprehensive Employment and Training Act. This agency provided her with a staff some fifteen strong. They began cataloging the entire eight-hundred-plus buildings in the soon-to-be Miami Beach Historic District.

Such a district, amazingly, had been suggested even earlier to the City of Miami Beach by Barbara's future friend: architect, author, and teacher Denise Scott Brown. It was Denise and her husband, Robert Venturi, who first wrote about the lessons to be learned from 1950s Las Vegas, Nevada.

Ms. Scott Brown's 1973 idea for a Miami Beach Art Deco district was ignored until it independently dawned upon Barbara Capitman and her friends. After first hearing from Barbara, U.S. Department of the Interior official Chris Delaporte and his associates in Washington kept the project moving along. Then the State of Florida's Office of Historic Preservation got into the act. Soon, Barbara had her district. It was the first historic district in the United States to enshrine architecture from the twentieth century. The Miami Beach district was entered into the National Register of Historic Places on May 14, 1979 on one of Barbara's proudest and happiest days.

This was not enough. Barbara wanted to recognize Art Deco buildings everywhere. She began an Art Deco odyssey with her friend the designer Leonard Horowitz. She agreed to keep a journal of the entire experience and received a promise from *Miami News* editor and esteemed Miami historian Howard Kleinberg to publish her story in a series of columns on her return. These articles, entitled "Travels with Barbara," delighted Miami readers and established Barbara as an important figure on the local scene. Before embarking, she began her journal, recording the following thoughts:

Miami Beach, June 15, 1981—Preparing for this three-month designers' odyssey around the country with Leonard, I am reminded of literary accounts of travel and adventure. For example: Steinbeck's *Travels with Charley.* The selection of a vehicle; the traveling companion; the fitting out; the funding of the expedition; the itinerary; the ports-of-call; even the mileage which we are just beginning to face up to—something over 10,000 miles—are now becoming very real.

Preparing ourselves means poring through books and periodicals hoping we won't miss something significant because we simply didn't know where to look for it or whom to see. It means calling our network of editors, architects, preservationists. "What should we visit in Seattle? Would you go up to Austin or down to Galveston?"

We are going to be looking for early modern architecture across the U.S.A. We know it's there— the Junior League of Tulsa [Oklahoma] has just published a book on Tulsa Art Deco that is superb.

Perhaps Leonard and I, who have often been accused of not being academic enough or rigid enough, can bring to other places the same excitement and pride in the recent past that's sweeping

Miami. People here say continually, "My eyes have been opened." They say they see Art Deco all over South Florida, not just in the District. Perhaps we can show other places how to open their eyes. We were not sure that there was a treasure here ourselves five years ago. Then Carl Weinhardt, Director of Vizcaya Museum, met a band of us on the steps of the Amsterdam Palace Apartments for the now-historic "Walk through the District." A pioneer of Boston's Beacon Hill, he reinforced our uninformed hunches and said the buildings were unique, and, "Yes, they could be called Art Deco."

But more importantly, we want to show how other places, other cities are solving their urban-planning problems; how they are using cultural events, ethnic heritage preservation, and restoration to build economy, decrease crime, and to give their citizens a better lifestyle.

Eventually the intrepid duo returned to their Art Deco wonderland of Miami Beach. On returning, Barbara summarized their experience in her journal:

On our trip around the country, Leonard and I, approaching cities situated off to the side of the parkways and bridges, beyond the industrial muck of the outskirts, would see differentiated from the solid mass of tall buildings comprising the contemporary skyline one or more graceful spires or stepped-shape silhouettes. We would turn off the throughway and pierce the city aiming for that spire, secure in the assumption that it would be an important Art Deco building.

We had been tipped off about the Baton Rouge, Louisiana, state capitol by the son of its architect, Julius F. Dreyfous. (Also an architect, the son was busy at work on plans for the 1984 World's Fair in New Orleans.) As we approached the city, we could see the skyscraper capitol presiding over the city from far off. It was, of course, Huey Long's monumental achievement of 1934.

We saw other skyscrapers that took our breath away with their grandeur: the Bullocks Wilshire department store in Los Angeles; the Chicago Board of Trade building with its black corbels and silver-relief sculptures, where Ceres, goddess of agriculture, stands guard over La Salle Street, a sculptured figure atop the tower.

Guided by members of the Allied Arts of Seattle, who had already published their splendid 1979 booklet, *Art Deco Seattle*, we stood reverently in other temples of commerce, the Exchange Building and the Seattle Tower—their entrance lobbies of dazzling gold Art Deco ornament set against dark polished stone— reminiscent of movie palaces of the 1920s.

We were to see the great asymmetrical Art Deco state capitol building in Bismarck, North Dakota, created by the leading architects of the Midwest, Chicago's Holabird & Root. This Stripped Classic building had immense rows of shining bronze chandeliers shaped like sheaves of wheat, set against tall corridors of white marble.

In Minnesota's Twin Cities our guide was Charles Senseman, a prolific collector and designer, who had moved from Miami to Minneapolis in 1980. We toured a series of Art Deco towers there with memorable reliefs and sculptures, all connected by the city's skywalk. It was the skyscraper city hall in Saint Paul, however, that was the most astounding. The lobby was dominated by a Native American *God of Peace*, carved in onyx by Swedish sculptor Carl Milles. It was two stories high and revolved slowly and majestically.

Impressive skyscraper lobbies are to be found in many major cities. Invited to help inaugurate the recycling of the Union Depot in Tulsa, Oklahoma, as an office building, I was shown a series of splendid 1930s office buildings set among recent buildings, replete with gilded, coffered ceilings and custom chandeliers and marble walls. But in Tulsa the skyscraper that most excited me was a church, the Boston Avenue Methodist Church.

In some cities Art Deco enthusiasts already had created an awareness of the style. In other places, like the great rustic Art Deco Timberline Lodge on Mount Hood in Oregon by Gilbert Stanley Underwood, a sophisticated California designer, the style had not, heretofore, been appreciated. But after our visit, a firm friendship with the staff developed and their new understanding of this sensational WPA resource emerged.

When we reached Phoenix, we registered at the Arizona Biltmore under the expansive gold-leafed ceiling. Leonard swore it was "Deco heaven." We were inside one of Frank Lloyd Wright's great buildings—much like, we were told, his Imperial Hotel in Tokyo, long since demolished.

After our visit to the Arizona Biltmore, having met with Art Deco buffs all over the country and having been shown a staggering number of Deco architectural treasures from great skyscrapers and ornate theaters to humble main streets, we processed our slides of the trip and eventually stood before some two hundred designers in the beautiful Prairie-style lecture hall of the Chicago Architectural Foundation. Stanley Tigerman introduced us. Our rapt audience was amazed at the extent and beauty of American Art Deco, aghast at the demolition of Miami Beach's New Yorker Hotel, and delighted with insights we furnished about our own District.

We had them mesmerized—until we came to Frank Lloyd Wright and the Arizona Biltmore. What derision! Never! Only an ignorant sensation-monger would associate Chicago's Frank Lloyd Wright with the bizarre European style called Art Deco!

Of course, we were right, but it did come as quite a shock to most of the architectural establishment.

The following week we met with an enthusiastic group that formed the third Art Deco Society—the Chicago Art Deco Society, or CADS.

We traveled on through Indiana and Ohio, finally arriving at the nation's capital. We helped form the Washington, D.C. Art Deco Society, a group that proved to be instrumental in helping the national government understand the capital as the city of Art Deco apartments and Stripped Classic government buildings built under the aegis of the Roosevelt New Deal.

All told, on this incredible journey, Barbara and Leonard visited the following places:

Tampa, Florida; Tallahassee, Florida; Baton Rouge, Louisiana; New Orleans, Louisiana; Houston, Texas; Austin, Texas; San Antonio, Texas; Phoenix, Arizona; Tucson, Arizona; San Diego, California; Los Angeles, California; Monterey, California; San Jose, California; San Francisco, California; Portland, Oregon; Timberline Lodge, Mount Hood, Oregon; Seattle, Washington; Bismarck, North Dakota; Saint Louis, Missouri; Kansas City, Missouri; Minneapolis, Minnesota; Saint Paul, Minnesota; Chicago, Illinois; Indianapolis, Indiana; Cincinnati, Ohio; Atlanta, Georgia; Savannah, Georgia; Washington, D.C.

Subsequently, Barbara visited Boston, Massachusetts; Philadelphia, Pennsylvania; Tulsa, Oklahoma; Milwaukee, Wisconsin; and New York City.

Barbara continued:

Out of that summer's expeditions came a strong new conviction—the realization that Art Deco is a strong American style, present in almost every little town, but particularly evident in our great cities.

Meanwhile, the idea was spreading. Art Deco Societies were being formed completely independently in Detroit, Dallas, Los Angeles, Baltimore, and even Anchorage, Alaska. Brilliant newsletters were published with in-depth articles about Art Deco films, furniture, and buildings in trouble.

The success of the Art Deco District in Miami Beach, its coverage in the international press, its seemingly unstoppable development of restored hotels, apartment buildings, and commercial ventures, made it a magnet for world travelers who love the style. And the annual Art Deco Weekend became the place to be. Our annual lecture series introduced new thinking about design history and building types—from diners to amusement parks.

Speakers from the Art Deco Weekend went on

to lecture at the other societies. The original formula of the Miami Design Preservation League was copied: parties, tours, lectures, an Art Deco Weekend, a ball, fashion shows.

Since 1988, the Art Deco Societies have made an important impact on preservationists by becoming an affinity group at the annual National Trust for Historic Preservation (NTHP) conferences. With the support of Leonard Horowitz, Michael Kinerk, Dennis Wilhelm, Sharon Koskoff, and Evelyn Perlman, a major offensive was launched in Cincinnati, funded by the Miami Beach Visitors & Convention Bureau. Cincinnati, with its incomparable Union Terminal and Carew Tower, provided the societies and other interested participants with stunning Art Deco tours. There were wonderful lectures and an Art Deco high-rise hospitality suite in the Netherland Hotel, where hundreds of preservationists sipped Alexis Lichine's Art Deco wine and looked at slide shows.

Barbara continued with her crusade, focusing her efforts on educating the members of the National Trust for Historic Preservation, a group heretofore not generally used to considering twentieth-century sites as historic.

In 1989, Barbara's entourage was joined at the Philadelphia NTHP convention by Denis Russ and the Miami Beach Development Corporation, which had a booth in the trade show, ReHABITAT, and a table in the main hall of the convention. Hundreds of people approached with the same comment: "I love Deco." Barbara presented a seminar featuring Gersil Kay of the Philadelphia Art Deco Society and Paul Manship's son, John, with slides from his new book on his father's sculpture. A tour of Manayunk, the reclaimed factory town on the Schuylkill River in Pennsylvania, brought a busload of conventioneers to the offices of Robert Venturi and Denise Scott Brown. Representatives from the established Art Deco Societies also had been involved in preservation projects in the same year, lobbying as a group of fifteen people in Washington, where the Carlyle Suites hosted a cocktail party for us. Here, Sherry Muss made sure that we had a first-rate time in the nation's capital. The hotel itself, right off Dupont Circle near many foreign embassies, was a treat, having been converted to the purpose from one of the Art Deco apartment buildings, with which Washington is amply blessed.

Also in 1989, Barbara was pleased to note the progress of Tony Fusco in organizing the Boston Art Deco Society, and to promote the restoration of the Paramount movie palace on Washington Street. She joined the new society in the struggle to save the Coolidge Corner Theatre in Brookline. It was the major Boston architectural firm of Anderson Notter & Alexander that created a plan for its conversion into a community theater. This firm, previously known as Anderson, Notter Finegold, created the visionary and award-winning 1981 preservation-development plan for Miami Beach, which we followed closely to ensure the success of the Art Deco District.

Capitman, Kinerk, and Wilhelm worked very hard throughout 1990 to organize and establish the First World Congress on Art Deco. The "organizing conference" was held before Barbara's death. The first congress came just after.

In a 1990 report to the organizing conference for the First World Congress in Miami Beach, Barbara warned that Art Deco architecture is rapidly disappearing and that most societies need help as more and more cities are losing their character. She observed: "Despite the enormous strides we have made in the past decade in the recognition of the style, too many urban centers are rebuilding and destroying movie houses, office buildings, shops, and housing. It is time to come together to protect this vulnerable style and to use our combined strength to project our message."

The presence of Vyonne Geneve, who came to the 1990 organizing conference all the way from Western Australia, forced us to think on a global scale. We realized that once again Barbara had been a visionary. She had told us the 1990s would be the "Deco Decade"—a rediscovery of Art Deco worldwide. Now, three years into the 1990s, the clarity of her prediction seems startling.

After Barbara's death, Miami Beach civic activist Matti Bower agreed to head the First World Congress on Art Deco. She, along with Wilhelm, Kinerk, and MDPL volunteers Betty Gutierrez, Keith Root, Christine Maillebiau, Peggy Hogan, George Neary, Dahlia Beauchamp and Erika Brigham, saw to it that the 1991 World Congress on Art Deco became a reality.

Wilhelm invited delegates from around the world. Speakers made presentations on Art Deco (or whatever they called it in their own countries) in England, France, Australia, New Zealand, Indonesia, Canada, and South America. Perth's Art Deco Society of Western Australia agreed to host the 1993 World Congress, and England's Twentieth Century Society agreed to organize one in 1995. The realization came upon us like the dawn after the night: The 1990s *is* the decade of rediscovering Art Deco worldwide!

In 1992, in the interval between the biennial World Congresses, MDPL hosted the presidents of all the active Art Deco Societies in the U.S.A. In order to protect endangered buildings more effectively, they agreed to band together, forming the National Coalition of Art Deco Societies (NCADS). On hearing of this, societies in the other countries clamored for inclusion in the coalition, requesting that it become international. The exact nature and goals of this organization are still evolving.

A SECOND NATIONWIDE TRIP

In 1991, seeking somehow to finish this chronicle begun by Barbara, her surviving co-authors, Kinerk and Wilhelm, themselves pioneers of the Miami Beach Art Deco District since 1977, set out to see what Barbara had already seen.

Kinerk and Wilhelm followed in Barbara's and Leonard's footsteps to rediscover a rich world—bridges, churches, city halls, state capitols, stores, movie palaces, homes, and hotels—spread before their eyes from coast to coast. Relying on help from Barbara's original contacts, they easily found what Barbara and Leonard had discovered a decade earlier.

By this time, the historic magnitude of the undertaking was clear; each building, architect, sculptor, and muralist was duly noted and entered into a massive computerized database, "The Art Deco Database of the Barbara Baer Capitman Archives." By the time this book was being assembled, the database already contained over three thousand entries, and it was clear that this was only the beginning.

Here is how Dennis Wilhelm remembers the evolution of the Deco Database:

Returning to Miami Beach after our first whirlwind trip, we felt overwhelmed by the number of buildings we had seen and the notes and photos taken. If this seemed unmanageable after one trip, how could we expect to cope after many such tours? What would become of the vast amount of material? Would it sit in boxes for years until it was finally discarded as rubbish?

Our project became even more unwieldy a few weeks later when Randy Juster arrived from California with hundreds of photos from his vast archive. The idea was to select the images we wanted so he would have a clearer idea of what new shots would be required. Once again we were overwhelmed. How could we sift through hundreds of photos and not only remember which we had seen but also rank the subjects as to their importance?

Michael, with his background in computers, immediately suggested using the computer. This idea was met with little enthusiasm. Wouldn't that mean typing a description of every photo and wouldn't that take days? These questions came too late, for information about the slide currently in the projector was already being typed into the computer by Michael.

It took us an entire weekend to go through Randy's collection of images—describing, reviewing,

ART DECO BUILDINGS SURVEYED - BY YEAR

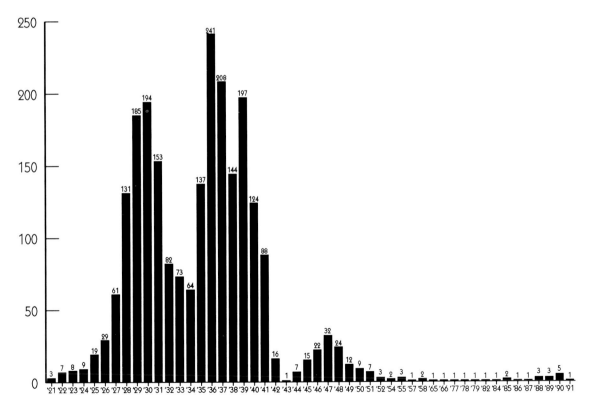

YEAR BUILT

ART DECO SITES SURVEYED - BY BUILDING'S ORIGINAL USE

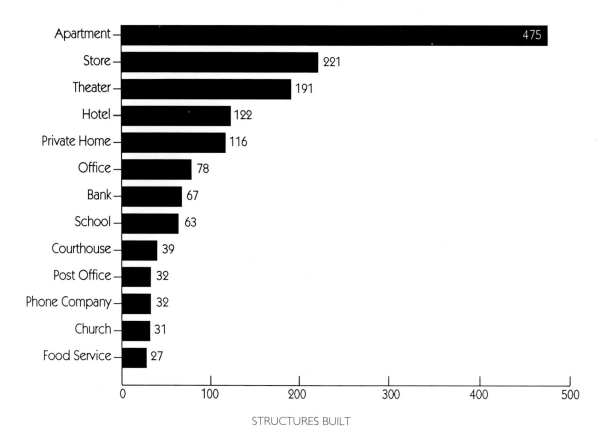

STRUCTURES BUILT

and ranking every photo. But in the end we all agreed it couldn't have been done any other way, and now we had an inventory of every photo and we could access the information in an instant. This spur-of-the-moment creation became the framework of a much-expanded database. All told, we surveyed nearly three thousand buildings during a two-year period of travels. With this cross-section we could compute how many buildings had been created each year in any city, what they had been used for, and who the architects had been. The possibilities were endless. Facts and figures, charts and graphs, the results of our technological voyage—in what we dubbed the Deco Database—can be seen in the succeeding chapters.

A NOTE TO OUR READERS

Throughout this book the authors have attempted to date buildings from the time the plans were first drawn. We view the time of creation as being the most relevant for purposes of exploring the Art Deco treasures of the United States. Sometimes the plans and the construction were accomplished within the same year, and sometimes they were not.

In some cases, projects were not built until months or years after the plans had been made.

Similarly, we have always used the original names of the structures when they are known. Original names do not change as current names do. In each case, where the *current* name is different and is known, we have included it within parentheses, for example: Boulder Dam (Hoover Dam).

We have also used a number of postcards dating from the time a building was constructed, in many cases because the postcard gives the only full view of the building exterior now available. Many Art Deco buildings stood proudly alone on the skyline when they were first built, but today they are hemmed in and obscured by taller structures. Also, we feel that these postcards add a delightful period flavor to this book. In no way do the cards detract from the outstanding work of our principal photographer, Randy Juster. On the contrary, most of the postcards used are from Randy's amazing collection of Art Deco material. We are indebted to Randy for far more than the splendid images you will see here. He is one of the foremost authorities on Art Deco whom we know, and he was selected by Barbara Capitman a year before her death as the only person with a single body of work suitable for this massive undertaking.

ART DECO BUILDINGS SURVEYED - BY CITY

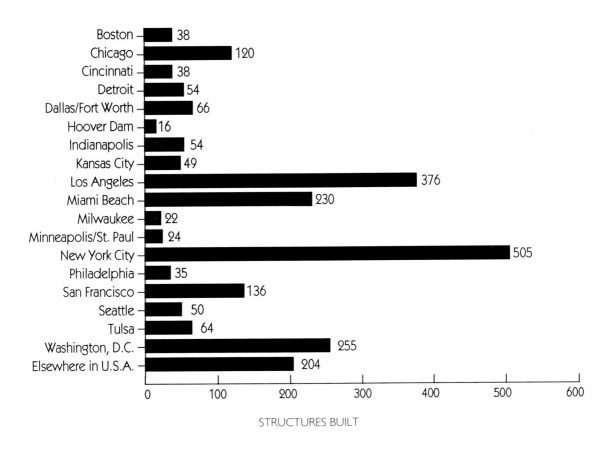

City	Structures Built
Boston	38
Chicago	120
Cincinnati	38
Detroit	54
Dallas/Fort Worth	66
Hoover Dam	16
Indianapolis	54
Kansas City	49
Los Angeles	376
Miami Beach	230
Milwaukee	22
Minneapolis/St. Paul	24
New York City	505
Philadelphia	35
San Francisco	136
Seattle	50
Tulsa	64
Washington, D.C.	255
Elsewhere in U.S.A.	204

STRUCTURES BUILT

THE
UNITED STATES
OF
AMERICA

REDISCOVERING ART DECO FROM SEA TO SHINING SEA

For those who are not trained, to mock the cultural judgment of those who are is highly unedifying . . . It is far better to risk a slight surplus of Art Deco here and there (especially in Miami Beach) than to stir up boobery throughout the land, even in defense of legitimate property claims.

—Oscar S. Gray, Professor of Law, University of Maryland, Letter to the Editor, *The New York Times*, March 11, 1981, in reply to William Safire's column of March 2, 1981 (Safire didn't like the Miami Beach Art Deco District).

EARLY IN THE PROJECT WE DECIDED TO USE THE Deco Database to learn who was most responsible for creating Art Deco buildings in the U.S.A. What companies, corporations, and businesses commissioned these buildings and why? Which architects achieved the greatest success?

Our data would support writing an entire volume on this subject. Here we attempt only to show examples of the larger and more important categories, according to our statistics.

Colony Theater (1,523 seats), 13116 Shaker Square, Cleveland, Ohio. ARCHITECT: John Eberson, 1937. After inventing the star-filled rococo "atmospheric" theater, the brilliant John Eberson subsequently created many Streamline Moderne interiors like this one. An incongruous feature of this theater is its neo-Colonial exterior.

AIRPORTS
SURVEYED: 25

In the early years of aviation Pan Am built bases near the water to accommodate the famous Sikorsky S-38 Clipper seaplanes. We found their seaplane terminals in Long Beach, California, in Miami, and on San Francisco's Treasure Island. Miami's was the earliest, built as the first international airport with flights to Havana. The best, however, is a Works Progress Administration (WPA) project built in Queens, New York, at the early airfield now known as La Guardia—the Marine Air Terminal. It has a huge interior mural, *Flight,* by James Brooks, which was painted over and not visible for years until resurrected by conservators in 1980.

As commercial aviation grew, many cities built municipal airports. A large number of these are still around, either lost and forgotten, tucked away on the grounds of our modern jet ports, or serving as executive or regional airports. We found the original terminal at Chicago's Midway at the very end of the modern one.

The best example we found is Lunken Airport, now an executive airport, on the outskirts of Cincinnati. Overall, the terminal is in its original state, with a pair of murals and a clock with wings in the lobby. Getting to it is an experience: the Columbia Parkway, built to connect the airport with downtown, is an icon of the 1930s with Art Deco viaducts, bridges, and retaining walls.

APARTMENTS
SURVEYED: 545

Developers used Art Deco in apartment-building design as a marketing tool to entice tenants. The 1920s Zigzag style symbolized elegance, luxury, and sophistication, and the Streamline styles of the 1930s evoked clean, carefree, up-to-date modern living. Due to building booms, the Bronx, Cincinnati, Manhattan, Miami Beach, San Francisco, and Washington, D.C., have more than their share of these buildings.

MUNICIPAL AUDITORIUMS
SURVEYED: 7

The Kansas City (Missouri) Municipal Auditorium has no rivals in this category. The multipurpose building occupies an entire city block, and its rich interior detail can be compared only to New York's Radio City Music Hall and the Paramount Theater in Oakland, California.

The Indiana University Auditorium also is noteworthy due to the two mural cycles by Thomas Hart Benton that illustrate the cultural and industrial history of Indiana.

The greatest municipal auditorium that is now lost, without a doubt, is the charred bulk of the Pan Pacific Auditorium in Los Angeles.

City Hall, 65 Niagara Square, Buffalo, New York. Architect: John J. Wade for Dietel & Wade, with Sullivan W. Jones, 1929. *This vintage postcard shows Buffalo's City Hall and adjacent McKinley monument lit at night. A twenty-eighth-floor observation deck overlooks Lake Erie from a height of 330 feet. Especially noteworthy is the Common Council chamber (not illustrated), with its Art Deco sunburst skylight.*

AUTOMOBILE INDUSTRY SHOWROOMS, FACTORIES, AND OFFICES
SURVEYED: 25

Most automobiles were severely streamlined in this era when speed was king. It is not surprising to find that Art Deco styling was also employed by the auto industry in its factories, offices, and showrooms. (See also: World's Fairs and Expositions.)

The best remaining example of these showrooms is now the Auburn Cord Duesenberg Museum in Auburn, Indiana. The exterior and interior French-style details have been lovingly preserved as the setting to showcase the museum's elegant automobiles that were made in Indiana before Detroit dominated the auto industry.

Other favorites, still serving their original purpose, are the Pierce Arrow (now Cadillac) Auto Showroom in Buffalo, and the Don Lee Cadillac showroom in San Francisco.

New York's Chrysler Building and Detroit's earlier Fisher Building are examples of automotive "power-skyscraper" headquarters. The auto imagery integrated into the Chrysler Building façade is exemplary.

Enormous automobile factories were constructed in the 1920s and 1930s, the majority designed by Detroit's Albert Kahn. Those he designed in the early 1920s are forerunners

"Sprite" from Chicago Midway Gardens now at Arizona Biltmore Hotel Gardens, 6000 South Cottage Grove Avenue, Phoenix, Arizona. Sculptor: Alfonso Iannelli; Designer: Frank Lloyd Wright, 1914. *Iannelli produced Art Deco–style posters in Los Angeles in 1911, and soon began to collaborate with Wright. The delightful "Sprites" at Chicago's Midway Gardens, where the integration of sculpture and geometry was a decade ahead of its time, resulted from this collaboration. The sprites were removed from their original site when the popular night spot was demolished in 1929. (Photograph by Michael D. Kinerk)*

of the Stripped Classic style, while later plants are more streamlined, perhaps as an outward indication of the speed and efficiency of the assembly lines within. We call these huge-scale buildings Industrial Deco.

BANKS
SURVEYED: 78

Banks can be divided into two types: skyscraper headquarters found in the downtowns of big cities and small-town or branch banks.

As the premier style of the skyscraper boom of the late 1920s, Art Deco quickly became the symbol of corporate power and wealth. Since this was the very image that banks wanted to portray, it isn't surprising that they were great patrons of the style. Most of these buildings still retain the original opulent details in the lobby and on the main banking floors and offices.

Our favorite big bank skyscrapers are: Second National Bank, Boston; Union Trust, Detroit; Title & Trust, Phoenix; Security First National Bank and Title Guarantee & Trust, Los Angeles; Bankers Trust, City Bank Farmers Trust, and Irving Trust, New York; and the Philadelphia Savings Fund Society, Philadelphia. Most of these are described in more detail in the city chapters.

Smaller banks almost always employed Stripped Classic or Greco-Deco styles. They presumably wanted to indicate they were modern and up-to-date but with the stability of the ancient Greek and Roman empires. Worthy of mention in this category are the seven branch banks built in Indianapolis in 1947 for Indiana National Bank.

Empire State Building, 350 5th Avenue, between 33rd and 34th Streets, New York City. ARCHITECT: William Lamb for Shreve, Lamb & Harmon, 1930. The magnificent Empire State is seen here during a laser-light show celebrating the buildings' fiftieth birthday in 1981. There hadn't been such excitement for the world-famous skyscraper since King Kong scaled its sides in 1933, or when a plane crashed into the seventy-sixth floor in 1945. Erected by the Starrett Construction Company, the building opened May 31, 1931.

Cincinnati Bell, 36 East 7th Street, at Elm and Plum Streets, Cincinnati, Ohio. ARCHITECT: Harry Hake for Hake & Kuck, 1931. Leaving no doubt as to the function of the building, the architects and designers employed images of the telephone and telephone equipment as decorative motifs throughout. This detail from a frieze on the stone façade shows old headsets and telephones. More views of this outstanding Bell edifice are included in the Cincinnati chapter.

WALDORF-ASTORIA HOTEL. – Park Avenue, New York City

Waldorf-Astoria Hotel, 301 Park Avenue, New York City. ARCHITECT: Schultze & Weaver, 1930; Restoration architect: Kenneth Hurd Associates, 1983. A vintage postcard of the hotel whose very name is synonymous with Art Deco elegance and class shows the main façade with its twin towers. Some scholars compare the design of these towers to that of the pyramid at Tikal, Mexico. Others compare them to Buck Rogers' spaceships. Whatever the influence, the hotel was elegant enough to get a mention in "You're the Top," Cole Porter's song enumerating the best things in the world, including a "Waldorf" salad. For years, the famed composer maintained an apartment here.

BARBER SHOP
SURVEYED: 1

While there may be quite a few barber shops in small towns with original chairs, sinks, and mirrors, most have disappeared from large cities. Surely none can surpass the one on the second floor of the Circle Tower in Indianapolis. It is emblazoned with black-glazed ceramic tiles and silver decorations of combs, clippers, and brushes. The details were lovingly preserved when the shop was expanded into a modern hair salon.

BARS
SURVEYED: 2

Many Streamline Moderne–style bars used structural glass, chrome, glass block, and neon. And they weren't complete without a jukebox! Few of these remain. Of the two we saw,

Yaquina Bay Bridge, Oregon Coast Highway 9, milepost 141.68, Newport, Oregon. ARCHITECT: Conde B. McCullough, state highway and bridge engineer, 1933. One of twelve WPA Art Deco bridges, all of which were built in Oregon by McCullough. This 3,223-foot bridge, which was opened in 1936, features fluted obelisk pylons flanking the entrance to the 600-foot arched central span. Oregon demolished one of these remarkable bridges in 1991. Others are now in danger.

one, the Elwood in Detroit, has been converted into an eatery. The other, Mac's Club Deuce in Miami Beach, has retained the original look.

BEACHES/SWIMMING POOLS
SURVEYED: 15

The New York City Parks Department wins hands down in this category. Through the determination of Parks Commissioner Robert Moses, many new swimming pools were created for New York's boroughs during the 1930s. Aymar Embury II was architect for several of these. The Joseph H. Lyons Pool in Staten Island is his best, for it is easily mistaken for the set of a Busby Berkeley movie. To add to the excitement, the pool, bathhouse, and terrace sit at water's edge, with a view of majestic lower Manhattan.

But the Lyons pool is just an old swimming hole compared to Long Island's Jones Beach, which the team of Moses and Embury had created earlier. Here they built a skyscraper tower, two pools with bathhouses (one holding 10,000 bathers and the other 5,400), a nautical-theme boardwalk along the five-and-one-half-mile beach and a thirty-four-mile-long four-lane parkway to get Manhattanites out to the beach. Of course, this was only a warm-up for Moses, who went on singlehandedly to create the site for the 1939 New York World's Fair in Queens by converting a swamp into a giant landfill.

BELL TELEPHONE SYSTEM
SURVEYED: 40

Two of the earliest Art Deco buildings in the United States were telephone-company headquarters. On the East Coast, Ralph Walker's 1923 Barclay-Vesey Building in New York City was commissioned by the New York Telephone Co. Its West Coast counterpart is Timothy Pflueger's monumental 1924 skyscraper for Pacific Telephone in San Francisco.

The critical success of these two buildings seems to have set a trend that led to the construction of major Art Deco telephone headquarters in virtually all cities. These were followed by a large number of smaller "switching stations" designed to fit into the residential character of outlying neighborhoods.

Three headquarters towers are notable for their artistic use of telephone imagery: Barclay-Vesey and Santa Monica's Associated Telephone (now GTE) both use communication as the theme for lobby murals. The headsets and phones in stone relief and the Oscar Bach metalwork of men stringing phone cable make the Cincinnati Bell tower a standout.

Several architects specialized in these buildings and received many commissions in their regions: Ralph Walker of Voorhees, Gmelin, Walker in the Northeast; Holabird & Root in the Midwest; and Irvin Ray Timlin in the Southwest. Adrian Smith's new sixty-story AT&T Chicago headquarters is an indication of continuing interest in the wonderful Bell System Art Deco style already so pervasive throughout the United States of America.

Coca-Cola Bottling Company (Indianapolis Public Schools Service Center), 801 North Carrollton Avenue, Indianapolis, Indiana. ARCHITECT: Rubush & Hunter, 1931, with additions in 1940 and 1949 by the same architect. This detail is an excellent example of one of the most familiar Art Deco motifs, the "Frozen Fountain" or Jet d'eau, as René Lalique called it at the 1925 Paris Exposition. This white glazed terra-cotta spandrel also contains a wealth of stylized flowers that are so typical of Art Deco style.

BIG BUSINESS SKYSCRAPER OFFICE BUILDINGS
SURVEYED: 96

Skyscrapers are America's unique contribution to architecture, and Art Deco took the American skyscraper to its zenith in the early 1930s. It was a perfect pairing—the newest, freshest, only truly modern style combined with the latest architectural thinking. These buildings became the symbol of corporate power, wealth, and sophistication. It was New York City's forward-looking zoning law of 1916 that was responsible for the stepped-back sculpture form that became the exterior hallmark. As New York went, so went the nation. No modern city was complete without a skyscraper.

A lavish, "drop-dead" lobby, the second requisite element dictated by the pioneers in New York, makes a walk-through a must. It is only here—amidst the splendor of exotic marbles, gleaming metals, magnificent chandeliers, heroic murals and sculpture, and the *de rigueur* artistic elevator doors and letterboxes—that one can feel the true splendor of the Machine Age.

Manhattan is the capital of this Skyscraper Style—entire books have been written on this subject alone. To experience properly the premier Art Deco metropolis requires careful planning, a good pair of walking shoes, and at least two full days. Los Angeles ranks second, with the best of its buildings in a few central areas. In both cities one can experience a critical mass of Skyscraper Style Art Deco unavailable anywhere else, although Chicago is also pretty wonderful.

Daily News *Building,* 220 East 42nd Street, New York City. ARCHITECT: Raymond Hood for Howells & Hood; Sculptor: René Paul Chambellan, 1929. Placed over the main entrance, this relief sculpture by Chambellan is animated with throngs of New Yorkers. These multitudes had made the Daily News the largest-circulation newspaper in the U.S.A., and in a tribute to them are carved words from Abraham Lincoln: "God Must Have Loved the Common Man . . . He Made So Many of Them." The carving is bracketed by superb lighting pylons.

BOTTLING PLANTS
SURVEYED: 14

As new technology made the bottling of soft drinks a science, many plants were constructed across the country to allow for regional distribution of national brands. Perhaps

Jones Beach State Park, West Bathhouse, South Façade, 34 miles southeast of Manhattan, Long Island, New York. ARCHITECT: Aymar Embury II and NYC Parks Department, 1932. Jones Beach, a 2,245-acre state park, is one of the largest Art Deco projects ever built, with two giant bathhouses and a Saarinen-like water tower. The West Bathhouse can hold 5,400 visitors. The larger East Bathhouse (not visible here) can hold 10,000. The complex also includes two swimming pools. The two-story windows seen here are in the dining room, allowing a splendid view of the Atlantic Ocean. (Photograph courtesy Capitman Archives)

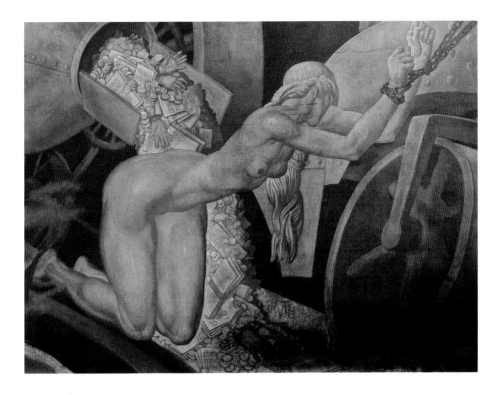

influenced by exhibits at world's fairs, many of these plants incorporated huge display windows, allowing passers-by to observe the assembly-line bottling process.

The king of soft drinks, Coca-Cola, created the finest plants. The Los Angeles headquarters probably is best known, being the textbook example of Nautical Moderne. The Indianapolis plant is a multibuilding complex with French Zigzag details carried throughout, giving it the appearance of a film-studio backlot. The streamlined example in Cincinnati was saved and adaptively reused, while a similar building in San Francisco may be in danger.

The memorabilia at the Coca-Cola Museum at Underground Atlanta clearly illustrates Coke's close association with Art Deco. Little wonder the plants were done in this style; everything else from graphics, displays, and promotional materials to the coolers and dispensers used Art Deco to create a unified image of Coke being *the* modern drink.

Many other companies from Pepsi to 7-Up had similar Art Deco bottling plants, vending machines, and associated market-identity techniques.

BRIDGES
SURVEYED: 28

San Francisco's Golden Gate Bridge is the leader in this category, recognized for its grace and beauty by all who see it. But few realize that the decorations on the piers and styling of the toll booths and lighting fixtures on the approaches are prime examples of the later Moderne phase of Art Deco. This "look" was determined as a result of an architect working with the requirements of a structural engineer. Although no other bridge can compare to the Golden Gate in sheer

Art Deco magnificence, there are other large-scale examples: New York's Triborough Bridge and the Oakland Bay Bridge.

Smaller, less well-known bridges are the most endangered Art Deco structures. Most have reached the age when they are in dire need of structural rehabilitation. Rehabilitation usually involves rerouting traffic. Governmental agencies avoid this by constructing new, bigger, styleless bridges nearby, then closing or demolishing the old bridge.

Twelve Art Deco bridges constructed from 1931–1933 on Oregon's Coast Highway 9 are a good example of the problem old bridges face. Built by the state's staff engineer, Conde B. McCullough, this is surely one of the largest group of Art Deco bridges ever built. McCullough used French–inspired decorative elements on spandrels, railings, stairs, and overlook platforms and plazas, with Paris Exposition–style pylons on several of the bridges. One, the Alsea Bay Bridge, was demolished by the state in 1991 despite an organized effort to save it.

Fountain County Courthouse Mural, *south entrance, 301 4th Street, Covington, Indiana. ARCHITECT: Louis Johnson; Muralist: Eugene Savage, 1937. The Works Progress Administration (WPA) was born of politics. From it came a remarkable profusion of buildings and art. In this detail, 1930s political turmoil boils into searing images. Savage, one of the most productive artists of the era, was from Covington. After the WPA constructed the courthouse in 1935, the Wabash River Sketch Club asked him to contribute to their mural project. He painted his two murals on canvas in his New York City studio, while several local artists painted theirs directly on the walls of the courthouse.*

Perhaps the Intermodal Surface Transportation Efficiency Act (ISTEA) of 1992 will offer hope for the remainder of these bridges. During the next six years $151 billion will become available to states and local governments for infrastructure improvements. Of this amount, $3 billion has been set aside for "enhancements," a category that includes historic preservation.

Architect Paul Philippe Cret is responsible for two of the outstanding bridges built within large cities. The Calvert Street Bridge and the Klingle Valley Bridge in Washington, D.C., are examples of Cret's refined style.

CHURCHES
SURVEYED: 45

We now know that churches can be counted among the pioneers in the use of Art Deco in this country. Architect Francis Barry Byrne was responsible for both Chicago's 1922 Saint Thomas the Apostle church (which has hints of Deco) and the adjacent school, a more developed example done several years later. Sculptor Alfonso Iannelli collaborated with Byrne on these buildings. Their work together reached an Art Deco maturity in 1926 with Tulsa's Christ the King Church.

Another pioneer was Douglas Ellington, who designed several early Art Deco buildings in Asheville, North Carolina. His First Baptist Church was done in 1925, the same year as the Paris Exposition.

The Boston Avenue Methodist Church in Tulsa can be termed a *Gesamtkunstwerk*, or unified work of art. Ada Robinson, although a Quaker, carefully designed sculpture, stained glass, and other decorative elements to incorporate imagery that would have symbolic meaning for the congregation. Her student, Bruce Goff, was the architect of record.

The two other "must-see" churches are by architect Henry J. McGill: Shrine of the Little Flower in Royal Oak, Michigan, and Church of the Most Precious Blood, Queens, New York.

CITY HALLS
SURVEYED: 20

Several cities with rapidly growing populations constructed new, larger government buildings to accommodate growing staffs. Two of the earliest were in Los Angeles and Asheville, North Carolina, in 1926.

One of the best is in Buffalo, New York. Constructed in 1929–1931, it is lavishly ornamented with art and stained glass, including an entry-portico frieze by Albert T. Stewart; sculptures by René Paul Chambellan and Bryant Baker; murals by William de Leftwich Dodge; and vaulted-lobby ceiling tile by the Rafael Guastavino

Company. The massing is a textbook example of symmetrical, stepped-back Skyscraper Style as promoted by Hugh Ferris in his book *The Metropolis of Tomorrow*.

Also notable are the municipal buildings in Kansas City, Oklahoma City, and Saint Paul. Both Kansas City's and Oklahoma City's are parts of civic-center skyscraper complexes. Kansas City's city council chambers are on the twenty-sixth floor. Saint Paul's skyscraper is a combined city/country building (see Courthouses).

The aluminum metalwork on the city hall at Fort Worth, Texas, makes it noteworthy, as do the Gladding, McBean Company tile decorations on the government center in Santa Monica, California. The most quaint and incongruous Streamline Moderne city hall is in Nevada City, a small California mountain town where the era of the Gold Rush is largely preserved.

CLUBS
SURVEYED: 12

Many clubs, if they have remained private organizations, are difficult to see, so we often know them only by their exteriors. Those that have been adaptively reused are easier to view, but the interiors often have been altered, if not destroyed.

The best remaining example, still serving its original purpose with interiors intact, is the Exchange Club (now City Club) on the tenth and eleventh floors of San Francisco's Stock Exchange.

Walter Chrysler's Cloud Club in the oddly shaped rooms at the top of the Chrysler Building is not in regular use. The Art Deco Society of New York has gained access to it from time to time and fortunately it has remained fairly intact.

An adaptive reuse worthy of mention is the former Women's City Club in Saint Paul (now the Minnesota Museum of Art). Its small-scale Moderne design is a wonderful contrast to the imposing Ramsey County Courthouse on

Shrine of the Little Flower Church and Tower, 2123 Roseland Avenue at North Woodward and 12 Mile Road, Royal Oak, Michigan. ARCHITECT: Henry J. McGill; Sculptor: René Paul Chambellan, 1927. Father Charles Coughlin, a fiery 1920s radio evangelist in Detroit, built one of the nation's handsomest Art Deco churches, with a façade boasting fine sculpture. The shrine's main feature is an impressive tower with a twenty-eight-foot-tall Christ on the Cross at its top. The tower was built in 1929 to create a symbol that would sustain fundraising efforts throughout the Great Depression. The large sanctuary was completed in 1933.

the opposite corner. Many original interior details were retained when it became a museum. It possesses sweeping views of the Mississippi River. The museum now counts the Paul Manship archive among its treasures.

COURTHOUSES
SURVEYED: 42

Many courthouses were funded, built, and embellished by one of the many Depression-era New Deal programs instituted by Franklin Delano Roosevelt. The majority are county courthouses, most in Stripped Classic design, as this style lent itself to symbolizing law, order, and institutional stability. Most imposing is the twelve-story Bronx County Courthouse that occupies an entire city block.

The Chicago firm of Holabird & Root did three of the best courthouses. They are the Jefferson County in Birmingham, Alabama, the Racine County, Wisconsin, and the showplace of them all, the Ramsey County in Saint Paul. Kansas City has not one but three Art Deco buildings in its civic center. The Jackson County building is the largest at twenty-three stories. Next is the nine-story Municipal Court followed by the four-story Juvenile and Police Courts.

As is the case in many cities, Kansas City also incorporated federal courts within its Art Deco post office. These are surveyed under the U.S. Post Office category below.

Fort Worth was lucky enough to receive funding for separate post office and U.S. Federal Courthouse facilities. The court building, restored in 1990, is of note due to the involvement of Paul Philippe Cret in its design.

Well outside the Stripped Classic tradition is the Cochise County Courthouse in Bisbee, Arizona. Its architect used regional imagery of the Wild West as a basis for his design in this copper-mining boomtown.

Louisiana constructed nineteen parish courthouses during the period, most emulating the look of the magnificent state capitol, with decorative references to the state's flora, fauna, and industries. One of the best is the Iberia Parish Courthouse in New Iberia that includes a stylized brushed-aluminum pelican, the state bird.

DAMS
SURVEYED: 7

Dams were the engineering feats of the 1930s, made possible by modern technology. They are examples of collaboration between engineer and architect. Best known and most spectacular is Boulder Dam (now Hoover Dam), dubbed the "Eighth Wonder of the World" when it was built. Due to its importance and isolated location, we gave it a chapter of its own.

We classify dams as Art Deco for several reasons—when architects used geometric forms of the style, blowing them up to monumental proportions; or when their enormous concrete surfaces were enlivened by slight variations ("banding") in the color of the concrete, a technique first used in Art Deco skyscrapers by varying the color of the brick; or when large-scale auxiliary components—bridges, approaches, overlooks, gantry cranes, intake towers, locks, power turbines and machinery—give the projects a futuristic Machine Age look.

Many dams were projects of the Tennessee Valley Authority (TVA), a New Deal project established by President Roosevelt in 1933. Roland Wank, who earlier worked on the Cincinnati Union Terminal for the firm of Fellheimer and Wagner, became the chief architect for the TVA. Two of his many designs are the Hiwassee Dam in North Carolina and the Norris Dam in Tennessee.

DINERS
SURVEYED: 19

Once found from one end of the country to the other, many diners died when the federal interstate system killed traffic on the state and U.S. routes where they were often located. Others were supplanted by fast-food outlets. Thus, not many are found operating in their original locations. Luckily, a number of diners have been relocated to areas more heavily traveled. A good example is the former Olympic Diner from Wilkes-Barre, Pennsylvania, which is now the 11th Street Diner in Miami Beach's Art Deco Historic District. As is often the case, the seating capacity was expanded to make it economically viable. In historic Savannah, Georgia, Richard Rowan's School of Art and Design moved and restored two diners for use as campus dining facilities.

Favorites we found in our travels are Mickey's in Saint Paul and the Empire Diner in Manhattan, the latter unique for its elegant atmosphere with live music emanating from a piano that was somehow squeezed in.

Butler Mansion (Kragie/Newell Advertising), 2633 Fleur Drive, Des Moines, Iowa. ARCHITECT: *George Kraetsch for Kraetsch & Kraetsch, 1936; Renovation architect: Doug Wells for Wells, Woodburn & O'Neil, 1988. This Bauhaus-style home was the General Electric House of the Future, a multilevel 13,000-square-foot house, with steel-reinforced concrete, cylindrical third-floor tower, observation deck, and nautical deck railing. Billed as fire-proof, earthquake-proof, termite-proof, and tornado-proof, it included garbage disposal, air conditioner, and electric garage door. The mansion is listed in the National Register.*

EXPOSITION & WORLD'S FAIR SITES SURVEYED: 32

Expositions were important purveyors of the Art Deco style to the masses, serving as showcases for the newest industrially designed products. By adopting Streamline Moderne as the style for the majority of the pavilions, virtually all 1930s fairs played an important role in popularizing the style.

Leading architects and industrial designers of the day created striking pavilions for both the fairs' governing bodies and the participating corporations. This fantastic, bigger-than-life architecture meant to captivate, entertain, and leave a lasting impression on the public Unfortunately, few of these buildings survive, as all but one of the fair sites were cleared and reused at the end of their runs.

Here are the major Art Deco expositions and an account of their surviving architecture:

Sesqui-Centennial Exposition, Philadelphia, 1926
Entrance gates were twenty-five-foot-tall pylons entitled "Heralds of the New Dawn," reminiscent of the *Porte de*

Honneur gate at the 1925 Paris Exposition. Nothing survives.

Century of Progress Exposition, Chicago, 1933
Six futuristic houses were floated across Lake Michigan on a barge at the close of this fair, and they now comprise the Beverly Shores/Century of Progress Architectural District at the Indiana Dunes National Lakeshore.

California Pacific International Exposition (CPIE), San Diego, 1935
The Ford Pavilion, a unique auto-exhibition building, and the ship-prowed Palace of Electricity and Varied Industries still are used as a museum and a gymnasium, respectively, in Balboa Park.

Texas Centennial Exposition, Dallas, 1936
Because it is the only entire exposition to remain intact, this provides a thrilling step back in time. (See the Dallas–Fort Worth chapter.)

Great Lakes Exposition, Cleveland, 1937
Cleveland's biggest moment in the Art Deco limelight. Streamline Moderne pylons marked the entrance to the fair. Nothing survives.

Golden Gate International Exposition, San Francisco, 1939
Cast-concrete sculptures from the Fountain of Western Waters and fragmentary ceramic elements of the Gladding, McBean Company's Pacific Basin Fountain are all that remain outside the Pan-Am Clipper Air Terminal that served Treasure Island during the fair. The terminal houses the Navy's Treasure Island Museum, now mostly military related, although a section is devoted to the exposition.

World of Tomorrow, New York World's Fair, 1939
This was the fair designed to show the way to a brighter, better future. Only two structures survive from this epic fair: the former New York Pavilion now houses the Queens Museum. On display here is an updated version of the fair's

Ford Pavilion (Aero-Space Museum), *California-Pacific International Exposition, Palisades Area, Balboa Park, San Diego, California.* ARCHITECT: *Walter Dorwin Teague, 1935. Teague, America's master industrial designer, created this demonstration Ford factory to resemble engine parts, with skylights over the assembly lines and blue neon stripping outside. This is a rare example of an exposition pavilion that was* not *demolished after the fair closed. A "V-8" fountain is visible in the center courtyard. (Photograph courtesy the San Diego Historical Society, Ticor Collection)*

giant "Panorama of the City" with 835,000 of New York's buildings in miniature.

The other survivor of the 1939 fair has an odd history. The Belgian Pavilion was designed by Victor Bourgeois and Leo Stijen under supervision of Henry van der Velde. At the fair's close in 1940 it was carefully disassembled and prepared for shipment to Belgium. The outbreak of World War II interfered with these plans, so the Belgian government gave the building to Virginia Union University in Richmond,

Veterans Hospital, 4150 Clement Street, San Francisco, California. ARCHITECT: Veterans Administration Staff, with Treasury Department Supervising Architect, 1934. Art Deco projects were often built by the government during the Great Depression. Many cities had veterans hospitals, but few were as imposing as this example or had its appealing ocean view. The main hospital building has a dominant central tower and many setback sections contributing to an overall character and complexity that later buildings would lack. The surrounding campus has many additional small buildings for staff and physical support functions, all designed in the same style. Later additions, however, have been considerably less compatible with the original design. (Photograph courtesy Historic Preservation Office, Department of Veterans Affairs)

Lobby Letterbox, 29 Broadway Building, 29 Broadway at Morris Street and Trinity Place, New York City. ARCHITECT: John Sloan and Markoe T. Robertson, 1930. Here is a tribute to form and function in cast aluminum. Public confidence in the U.S. Postal Service undoubtedly was bolstered by the idea that planes and trains would certainly speed the mail. Similar letterboxes are common in Art Deco office buildings.

Advertisement for ALCOA, Fortune *magazine, January, 1935. This advertisement for the Aluminum Company of America extolls the wonders of aluminum, for it announces the inauguration of Union Pacific's second all-aluminum six-car train, which crossed the U.S.A. in just under fifty-seven hours, thus beating the previous record by fourteen and a half hours. Cheaper and lighter than steel, aluminum quickly became a metal of choice for Art Deco architects and designers.*

where it stands today. The survival of these buildings is remarkable because the site was reused for the 1964 New York World's Fair. Most structures from that fair have also been demolished. At the center of the fairground today is the 1964 Unisphere Globe, right on the spot where the legendary 1939 Trylon and Perisphere once mesmerized millions. The 1939 New York World's Fair marked the end of the Art Deco glory days. By 1940, several countries had withdrawn as their home soil was consumed by the flames of war. Attendance at the fair was down and it operated at a loss. Building for a better future was put on hold.

FACTORIES
SURVEYED: 17

Small manufacturing companies often used the clean lines of the Moderne in their factories to signify they were up-to-date. Many of these still can be found in out-of-the-way industrial sections, where they often have fallen on hard times. Many attempt to rise above the ordinary by using a vertical tower or pylon over the main entrance, or by adding interest with glass block. Others are so nondescript that we coined the term "Plain Jane Deco" to identify them.

FILLING STATIONS
20,000 BUILT; FEW SURVIVING

Automobile travel boomed in the 1930s and competition between oil companies became fierce. The United States was blanketed with stations, each trying to capture the motorist's eye and business. Those in the Art Deco class ranged from Zigzag to Nautical, and from Pueblo Deco to Fantasy. One station, however, was so well designed that it captured the market, allowing the Texas Oil Company—Texaco—to become the greatest patron of Art Deco. Texaco hired noted industrial designer Walter Dorwin Teague to develop prototype stations to fit a variety of locations. Teague produced a streamlined design that could be mass produced. The elements could be easily reconfigured to create five variations, making the station adaptable to any site or market. In order to establish the company's identity coast to coast, Teague specified clean white enamel panels with a simple band of red Texaco stars. To build market share, Teague specified tile-lined, easily cleaned indoor restrooms—an unheard-of luxury along most highways, and a feature that proved irresistible to weary customers.

The success of the stations was immediate. According to records in the Texaco archives, over 10,000 of these Teague-designed stations were built from 1934 until 1960, when they were phased out. Once found everywhere, they are now an endangered species.

FILM INDUSTRY BUILDINGS
SURVEYED: 22

The importance of distributing the products of Hollywood grew as movie theaters were constructed in even the smallest towns. Central distribution centers were built in larger cities; usually they were Art Deco. Many used glass block, shiny metal canopies, and light sconces at the street entrance with the studio's nameplate prominently above the door. The flagship Art Deco film industry building was Howard Hughes's Multi-Color Lab in Los Angeles. This building, with its elegant gates, railings, lighting, and etched glass, was saved and restored when a new owner purchased the building in the 1980s.

FIRE HOUSES
SURVEYED: 16

The best we saw was the Central Fire Station in Fort Worth, Texas, designed by Hermann Koeppe, architect of many of the city's Art Deco treasures. Canvas fire hoses were dried by hanging them from the tall towers that once were part of all firehouses. Indianapolis may hold a record with its four

firehouses built by the WPA, some now in danger of demolition. Also fire-related is the wonderful Tulsa Fire Alarm Company with its terra-cotta imagery of fire fighters and fire-breathing dragons. And finally, one listed on the National Register is the Coney Island Fire Pumping Station.

FOUNTAINS AND ESPLANADES
SURVEYED: 9

The most famous Art Deco fountain has to be Paul Manship's *Prometheus*, which presides over the skating rink at New York's Rockefeller Center. This gilt-bronze demigod, who brought fire and the arts to mankind, has been seen by millions of people over the years. Another notable example is the 1937 *Fountain of the Pioneers* in Michigan, at Kalamazoo's Bronson Park, across from the city hall. This creation by Alfonso Iannelli could be mistaken for the work of Frank Lloyd Wright, because there is a strong resemblance between the work of these two artists, ever since their famed collaboration at Chicago's 1914 Midway Gardens.

Texaco Oil Company filling station. ARCHITECT: *Walter Dorwin Teague, 1936. In 1934, Teague won a contract to standardize the design of the Texas Oil Company's service stations. This is one of the 10,000 Texaco stations that resulted from the commission. This ubiquitous building may well be the best-known Art Deco design in the U.S.A. Teague used marketing research to establish the essential features of his design. Among innovations he pioneered were the front office with the spacious window display space. Undoubtedly, he attracted new customers with the "clean restrooms" concept that was widely advertised. He provided Texaco with five basic designs, "A" through "E," for different lot sizes and configurations. The designs were used well into the 1960s. Pictured here is the "A" design. (Photograph courtesy Texaco Inc.)*

Gulf Refining Company filling station (illustration in Fortune *magazine), Pittsburgh, Pennsylvania, c. 1930. Pittsburgh-based Gulf used Art Deco styling in its gas station of the future. This ad praises the design as the ". . . most complete and luxurious . . . anywhere in America. Its beauty is unusual . . . . . an indication of what tomorrow may bring. . . ." Most gas companies jumped on the bandwagon and built stations using Art Deco design. While Gulf used a French zigzag approach in this example, Texaco built thousands of stations in an even more popular design by Walter Dorwin Teague.*

27

FRATERNAL ORGANIZATIONS
SURVEYED: 18

Fraternal organizations often aligned themselves with the exoticism of ancient cultures in the Far East and Egypt. Since Art Deco borrowed elements from the same sources, early 1920s fraternal buildings have strong links with Art Deco. By the 1930s many had graduated to the Stripped Classical style. One adaptive reuse is worth mentioning here. The Medinah Club in Chicago is now a Hotel Inter-Continental, and its proto-Deco Assyrian decorations can be viewed close up. The architect, Walter Ahlschlager, progressed from this to the French Art Deco he used for Cincinnati's Netherland Plaza Hotel.

GREYHOUND BUS TERMINALS
SURVEYED: 26

Greyhound assumed an image of efficiency and speed by adopting Streamline Moderne as its company image. The firm built a network of terminals to serve their streamlined buses criss-crossing the country. Architect W.S. Arrasmith of the Louisville firm of Wischmeyer, Arrasmith & Elswick designed many of these. Largest and most sophisticated of his designs is the Washington, D.C., terminal, which no longer serves buses, but has been preserved intact in its new function as the lobby of a modern high rise. Other notable examples are in Evansville, Indiana, and Columbia, South Carolina.

HOSPITALS
SURVEYED: 25

The U.S. Government was responsible for several of the best Art Deco hospital complexes. Each has a large central stepped-back building surrounded by a group of smaller support buildings. We found three, two of which use French Zigzag decorative elements: The U.S. Marine Hospital on New York's Staten Island and the Veterans Administration Hospital in San Francisco; the third, Seattle's U.S. Marine Hospital, is more streamlined. The U.S. Naval Hospital in Philadelphia broke the multibuilding mold by combining all activities under the roof of a huge thirteen-story tower, but that was quickly outgrown and the site now is crammed with new additions.

The most unusual of these buildings must be the Albuquerque Indian Hospital, which was designed in the Pueblo Deco style. Familiar American Indian motifs were employed to allay fear of seeking medical treatment in such a place.

Greyhound Bus Terminal, 102 Northwest 3rd Street, Evansville, Indiana. ARCHITECT: W. S. Arrasmith for Wischmeyer, Arrasmith & Elswick, 1938. Greyhound built a nationwide motor-transportation network during the Machine Age that was unprecedented. Many of their terminals were designed by this Louisville firm. The familiar streamlined Art Deco look in city after city helped give Greyhound a popular up-to-date identity. The buses also were streamlined, further reinforcing the image of speed and efficiency.

28

HOTELS
SURVEYED: 132

The many small hotels in Miami Beach's famous Art Deco Historic District helped put the hotel category in the Top Five. Preservationists struggled for years to promote these Deco Delights, but it was only after the producers of the popular "Miami Vice" television program "discovered" them that they gained international fame. A stay in the Deco District is a must for anyone interested in Art Deco or design history.

Outside of Miami Beach, four hotels reign when it comes to Art Deco elegance: the Waldorf-Astoria, New York; the OMNI Netherland Plaza, Cincinnati; the Arizona Biltmore, Phoenix; and the Saint James Club, Los Angeles. Their splendor is so lavish that entire books could be written on each, for they're the Tops.

Other hotels where one still can catch the spirit of the times are: the Shangri-La, Santa Monica, California; Carlyle Suites, Washington, D.C.; Hotel Edison, New York; and Lake Merritt Hotel, Oakland.

LIBRARIES
SURVEYED: 20

Washington, D.C., has two outstanding examples in this category. The Folger Shakespeare Library stands as the supreme example of a Stripped Classic façade. Appropriately enough, it was designed by the style's greatest proponent, Paul Philippe Cret. The Library of Congress Annex, on the other hand, is known for its lavish interiors. Also of note is the Indiana State Library in Indianapolis, a city that boasts a 1919 Paul Philippe Cret Neo-Classical public library. Chicago's Loyola University has the little-seen Cudahy Library with original interiors and a wonderful John Norton mural. Miami Beach's Bass Museum—one of the best examples of Tropical Deco—originally was a public library. And finally, the Public Library in Lake Forest, Illinois, has an astonishing Art Deco interior hidden behind a Neo-Georgian façade.

Time and the Fates of Man *sundial at Brookgreen Gardens*, *1931 Brookgreen Gardens Drive, Murrells Inlet, Georgetown County, South Carolina. Sculptor: Paul Manship, 1939. Brookgreen Gardens contains the largest collection of Art Deco–era sculptures in the country. The Manship sundial is a bronze cast of the one created for the center court of the fabled 1939 New York World's Fair, where it was placed beside the signature landmarks the Trylon and Perisphere. This work is almost twelve feet high and eleven feet long. The sculpture collection includes works by such artists as Bohland, Jennewein, Lachaise, Nadelman, the Piccirillis, Tennant, and many others. (Photograph by Gurdon L. Tarbox, Jr. courtesy Brookgreen Gardens)*

LODGES
SURVEYED: 3

On first encounter, what we term Rustic-Deco seems an incongruity. Here in the U.S.A. we associate Art Deco with mass production and the Machine Age. However, Art Deco's origin was in the craftsmanship of the European workshops. Even the products of the famed Bauhaus were handmade. With this in mind, hand-carved chairs sporting stylized buffaloes or intricate geometric lighting fixtures of hand-forged iron can be seen in perspective and given a place within the style. Gilbert Stanley Underwood, architect for both the Ahwahnee Hotel (Yosemite National Forest, California) and Timberline Lodge (Mount Hood, Oregon), collaborated with accomplished artists on both projects. A third example is the Naniboujou Lodge on Lake Superior in Minnesota.

MATERIALS: VITROLITE
SURVEYED: 3

Finding intact interiors or exteriors in original Vitrolite or Carrara Glass is getting increasingly difficult. The Forum Cafeteria in Minneapolis is by far the most impressive example, with nearly every square inch of wall space sheathed with Vitrolite Structural Glass panels. The entrance lobbies in the Hoover Dam are lined in beautiful Vitrolite Structural Glass sheets. And we even found a Chicago bungalow, belonging to our friend Peter Miller, former manager of the Chicago Theatre, where the entire kitchen and all baths were paneled in Vitrolite in an Art Deco updating. When we told our Miami Beach friend Richard Hoberman, past chairman of the Miami Design Preservation League, about this Vitrolite find, he was so inspired he located nearly impossible stocks of virgin Vitrolite sheets and had his own kitchen completely made over in this unique decorative-glass material. For kitchens and restaurants it is perfect— easy to clean and always bright and shining. (See also the Minneapolis chapter.)

MARTS AND EXCHANGES
SURVEYED: 3

The Merchandise Mart in Chicago, the largest retail building in the world, and the Western Furniture Exchange in San Francisco fall into this category. Each of these has lavish decorations and fixtures that have been preserved during recent adaptive reuses.

MEDICAL/DENTAL BUILDINGS
SURVEYED: 17

Several large buildings were constructed in downtown areas to capture the health-care market by combining doctors, dentists, labs, and other related businesses under one roof. The one with the best Art Deco medical imagery, including the caduceus in relief on the façade, is Atlanta's W. W. Orr building. In 1928, architect Timothy Pflueger designed the Four Fifty Sutter Medical-Dental Building in San Francisco. The unusual Mayan-inspired geometric decorations covering the entrance and spandrels give the building an immediate identity. Less noticeable from the street are the rounded bay windows running up the corners of the thirty-story building, giving the offices wonderful views and making this the first skyscraper that can be called Streamline Moderne.

MEMORIALS/MONUMENTS
SURVEYED: 9

In 1921 H. Van Buren Magonigle, winner of a national competition, designed the Liberty Memorial in Kansas City. A pair of monumental Egypto-Deco sphinxes, Memory and Future, guard the base of the 217-foot Torch of Liberty completed in 1926. A very early example of Art Deco, the memorial became even more so when large relief panels, sculpted steps, and a fountain were added between 1926 and 1933. Washington, D.C., city of monuments and memorials, has two worth special mention: the 1931 Titanic Memorial by Lincoln Memorial architect Henry Bacon, with sculpture by Gertrude Vanderbilt Whitney, is in a style that has been called Greco-Deco; and the 1941 Guglielmo Marconi Memorial, with a bronze sculpture of a nude woman speeding through the clouds above a smaller bust of Marconi, was a collaborative effort by Joseph Freedlander and Attilio Piccirilli.

MILITARY BUILDINGS
SURVEYED: 10

Most common in this category are National Guard Armories, which often have outlived their original purpose. Several, such as the Minneapolis Armory, are in danger of demolition. The West Palm Beach, Florida, Armory was converted into an Art Center, after a concerted effort by Sharon Koskoff and the Art Deco Society of the Palm Beaches. One of San Francisco's most charming small-scale buildings also is endangered. Built in 1941 as the U.S.O. Hospitality House, it now sits on a coveted site in the Civic Center. Activists are trying to convince the city it should be moved to a park where it could serve in some new capacity.

MORTUARIES/CEMETERIES
SURVEYED: 11

The outstanding cemetery is the National Memorial Park in Falls Church, Virginia, which has a large number of Art Deco mausoleums and memorial statues. Another excellent example of funerary Art Deco is Memorial Park Mausoleum in

Vitrolite Promotional Brochure, L-O-F Glass Company, Toledo, Ohio, c. 1930. Libbey-Owens-Ford manufactured panels of its Vitrolite Structural Glass in every color of the rainbow. This is a sample page from one of the company's brochures. The other big glass company, Pittsburgh Plate Glass (PPG), made a similar product called Carrara Glass.

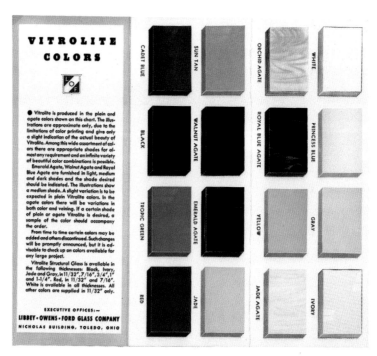

Niagara Hudson Building (Niagara Mohawk), 300 Erie Boulevard West, Syracuse, New York. ARCHITECT: Clayton B. Frye and Albert A. Rumschik for Bley & Lyman, with Melvin L. King, 1930. "Gas" is one of four Vitrolite panels in the lobby. The subject of each panel pertains to electricity. Natural gas was used to make steam for the generators' turbines. These images were produced by sandblasting and heat-fusing colors into the glass panels. The other panels are "Illumination," "Generation," and "Transmission."

Skokie, Illinois. Its most striking feature is a tiered-glass ceiling, somewhat like an Art Deco wedding cake. Also, a 130-foot mausoleum built for William Wrigley, Jr., on his California island retreat, Santa Catalina, is an outstanding example. The Wrigley family moved his body to the mainland long ago, but the monument is still in place at the head of Avalon Canyon. The island is also home to the Avalon Casino (see the Los Angeles chapter).

MOTELS
SURVEYED: 3

Coral Court Motel in suburban Saint Louis uses streamlined design with eye-catching glass block. Each bungalow provides two separate "cabins" with attached garages.

MUSEUMS
SURVEYED: 11

Only a few museums have been bold enough to commission Art Deco edifices to house their collections. The front façade of the elegant Norton Gallery of Art in West Palm Beach is adorned with a pair of Paul Manship bronzes, *Diana* and *Actaeon*. The Art Museum in Seattle's Volunteer Park is

beautifully proportioned and features French-style metalwork. The Panhandle Plains Historical Society Museum, off the beaten path in Canyon, Texas, is an excellent example of Pueblo Deco architecture and perfectly suits the museum's collection. Our favorite is the Bass Museum (formerly the Public Library) by Russell T. Pancoast in Miami Beach.

MOVIE THEATERS
SURVEYED: 217

It was undoubtedly through the enchanted kingdom of the cinema that Art Deco was most popularized across the U.S.A. Movie-set designers imprinted the style in the minds of the public as the embodiment of both sophistication and glamour. Theater owners and their architects used the sleekness and richness of Art Deco to lure patrons into a fantasy world of escape. As awareness of the style began to reawaken in the 1970s, it was often in association with movies that the term "Art Deco" was first heard by many. Fred and Ginger, Busby Berkeley, *Grand Hotel*, Radio City Music Hall—we were told that these were Art Deco. If they were, then our local theaters—the Warners, the Lakes, the Towers—seemed custom-made to go with them. Today, many of our great movie theaters have become performing-arts centers. Two are Deco Meccas to which a pilgrimage is mandatory: Radio City Music Hall in New York and the Oakland Paramount. Of the architectural firms that specialized in the style, several must be mentioned: John Eberson, Liebenberg and Kaplan, Rapp and Rapp, Thomas Lamb, and S. Charles Lee.

OPERA HOUSES
SURVEYED: 2

Chicago and Saint Louis have the two main examples: The Civic Opera House in Chicago has fine interior detailing but is fairly restrained. The Kiel Opera House in Saint Louis makes a much stronger statement. Both have excellent Art Deco lighting fixtures, plaster detailing, and metalwork.

PUBLISHING BUILDINGS
SURVEYED: 23

Many newspapers were making so much money and growing so fast by 1929 that they were forced to consider new homes. Many publishers knew that a building's reliefs, murals, and sculpture could serve a higher purpose, just as they believed that their newspapers did. They wanted decorations that not only looked handsome but also stood for something or told a story. This heroic purpose (often found in govern-

Mountain Lake Singing Tower (Bok Tower Gardens), U.S. 27 at State Road 60, Lake Wales, Florida (3 miles north). ARCHITECT: *Milton B. Medary; Landscape: Frederick Law Olmstead, Jr.; Metalwork: Samuel Yellin; Sculptor: Lee Lawrie, 1927. The inspirational Bok Singing Tower is set in a 140-acre garden designed by Frederick Law Olmstead, Jr., in the heart of Florida's orange country. Its silhouette resembles a Gothic tower, but a closer look reveals Tropical Deco detailing, especially in Lawrie's carvings. Built on a 300-foot hill, the highest elevation for miles, the tower houses a splendid ("singing") carillon that is played daily. (Photograph courtesy Bok Tower Gardens)*

Mountain Lake Singing Tower (Bok Tower Gardens), U.S. 27 at State Road 60, Lake Wales, Florida (3 miles north). ARCHITECT: *Milton B. Medary; Landscape: Frederick Law Olmstead, Jr.; Metalwork: Samuel Yellin; Sculptor: Lee Lawrie, 1927. Lawrie's Young Man Watering Plants is an appropriate theme for this Florida garden oasis. The grillwork is carved from gray Georgia marble. The site is a National Register Landmark with its majestic fifty-seven-bell carillon in a 205-foot Gothic-Deco tower. (Photograph by Charlene W. Johnston, courtesy Bok Tower Gardens)*

ment buildings too) is what set these buildings apart, giving them a special place in the public's mind. The *Cincinnati Times-Star* has a tower surmounted by figures representing four essentials of a newspaper: Truth, Patriotism, Progress, and Speed. The building of the now-defunct *Chicago Daily News* illustrates its intended purpose via three enormous John Norton ceiling murals: Gathering, Printing, and Transporting the News. Two examples of the work of industrial architect Albert Kahn can be seen in *The Detroit Free Press* building of 1923 (Gothic, but with the symmetry and massing of Art Deco) and *The New York Times's* 1929 Brooklyn printing plant, with its large factory-style windows allowing passers-by to observe the presses at work. A newspaper's mandate to bring home the news from all over the world is symbolized by the massive globes dominating the lobbies of the *Los Angeles Times* and *New York Daily News*. The latter, designed by Raymond Hood, is the most honored building in this class, having gained National Landmark status in 1989.

RECREATION CENTERS
SURVEYED: 15

Many amusement parks in the 1930s added streamlined pavilions and rides, a number of them outlined with brightly colored neon. The best park, however, is Playland in Rye, New York, which dates from 1927. The architects, Walker & Gillette, chose the French Zigzag style for the buildings, not only to amuse, but also to lure prospective residents to this suburban county. The pavilions flanking the lushly landscaped mall and the landmark Music Tower have been well maintained through the years by Westchester County. The park was placed on the National Register in 1984. Also listed on

Coral Court Motel, 1 mile southwest of Saint Louis on Watson Road (old U.S. Route 66), Marlborough, Missouri. ARCHITECT: Adolph L. Struebig, 1941. Duplex Moderne cabin units like this example are scattered over an eight-and-one-half-acre wooded lot near Saint Louis. Finished in yellow glazed tile with burgundy trim, each unit has large curving expanses of glass block and its own remote-control garage door with interior entry, providing complete privacy and earning it the sobriquet "Saint Louis's Little Sin." (Photograph by Bob Barrett)

the National Register is the Glen Echo Amusement Park in Glen Echo, Maryland.

One great amusement park now lost is Chicago's Midway Gardens, designed by Frank Lloyd Wright and with sculpture by Alfonso Iannelli, who had done early theater posters that helped carry Abstractionism and Cubism into advertising and architecture. Wright had always been engineering-minded; he envisioned systems and techniques for building that didn't quite exist yet. Much like Leonardo da Vinci's unbuilt helicopter, Wright's buildings looked to the future for their realization. In the "Sprites" that were designed by Wright and sculpted by Iannelli in 1914, both men were striving to bring delight and playfulness to the park. Collector Mitchell Wolfson, Jr., acquired two of these Midway Gardens sprites for his Wolfsonian Foundation museum in Miami Beach. Several others have found a home in the gardens of the well-known Arizona Biltmore in Phoenix.

This category wouldn't be complete without mentioning a modern-day wonder that uses Art Deco as a signature statement. The Disney-MGM theme park at Orlando not

Tower Theater (1,206 seats), 2508 Land Park (now 16th Street and Broadway), Sacramento, California. ARCHITECT: William David, 1938. Sacramento was blessed with several wonderful Art Deco theaters. The Esquire and Crest were downtown near the capitol on the K Street Mall. This one, the Tower, neon-embellished at twilight, is a neighborhood theater just off Interstate 80. Partly to preserve the theaters, an Art Deco Society was established here in 1991.

Lake Theater (1,464 seats), 1020 Lake Street, Oak Park, Illinois. ARCHITECT: Thomas W. Lamb, 1936. Dramatically lit at night, this splendid movie house is by one of America's greatest theater architects. The round lower lobby features terrazzo in geometric interlocking circular patterns. This is just one of many Art Deco buildings on the main street of this city, which is better known for Frank Lloyd Wright's work, including his home and studio, Unity Temple, and many private residences.

Marianne Theater (640 seats), 611 Fairfield Avenue, Bellevue, Kentucky. ARCHITECT: Unknown, c. 1942. Capturing Hollywood's own Moderne look, this little movie house adds its own glamour to this Cincinnati suburb.

Marianne Theater, 611 Fairfield Avenue, Bellevue, Kentucky. Oil painting, 1992. Another view of this theater conveys the impact upon the surrounding streetscape of its brilliant glazed tile, terra-cotta brick, and flashy marquee. But this is not a photograph! Hyperrealist artist Davis Cone captures the excitement and glamour such a small theater can lend to the city by portraying it at twilight, when the marquee has just been lit and patrons have parked their cars nearby. Cone is well-known for his paintings of small-town Art Deco theaters across the U.S.A. (Photograph courtesy Laurie O'Steen)

only has re-created a version of the mostly destroyed, fire-charred Pan Pacific Auditorium as its entrance gates, but also features reproductions of scores of other Los Angeles Art Deco buildings along its Main Street. This design format is fitting, since Disney himself hired famed designer Kem Weber to create his original 1939 film studio and office in Burbank, California. The new Post-Modernist hotels and offices at Disney World, commissioned by Michael Eisner, incorporate many of the whimsical and artistic elements found in Art Deco. We might refer to this as Disney Deco.

RESIDENCES
SURVEYED: 145

Most research into Art Deco has been confined to the core of cities where buildings often are in danger of alteration or demolition. This has left residential architecture as unexplored territory. Even in Miami Beach, a city known for its Art Deco, almost no research has been done into the large number of Nautical and Moderne houses to be found in residential areas. For that reason, a bit more space will be devoted to this category here in hopes it will promote further investigation into this fertile area.

Many books have been written on the work of Frank Lloyd Wright, so we will merely mention those residences that stand out among the dozen or so we visited. Of his earlier works using his famed "textile block" construction, the Ennis, Freeman, Hollyhock, Millard, and Storer residences in the Los Angeles area are the most noteworthy. From the more Moderne period that followed, Fallingwater (now a museum) was built for department-store mogul Edgar Kaufmann, Sr., and Wingspread, the house built for Johnson Wax tycoon Herbert F. Johnson, now houses the Johnson Foundation. The outstanding private residence from this later period is Westhope in Tulsa, featuring wonderful stepped-glass atriums.

In the mansion category two stand out: George Kraetsch's 1937 Butler mansion in Des Moines, which recently was converted into an office for an advertising agency; and the little-known William Rankin villa in Louisiana, begun in 1938 by a "shady" state commissioner, but never completed due to his incarceration. Justin Wilson of cookbook fame recently purchased the property with the intention of completing the grand project.

The house that best captures the lavish, sophisticated style popularized in Deco-era films is actually the one a famed Hollywood set designer built for himself. In the Cedric Gibbons house in Santa Monica the designer employed all the tricks of his profession to create one of the most dramatic party settings in Hollywood.

Fore and Aft, a home on the intracoastal waterway in Palm Beach, is a textbook example of Nautical Moderne by architect Belford Shoumate. It bears a striking resemblance to the ocean liner set used in the revival of Cole Porter's musical *Anything Goes*. Saved from a planned remodeling, it was restored by its owner, socialite and serious preservationist Kirby Kooluris.

In Miami Beach architect Robert Law Weed designed the Eastman house, quite similar to his Florida Tropical Home in the 1933 Century of Progress Exposition in Chicago (now part of the Beverly Shores Historic District at Indiana Dunes park). The house included a massive Tropical

Vitrolite Promotional Brochure, L-O-F Glass Company, Toledo, Ohio, 1938. From the Libbey-Owens-Ford Vitrolite sample book comes this ad, "Restaurants That Win," showing three interiors and touting both Vitrolite and the lesser-known and shorter-lived product, Vitrolux. In the early 1920s, Vitrolite was an independent Chicago company. L-O-F acquired it during the Great Depression.

Playland Amusement Park, Music Tower, Playland Parkway, Rye, New York. ARCHITECT: Walker & Gillette, 1927. Rising above the bizarre and wacky attractions below is this central Music Tower set in the middle of the first Art Deco amusement park. Built by the Westchester County Parks Department, and still in operation, the original purpose of the 200-acre park was to lure new residents. According to the architects' careful plan, rows of structures symmetrically flank a wide central mall. The tower's role was to present a single musical program and thus avoid the cacophony and shrillness experienced in other parks. Playland was listed in the National Register in 1984. Walker & Gillette also designed the Fuller Building in Manhattan (see New York chapter).

Deco stone frieze in its entrance, neon ceiling-cove lights, glass-block walls, and an early laundry room with electric machines rather than washtubs. The Eastman house now is the winter residence of Art Deco collector Annella Brown, M.D. From this house, on a straight shot across the golf course, is the MacKenzie residence by Robert Fitch Smith. It has beautiful iron grillwork, glass-block walls, terraced roof decks, and two charming cottages for in-laws.

RESTAURANTS
SURVEYED: 45

Restaurants of the period used newly available materials to stress their immaculate cleanliness. Stainless steel, aluminum, glass block, enameled porcelain, and Carrara and Vitrolite structural glass were among the favorite materials. The best example in this category is the old Forum Cafeteria (now Mick's at the Forum) in Minneapolis. The Forum Cafeteria chain, based in Kansas City, used Vitrolite panels extensively in the interior of their restaurants, of which this may be the last one in existence.

ROADS
SURVEYED: 7

As with bridges, Art Deco roadways are very much in danger if they haven't already been modernized beyond recognition. Cincinnati's Columbia and Eastern Parkways are fairly intact with viaducts, retaining walls, stairs, and fences constructed of a textured cement. Also, the Merritt Parkway in Connecticut is an outstanding surviving example, but it is under seige by the Connecticut Highway Department, which wishes to make its unique, charming, and artistic bridges "safer" by destroying them. It is, after all, a Parkway—not an expressway. (More on this in the Boston chapter.)

SCHOOLS
SURVEYED: 84

In the 1920s and 1930s a great many public-school districts replaced crowded out-of-date schools with larger complexes containing classrooms, gymnasiums, and auditoriums. San Francisco takes top honors with five excellent examples: George Washington and Gompers High Schools, Roosevelt Junior High, and James Lick and Marina Middle Schools. Many Art Deco schools were built by the Federal job programs of the Depression. Outstanding examples are: Bloom High in Chicago Heights; Hollywood and Thomas Jefferson High Schools in Los Angeles; Berkeley High in California; Hermann Ridder and Joan of Arc Junior Highs in New York City; and Daniel Webster and Will Rogers High Schools in Tulsa. Also noteworthy is the school in Greenbelt, Maryland, the only one of three experimental communities to employ Art Deco styling. Two famous and influential schools of design also fall in this category: Cranbrook Academy's multi-building complex by Eliel Saarinen in Bloomfield Hills, Michigan, and New York's Beaux Arts Institute of Design, which features a beautiful Art Deco façade.

SHOPPING CENTERS
SURVEYED: 14

Shopping centers were a new building type made possible by the increasing use of the automobile. The flashiest is Los Angeles's ship-shaped Crossroads of the World. Atlanta's small Streamline Moderne–style Plaza Center with a movie theater as the star attraction has been well maintained over the years. Washington, D.C., and its suburbs had many examples, the best being the Silver Theater and Shopping Center in Silver Spring, Maryland. The center was designed by architect John Eberson, who is best known for the hundreds of theaters he designed in the Atmospheric and Streamline Moderne styles. The Silver Shopping Center is a rare example of his non-theater work and has been under threat of demolition since 1984. Richard Striner and the Art Deco Society of Washington have been trying valiantly to preserve this treasure by convincing developers and city officials that it should be preserved as part of a larger new complex.

STATE CAPITOLS
SURVEYED: 4

There were nineteen state capitols built in this century. The one in Lincoln, Nebraska, begun in 1919, was the first to use a skyscraper tower, a potent symbol of authority on the flat Nebraska plains. This work by Bertram Goodhue broke the mold for public buildings. It was neither Grecian nor Victorian. It was quite a shock, towering over low-rise Lincoln, and was visible for miles. American Indian themes were chosen for the bountiful sculpture and mosaics by Lee Lawrie and Hildreth Meiere, respectively.

The next skyscraper capitol to be built was the 1931 Louisiana State Capitol in Baton Rouge, designed by Weiss, Dreyfous & Seiferth. This capitol is surely the most colorful both architecturally and historically. While the architects owe a lot to Goodhue, they also have Paul Philippe Cret to thank. It was Cret who taught his Stripped Classic "Beaux Arts Modern" doctrine to a young University of Pennsylvania student named F. Julius Dreyfous. Cret's exhortation to budding architects not to abandon classic Greek and Roman proportions and details in their quest of the purity of Modernism undoubtedly led to Dreyfous's incorporation of a faux-Greek temple, designed by Lee Lawrie, at the apex of the Louisiana capitol's spire. It is best viewed from the 27th-floor observation deck below.

The Louisiana capitol was made possible by its legendary megalomaniac governor, then senator, Huey P. Long. The opulent building tried to be many things at once. It is filled with splendid work by many different artisans. Themes of Louisiana industry, agriculture, flora, and fauna are expressed in the sculpture and decorative details of this most

The fourth Art Deco capitol, in Salem, Oregon, was designed in 1936 by Francis Keally of New York, with Trowbridge & Livingston. Winning the competition against one hundred twenty-three other firms, their design featured an unusual "lantern top" in the center of a cylindrical atrium. A PWA project initiated after the old capitol burned, it was the last of the 20th-Century Modern statehouses to be built. While done on a smaller scale than the others, it has perfect classical proportions and fine details.

lavish of the Art Deco statehouses. It also is the tallest capitol, having thirty-four stories. Governor Long had the capitol built in a single year so he could go off to the Senate in Washington with his impressive statehouse complete. He was running for president against FDR when, in 1935, his career was cut short by an assassin's bullet —fired in the very Art Deco capitol he had built. The opulent tower instantly was converted into the world's largest monument. Long was buried in the capitol gardens. Standing on a pedestal over the grave is a statue of Long perpetually facing his beloved capitol.

Less flashy is the North Dakota capitol in Bismarck, designed in 1931 by Chicago's Holabird & Root. Functions of government and bureaucracy were divided, with the legislature's earth-hugging building connected to the tall office tower by a shared lobby.

STATE FAIRS
SURVEYED: 4

This category wasn't fully surveyed, as most fairgrounds are situated outside of large cities. An outstanding example is the exhibition building at the Tulsa State Fairgrounds with farm animals depicted in polychromed terra-cotta.

STORE: DEPARTMENT
SURVEYED: 45

Department stores were very influential in promoting Art Deco as a new style for the modern home. Many stores created window displays and organized model rooms and exhibits to showcase the style to the public. In Los Angeles,

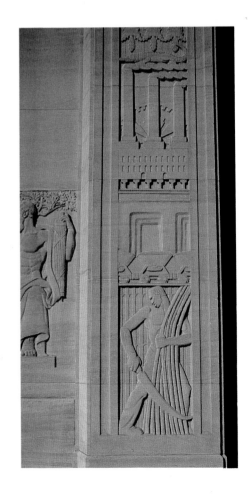

Nebraska State Capitol, *1445 K Street, Lincoln, Nebraska.* ARCHITECT: *Bertram Goodhue; Sculptor: Lee Lawrie; Mosaics: Hildreth Meiere, 1919. This is considered the most influential state capitol built in the twentieth century. Goodhue placed a classical dome atop a soaring streamlined tower, and removed most classical detail, thereby enunciating an exciting new stripped-clean Modernism. Lawrie, the capitol's sole sculptor, focused on Nebraskan themes and symbols of Native Americans. Construction of the capitol was not completed until 1932, eight years after Goodhue's death.*

Louisiana State Capitol, *1 State Capitol Drive, Baton Rouge, Louisiana.* ARCHITECT: *Weiss, Dreyfous & Seiferth, 1931. Louisiana's thirty-four-story capitol is the tallest in the U.S.A. It is topped by Lee Lawrie's classically inspired "civic temple" in Classic Moderne style. A popular twenty-seventh-floor observation deck overlooks the nearby Mississippi River, sugarcane fields, and a splendid twenty-seven-acre formal garden. A monument and grave for Louisiana's Senator Huey P. Long was added in the gardens after his assassination in the capitol's corridors. Long's determination and vision as governor enabled the capitol to be erected in a single year.*

Louisiana State Capitol, *1 State Capitol Drive, Baton Rouge, Louisiana.* ARCHITECT: *Weiss, Dreyfous & Seiferth; Sculptors: Lee Lawrie and Adolph A. Weinman, 1931. Low reliefs designed by Lawrie surround the main entrance. These celebrate Louisiana's people, parishes, and industries, which are represented by smokestacks, mining equipment, and a sugarcane cutter. Weinman and Lawrie were among the project's many sculptors. The fragment at left is an allegory on law, order, and justice by Weinman.*

Bullocks Wilshire is the outstanding example built in the style, and one of the few that hasn't been "updated" over the years. The architect and designers skillfully integrated in the building many of the various phases of Art Deco, from French, to Frank Lloyd Wright, to the strictly Moderne. Other stores worthy of mention are Burdines in Miami, Shillito's in Cincinnati, and Bloomingdale's and Macy's in New York. The outstanding landmark Rosenberg's in Santa Rosa, California, is abandoned and in danger of demolition.

STORE: SEARS
SURVEYED: 14

Sears, Roebuck & Company pioneered the art of mail-order sales and became tremendously successful. After only a brief stay in Minneapolis the headquarters was moved to more centrally located Chicago, where it remains to this day. As the company grew and much of the population shifted to the cities, Sears began opening retail stores. In the late 1920s, Sears commissioned the Chicago firm of Nimmons, Carr & Wright to design a number of stores and distribution centers around the country. The firm chose to use a large tower with a vertical illuminated Sears sign in order to give the stores an identity, the store thus becoming a huge bill-board. Decorative details were done in the French Zigzag style. Only a few of these rarities remain today. Among the largest is Boston's now-closed sprawling nine-story mail-order distribution center with its slender fifteen-story tower. Another beautiful example is on Biscayne Boulevard in Miami. Sears abandoned the Biscayne Boulevard store and it has been crumbling ever since. This tale is taken up in the Miami chapter.

By the 1930s, the Sears stores took on a more streamlined look. Large stores were built in cities, with smaller ones in less-populated areas. This was the Sears style well into the 1940s and 1950s. An outstanding example is the Brooklyn store on Bedford Street just behind the once-glorious Loew's Kings Theater on Flatbush Avenue.

Sears, Roebuck & Company, 1300 Biscayne Boulevard, Miami, Florida. ARCHITECT: Nimmons, Carr & Wright, 1929. Sears apparently erected stores with the same speed and efficiency with which it delivered sewing machines and watches. Most of the stores were by the same "house" architectural firm. As seen in this early example, they featured a prominent tower with "Sears" on top and a long vertical illuminated signage strip displaying Sears's full name. One of the first Art Deco buildings in Miami, this was donated to Dade County in 1990 to become part of a proposed performing arts complex. Preservationists are worried about its future, but the Miami Design Preservation League has mobilized to save it.

STORE: S.H. KRESS
SURVEYED: 19

This chain store, more than any other, was responsible for bringing Art Deco to Main Street U.S.A. In 1931, Kress hired Edward F. Sibbert as in-house architect, and he quickly redesigned the chain's image. Sibbert frequently used regional imagery in his decorative details, specifying polychromed terra-cotta in order to enliven the store façades.

The best example we found was in the Church Street Station historic district in downtown Orlando, Florida. The building is L-shaped with two façades, each slightly different, on each of Orlando's two main streets. It is no longer a

Kress store, but still provides attractive downtown retail space. Another great former Kress enjoying another life is the one in Los Angeles's southern seaport neighborhood of San Pedro. Here Sibbert used aerial views of ships entering port on the decorative panels. Probably the most visible of the remaining Kress stores is the one now housing the Frederick's of Hollywood business.

Other Kress stores listed on the National Register are: Anniston, Iowa (NR 1985); Huntsville, Alabama (NR 1980); and Sarasota, Florida (NR 1984).

F.W. Woolworth Company, 301 Pike Street, Seattle, Washington. ARCHITECT: Harold B. Hamhill, 1938. A special creamy-white terra-cotta was made from Washington state clay by Gladding, McBean of Lincoln City, California, expressly for the Woolworth stores. The firm is the only survivor from dozens of terra-cotta factories operating between the world wars. This Woolworth store opened in 1940. Similar stores were found in almost every city in the country. (Photograph by Leonard Horowitz courtesy Capitman Archives)

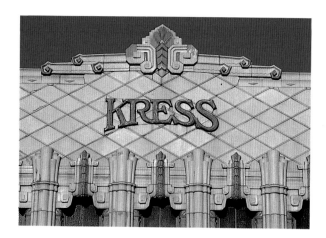

S.H. Kress (Wonder Store), 580 Central Avenue, East Orange, New Jersey. ARCHITECT: Edward F. Sibbert, 1932. Terra-cotta façades like this, with the company logo (now removed), were common across the country. Sibbert, a Cornell graduate, was corporate architect and vice president for the well-known New York retailing firm from 1929 to 1954. He directed the chain's conversion from a Beaux Arts to an Art Deco look.

Rosenberg's Department Store, 4th and A Streets, southeast corner, Santa Rosa, California. ARCHITECT: Hertzka & Knowles, 1937. This award-winning historic department store has movie palace–style finial signage, frosted glass panels, and glass-block bands. Closed in 1990, it is abandoned and in danger of demolition.

STORE: WALGREEN
SURVEYED: 2

Walgreen's was one of the first chain drugstores. The firm built Art Deco buildings in most cities, but many have been lost as new stores opened in the suburbs and the center-city stores, often on prime real estate, were sold and relocated. The best example we found is the store on downtown Miami's Flagler Street.

TERRA-COTTA
SURVEYED: 130

Terra-cotta, which means baked earth, is a very strong and durable building material that has been used for centuries. Compared to stone it is lighter and much less expensive, factors that led to its increasing use in the United States as skyscrapers grew taller and taller, thus giving architects an inexpensive, yet artistic, means to enliven their buildings.

A surprising factor is the pervasive use of brilliant colors in these Art Deco designs. Over and over the colors—seafoam green, copper, gold, coral, turquoise, forest green—show up. Leonard Horowitz, when he began splashing the Miami

Walgreens, 200 East Flagler Street, Miami, Florida. ARCHITECT: Zimmerman, Saxe and MacBride, with E.A. Ehmann, 1936. Some commercial archeologists have hailed this as the all-time best Walgreens store. This streamlined store survives on a busy corner in the heart of downtown Miami, across from Gusman Center for the Performing Arts. Its once-glorious interior has been remodeled into a horrendous mess. (Photograph by Steven Brooke, copyright © 1991. Used by permission.)

Beach buildings with color, was reacting to the many panels and walls with these colors in glazed terra-cotta that he and Barbara had seen. Architects such as Joseph Urban, Le Corbusier, Belford Shoumate, and others, often used these colors, but they have been repainted, or faded by the sun and lost. Only under the unyielding sheath of oven-fired glazes can the colors of the Art Deco period come through to us today, brilliant, undiminished, and authentic.

These techniques in glazes and color were an industrial byproduct of an innovation in the world of art, specifically

Essex Market Decorative Turkey Panel, 138 Washington at end of Linden Street, Newark, New Jersey. ARCHITECT: F.H. Koenigsberger, 1931. This terra-cotta gobbler sat prominently over A.J. Walker's poultry stand in the Essex Market, which opened in 1932. Previously, this had been the site for various schools since 1873, when a public school was first built. Shortly after 1930 the school system abandoned the site and it became a market, at which time the turkey and other decorations were created to suit its new purpose.

Union Station (Western Heritage Museum), 801 South 10th Street, Omaha, Nebraska. ARCHITECT: Gilbert Stanley Underwood, 1929. Native American themes abound in the sculpture on the glazed terra-cotta façade of this Pueblo Deco landmark. It also has Paris Exposition–style relief panels above and below the windows. A distinguished architect, Underwood worked throughout the West, designing Yosemite Park's Ahwanee Hotel (see Hoover Dam chapter) and the Wilshire Tower (see Los Angeles chapter).

ceramics. The work of Louis Comfort Tiffany and others in glass chemistry undoubtedly influenced and spilled over into the ceramic glazes and colors. The worldwide impact of the work of De Stijl, Piet Mondrian, and Paul Klee was seen in brilliant primary colors on building façades. Art Deco terracotta façades are represented in many all-black, all-green, black-and-gold, or shocking-blue examples.

In Kansas City the quality of the terra-cotta façades is the finest. Many of the finest façades in the Midwest were done by Chicago's Northwestern Terra Cotta Company, which thrived for a time when glazed terra-cotta façades were the norm in "modern" buildings. The popularity declined when the later phase of Art Deco began to emphasize volume and form over color and decoration.

TIRE & RUBBER COMPANIES
SURVEYED: 5

Firestone is the big name in this category and the design of the outlets run from the frilly Zigzag to the Streamline. Two on the National Register are: Evansville, Indiana, and Phoenix, Arizona. Los Angeles's monstrous Samson Tyre and Rubber Company, a rare example of Art Deco based upon Assyrian ziggurats, has been restored and incorporated into a massive thirty-five-acre mixed-use complex.

TRAIN STATIONS
SURVEYED: 27

Fellheimer and Wagner, a New York firm specializing in industrial architecture, designed the best Art Deco train stations. The most outstanding example in America is the 1930 Cincinnati Union Terminal. Two of their early works are Boston's North Station and Buffalo's New York Central Station. The Buffalo station is similar to Saarinen's 1905 Helsinki Station in its use of two essential elements: a tall streamlined tower and a semicircular arched façade. Others worthy of mention are the 30th Street Station in Philadelphia, the Texas & Pacific Terminal in Fort Worth, and the Union Passenger Terminal in Los Angeles, which is a skillful combination of Spanish Mission and Art Deco. Memorable on a much smaller scale are Chicago's three Moderne elevated-train or "L" stations, as they are called.

TUNNELS
SURVEYED: 5

The entrances to the 3,000-foot Broadway Low-Level Tunnel running between Berkeley and Orinda are marked by fluted columns designed by consulting architect Henry M. Myers hired to beautify this engineering project. Many tunnel-entrance portals are Art Deco, including those in San Francisco's Presidio, Los Angeles's Pasadena Freeway, and the Lincoln Tunnel in New York City.

URBAN COMPLEXES
SURVEYED: 2

Cincinnati's multi-tower Carew complex was built first, but the greatest of all, of course, is Rockefeller Center, the most Art Deco place in the world. Nothing ever topped it, nothing ever will. The RCA building, Radio City Music Hall, The Rainbow Room, the Rockettes, the statues of Prometheus and Atlas, television and radio studios of NBC, the Channel

Outstanding color examples are found at Tulsa's Farmers Market; the Tulsa State Fairground Pavilion; a Chicago apartment building at 10 West Elm; and a bountiful collection of beautiful buildings in Kansas City, Missouri.

There was a special shade of green most associated with Art Deco and called in the 1930s Chantilly, Sulfate, or Serpentine green. Three outstanding examples of buildings clad with terra-cotta in these hues are: Raymond Hood's McGraw-Hill building in New York; and in Los Angeles, the Pellissier/Wiltern Theater and the Eastern-Columbia building. Each of these reigns over its environs with a special majesty—and there can be no doubt that the serene color is part of the attraction. The Eastern-Columbia building has its green façade accentuated with gold-glazed highlights, giving it a regal presence.

A few of these incorporated regional traditions: the Pueblo Deco post office in Gallup, New Mexico, and the Nautical-style Rincon Annex in San Francisco, are good examples. But the majority were either Stripped Classic or Streamline Moderne. These clean, sensible styles were perfectly suited to Depression-era projects.

The Chicago firm of Graham, Anderson, Probst & White did two large facilities. One was in their hometown of Chicago and the other in Philadelphia. The Miami Beach Post Office, a perfect example of the small-scale local office, was the first major building to be restored in the National Register Art Deco District.

U.S. Post Office, 1300 Washington Avenue, Miami Beach, Florida. ARCHITECT: Howard L. Cheney; Muralist: Charles Hardman, 1937; Restoration architect: Frasuer Knight; Design oversight: David Feinberg, 1979. Cheney designed post offices in several cities. Undoubtedly, one of his most appealing is this WPA project in Miami Beach, with the Federal Art Project mural in the rotunda. U.S. Department of Interior official Chris Delaporte helped find $200,000 to make it the first major restoration project in Miami Beach's Art Deco District. The Post Office Department recognized the work of Barbara Capitman and her fledgling Miami Design Preservation League (MDPL), for they requested and got design oversight from members of the MDPL board, many of whom were designers or architects.

Gardens, multinational consulates—the list is staggering. This is the spot to linger in, to savor the arts in all forms: murals, sculpture, mosaics, metalwork, glasswork, music, and dance. And let's not forget architecture, for here are the most harmonious and beautifully sculpted skyscrapers ever built.

U.S. POST OFFICES
SURVEYED: 39

U.S. post offices rank with courthouses as the major group of buildings contributed by the Federal government. Many were products of FDR's New Deal programs. In fact, this would be an exceptionally broad category if we were to factor in all the Art Deco murals commissioned by New Deal programs for non-Deco post offices around the country. Post offices can be broken into two subcategories: large-scale central postal facilities and small-scale local post offices. The Department of Treasury's architects James A. Wetmore and Louis A. Simon supervised all new construction. One or the other of these names can be found, along with the local architect, on dedication plaques in post offices from coast to coast.

UTILITIES
SURVEYED: 32

The Niagara Hudson Building (now Niagara Mohawk Power) in Syracuse, New York, is not to be missed. From its name, which evokes the force of the great river and falls, to the sculpture titled *Spirit of Light* above the entrance, and the glass murals lining the interior, all elements combine to say—power. The Kansas City Power and Light and the Milwaukee Gas Light also are excellent examples of utility-company skyscraper headquarters.

ZOOS, AQUARIUMS, PLANETARIUMS
SURVEYED: 3

The Paul Rainey Memorial Gates to the Bronx Zoo by Paul Manship, Chicago's Shedd Aquarium and Adler Planetarium, and the Griffith Park Observatory overlooking Los Angeles are rare sites that are intended to be enjoyed by the public. Each has outstanding merit architecturally and artistically, as well as offering scientific and educational programs throughout the year.

MODERN ARCHITECTURE IN THE DECO STYLE: "NEO-DECO"

Adrian Smith is the heir-apparent to the Art Deco tradition. Much Deco-style architecture built after the revival of interest in the 1970s and 1980s has an air of artificiality to it. It is only a faint echo. Seldom today can architects afford to use the now-expensive woods, metals, and glasswork that were common in Art Deco buildings, and the sculpture and murals are scarcely possible in a modern building project. But there are some attempts; and a few of them are successful.

Smith is the best of the new breed of architects continuing in the Skyscraper Style tradition. Unlike several others whose attempts lack the aura of craftsmanship and have thus been labeled "Deco Echo," Smith has mastered the vocabu-

lary. Perhaps his work marks the beginning of an Art Deco—or neo–Art Deco—revival. Notable are his twenty- nine-story NBC Tower in Chicago's Cityfront center, which pays homage to Rockefeller Center's RCA Building, and his sixty-story AT&T Corporate Center, also in Chicago.

Niagara Hudson Building (Niagara Mohawk), 300 Erie Boulevard West, Syracuse, New York. ARCHITECT: Clayton B. Frye and Albert A. Rumschik for Bley & Lyman, with Melvin L. King; Sculpture execution: Machwirth Brother Company, Buffalo, New York, 1930. The monumental figure Spirit of Light stands watch over the entrance of this outstanding Art Deco electric-utility headquarters. This unusual stainless-steel sculpture is among the finest in the U.S.A. So far, attempts to bestow historic-landmark status upon this masterpiece have been resisted by its owners.

United Shoe Machinery Building (The Landmark office condominium), 34-66 High Street; new address: 160 Federal Street, Boston. ARCHITECT: Parker, Thomas & Rice with Henry Bailey Alden, 1928; Restoration architect: Elliot Jon Schrank for Jung/Brannen, 1986. Very elaborate bronze grillwork over the main entrance features stylized nudes, shoe machinery, and other sculptures, including the ubiquitous Frozen Fountain motif. The building was listed on the National Register in 1980. (Photograph by Robert Four)

United Shoe Machinery Building (The Landmark office condominium), 34-66 High Street; new address: 160 Federal Street, Boston. ARCHITECT: Parker, Thomas & Rice with Henry Bailey Alden, 1928; Restoration architect: Elliot Jon Schrank for Jung/Brannen, 1986. A shoemaker, kneeling in a heroic pose, romanticizes his craft in this detail from a bronze panel over the main entrance. This twenty-four-story tower is Boston's most celebrated adaptive-reuse project. A new and old building were bound up into a single downtown project. As part of the complex, developers Meredith and Grew restored this building while erecting a new skyscraper on an adjoining lot on Federal Street. (Photograph by Robert Four)

2

BOSTON

ACADEMIC CENTER OF MODERNISM

Time present and time past
Are both perhaps present in time future,
And time future contained in time past.

—T. S. Eliot
Four Quartets: Burnt Norton, 1938

BOSTON CONJURES UP IMAGES OF COLONIAL America, not Art Deco. Although Boston did not experience a spurt of growth in the 1930s, as did many other cities we visited, many high-quality buildings were constructed during this period. More significantly, Boston became the home of Walter Gropius, founder of the Bauhaus, when he fled Nazi Germany. Of course, by the time Gropius arrived here, his profound influence had already made a lasting impression upon American architecture. That is precisely why he was welcomed at Harvard University in Cambridge, where he became head of the School of Architecture. The Modernists—and the Great Depression—forced the highly decorated early Art Deco to undergo a mitosis into the sleek, stripped Moderne style that dominated and then entirely supplanted the earlier periods of the Art Deco era. It is hard to know which influence on architecture was greater—that of the Bauhaus or that of Le Corbusier. Interestingly, it is only in Boston's environs that we can compare the work of these two masters. In suburban Lincoln, on land provided by the influential Mrs. James J. Storrow, is Gropius's own home. And nearby, in Cambridge, on the campus of Harvard University, is Le Corbusier's only American construction, the 1961 Carpenter Center for the Visual Arts.

While neither of these buildings is Art Deco, nevertheless their existence in metropolitan Boston serves to under-score the impact their creators had on architecture in this

50

country. It is not only the buildings themselves that deserve our attention, but the inevitable interest they aroused in the European Modernist movements. Without the pioneering work of Gropius and Le Corbusier, Art Deco might have been far different during the Depression years, or might not have developed at all. Their teaching in this country—stripping decoration from architecture—ultimately forced Art Deco into eclipse, and the International Style became dominant.

Boston owes a lot of its fascinating atmosphere to the fact that it has long had public organizations engaged in preservation. Fortunately, the Gropius house of 1938 is now preserved by the Society for the Preservation of New England Antiquities. It is operated as a historic home by the society, which owns thirty-three other properties. But none of these is as startlingly modern.

Barbara Capitman finally, and happily, made a pilgrimage to this site in 1989 with her younger son, John, and her grandson, Jason. She lingered, they reported, for nearly an hour in Gropius's study, taking in every detail of his desk and work area at the front of the house. Like Frank Lloyd Wright, Gropius maintained a business office in his residence. This front room had two desks under a wall of windows. The double desk, like much else in the house, was designed by Gropius's Bauhaus colleague Marcel Breuer. From this desk, Gropius could survey the rolling Massachusetts hills as they fell away from the commanding site of his rather small and modest, yet revolutionary, house. Of this experience Barbara wrote:

> In the springtime-flowering orchards surrounding the Walter Gropius house the visitor finds one of the most esthetically pleasant and together treats of modern architecture. The exterior, the interior, the siting of this small personal house are of one low-key perfect piece. Works of the Master's friends—famous modern artists all—hang on the walls. Here and there, amongst the new industrial materials, glass block, cork floors, are found the custom-designed pieces he was able to bring from Germany. All suggest something loved and carefully preserved through the decades.

New England Telephone & Telegraph, 6 Bowdoin Square, Government Center, Boston. ARCHITECT: Densmore, LeClear & Robbins, 1930. This eleven-story tower, with stepped-back massing, has a compatible 1970 addition, visible at right rear. Some original window bays have been sealed. In cities across the U.S.A., this combining of 1930s Art Deco with 1960s and 1970s additions is typical. The result of unrelenting growth within the telephone system, the building demonstrates how well the Bell system was planned for growth: most of the Art Deco buildings did not need to be enlarged for nearly thirty years. (Photograph by Robert Four)

In Boston, the predominant experience is the legendary Freedom Trail. The Old North Church, the home of Paul Revere, the road to Lexington and Concord, King's Chapel, the 1712 Old Royal State House, Ben Franklin's birthplace, Boston Common (the country's oldest park, reserved for the use of the public since 1640), and, of course, the celebrated harbor, where some eighty "Mohawk braves" held a very famous tea party—these hold the visitor in awe and wonder.

The city has been a major port since the birth of the nation. By the dawn of the twentieth century, Boston already had a splendid heritage. Before Gropius arrived, the rich architectural fabric of the city had already been augmented by several important Art Deco buildings. To this day, most Bostonians fail to take any notice of their twentieth-century buildings.

Thus is the task of the Art Deco Society of Boston doubly arduous. The ADSB, as it is called, had its first meeting on May 9, 1989. Surprisingly, in a city thought of as being totally traditional, the society has become, in its brief existence, one of the most active of the Art Deco Societies. The ADSB has sponsored lectures, walking tours, and a number of preservation-related activities, such as a "Deco Dig," in which members walked through Boston in order to inventory all the Art Deco buildings. Its founding president, Tony Fusco, has become one of the most widely respected Art Deco forces in the U.S.A.

The ADSB sought to verify and update a list of buildings first identified in a 1974 Art Deco Walking Tour brochure published by the Institute of Contemporary Art. This was the first attempt in Boston to raise public awareness for Art Deco architecture. The ADSB discovered several new buildings that they could add to the list as they fanned out to find suburban Art Deco as well. All were photographically documented by Robert Four and several other members.

From its inception, the ADSB took an active role in the successful fight to save the Coolidge Corner Theatre in nearby Brookline. It was a 1906 church that Ernest Hayward remodeled into an Egypto-Deco movie house in 1933. David Kleiler founded the nonprofit Coolidge Corner Theatre Foundation, which purchased the theater in 1989 and converted it into a multipurpose community arts facility.

The ADSB also publishes a quarterly newsletter, *Motif.* The newsletter reports on preservation issues and the Art Deco arts of the 1920s and 1930s, carrying not only local stories but also national and international information about the field.

Several downtown buildings have been restored and rehabilitated. Most notable is the restoration and compatible "twinning" of the Second National Bank (later known as the State Street Bank & Trust). This building now is known by the address of its new adjacent addition, 75 Federal. The original twenty-one-story tower was designed in 1929 by Frank H. Colony for the firm of Thomas M. James. It is Boston's finest Art Deco skyscraper. Its beautiful marble, abundant sculpted-metal panels, and outstanding light fix-

tures gleam brightly anew since its thorough renovation and linking to the new, but totally neo–Art Deco, twin tower.

Another splendid renovation was done on Parker, Thomas & Rice's 1928 United Shoe Machinery Corporation Building. At one time, Boston was the shoe and leather capital of the world. United Shoe Machinery controlled an amazing ninety-eight percent of its market. The machinery shown in the bronze grilles symbolizes the Machine Age's ease of labor and manufacture. In 1980, the building was designated a Boston landmark, but the designation was vetoed by then Mayor Kevin White because the owner wanted to tear the building down. However, when it was nominated to the National Register of Historic Places by the Massachusetts Historical Commission and became eligible for federal tax credits, the owner had a change of heart. By 1986, the twenty-four-story office tower, with retail shops at the street level, had been completely restored by Elliot Jon Schrank. Under the new name The Landmark, it became home to such prestigious tenants as Price Waterhouse.

Arthur H. Bowditch's large and wonderful 1930 Paramount Theater has remained faded and dormant since 1976. It was to be renovated as part of "Commonwealth Center," a package deal worked out by the Boston Redevelopment Authority, but the failing finances of the late 1980s put the project on hold.

One restoration project that did work, however, is Brookline's elegant 1930 Boulevard Trust Company building, designed by J. William Beals' Sons. It was restored by Bay

Coolidge Corner Theatre (1,274 seats), 290 Harvard Street, Brookline, Massachusetts. ARCHITECT: Ernest Hayward; Engineer: Mark Linenthal, 1933; Restoration architect: Notter Finegold + Alexander, 1991. For this project, Barbara Capitman crisscrossed the country collecting signatures on petitions to help the Art Deco Society of Boston convince the people of Brookline to save this theater. (Photograph courtesy Notter Finegold + Alexander)

Bank in 1987. The classically derived details executed in a highly symbolic Art Deco style were restored by DRL Associates of Weymouth, Massachusetts.

Boston also is the home of two of the leading collectors in the United States of significant Art Deco objects. They are John Axelrod and Annella Brown.

Axelrod convinced the important Boston Museum of Fine Arts to include two rooms of Art Deco furniture, glassware, sculpture, and other objects, mostly from his own collection, in its twentieth-century decorative-arts department. Brown, a longtime admirer of Barbara Capitman, also purchased the 1936 Eastman "House of Tomorrow" in Miami Beach and maintains a residence in both cities. The astute activity of these two in the early 1970s contributed to the recognition of the importance of Art Deco objects after a long period of scorn and neglect. They were not exactly alone, however, as they often found themselves bidding at auctions against the likes of Andy Warhol and Barbra Streisand, two other early collectors of Art Deco.

Other notable Boston Art Deco landmarks include the following:

The second John Hancock Life Insurance tower, which was designed by Cram & Ferguson in 1939 but was not built until 1947, with an appropriate update in fenestration styling. Its definite Deco ziggurat top is crowned by a rocketlike weather beacon, beaming forecasts to all of Boston in coded light signals indicating clear blue, cloudy rain, or snow.

Cram & Ferguson, Boston's most successful Art Deco practitioners, were also responsible for the 1932 U.S. Post Office and Courthouse. This huge pile sits at one end of a triangular park, part of a splendid Art Deco vista that is unparalleled in the U.S.A. At the opposite end of this urban plaza is the New England Bell Telephone Headquarters building, which, when lit at night, is absolutely spectacular. This, too, was a 1947 Delayed Deco work of Cram & Ferguson.

Behind the famed Copley Plaza Hotel is an excellent eleven-story New England Power Company office which is now a school. It was designed in 1930 by Blackall, Clapp, Whittemore and Clarke, but not completed until 1937.

Across the Charles River in Cambridge is the massive BB Chemical Building, now the Polaroid Corporation. This building resembles a stately world's fair pavilion and was designed in 1937 by Coolidge, Shepley, Bulfinch & Abbott.

The first of the famed Art Deco train passenger terminals designed by the bellwether New York City firm of Fellheimer and Wagner was Boston's 1927 North Station. The firm is most famous for its Cincinnati Union Terminal and a similar earlier station for the New York Central in Buffalo, New York. Yet here, in Boston, they did their prototype terminal. The importance of this effort lies in its bold departure from the admittedly splendid but traditional Richardsonian and Victorian creations already found across the U.S.A.

Elsewhere in New England

Pioneer woman architect Eleanor Raymond graduated from the Cambridge School of Architecture in 1919 and received a master of architecture degree in 1936 from Smith College. In 1931, she designed a house for her sister in the Boston suburb of Belmont. *Architectural Forum* termed it the first modern house in Massachusetts. In 1933, she designed a superb Art Deco sculptor's studio for Amelia Peabody in Dover, Massachusetts. Her own 1937 office in Boston featured citron-yellow walls and black steel furniture, with bright green bookshelves and dark brown linoleum floors. While she did many fussy New England structures to keep her tradition-bound clients satisfied, she was able to produce a handful of outstanding Moderne buildings as well. Her Art Deco work was equal to that of her more famous male peers, and her use of color rivaled that of Le Corbusier and Joseph Urban.

The outstanding 1932 Art Deco Criterion Theater in the famous summer resort at Bar Harbor, Maine, is listed in the National Register.

The 1940 Merritt Parkway through Connecticut was listed in 1991 as a National Register of Historic Places Scenic Highway. It had been nominated to the National Register several times in the past, but vigorous lobbying by state officials always kept it off the register. It is renowned for its diverse collections of thirty-five bridges. A few are Art Deco and Moderne. The state's highway department has been hoping to rip down these "dangerous" old bridges and replace them with modern wider ones. But preservation-minded residents of the state have staved this off for sixteen years and have protected what may be the last of its type, a thirty-seven-mile picturesque green beltway, designed when travelers were thrilled to cruise along enjoying the countryside at a safer thirty or forty miles per hour. The roadway was originally designed by George Dunkelberger, with landscape design by W. Thayer Chase.

3

CHICAGO

Form ever follows function.

—Louis Henry Sullivan
"The Tall Office Building Artistically Considered"
Lippincott's Magazine, March 1896

IN UNRAVELING THE HISTORY OF ART DECO, WE come inevitably to Chicago, where the skyscraper was born. Chicago's tall steel-frame buildings, along with the thinking of its revered masters, Louis Sullivan, Daniel H. Burnham, and Frank Lloyd Wright, had such an impact upon the rest of the world that Chicago became the focal point of architectural evolution in the early twentieth century and therefore could well be viewed as the cradle of Art Deco in the U.S.A.

The direct contribution of the Chicago School to Art Deco is little known, but it includes the following: the elevation of urban greenbelt planning to a new level (Burnham); decoration free of historical precedent for modern-age buildings (Sullivan); pre-Columbian and Mayan detailing, influence on European architects through published works, and radical geometric massing never seen before (Wright).

It is not insignificant that Barbara Baer Capitman, whom architect Stanley Tigerman called in 1981 "the Jewish Mother of Art Deco," was born here April 9, 1920. She understood Chicago's history and returned here often during her lifetime. Barbara Capitman and Leonard Horowitz encouraged the founding of the Chicago Art Deco Society (CADS), one of the oldest in the country. Later, Barbara expressed surprise and delight in the splendid representation of Art Deco masterpieces to be found in her native city. Because she moved to New York City so soon after her birth, Barbara had forgotten—until returning in 1981—the extent and importance of Art Deco in Chicago. When it was announced that she would lecture, hundreds of people showed up, and Stanley Tigerman introduced her. It was a thrill for everybody.

Her visit spurred a revival of interest in the treasures of this period—in a city where, seemingly, both Art Deco and the Machine Age had entirely faded away. With the arrival in

Chicago Board of Trade, *141 West Jackson Boulevard, Chicago.* ARCHITECT: *Holabird & Root; Sculptor: Alvin Meyer, 1928. The famed eagle and clock are flanked by hooded figures over the massive stone entrance to Holabird & Root's best-known work. Meyer won the Prix de Rome in 1923 and soon headed Holabird & Root's sculpture department. The figures, holding sheaves of wheat and corn, represent commodity traders.*

Merchandise Mart, *350 North Wells, north bank of the Chicago River, Chicago.* ARCHITECT: *Graham, Anderson, Probst & White, 1928. In a city dominated by projects of the Field family, this topped them all. Containing 4.2 million square feet, the Mart remained the world's largest commercial building for many years. The Fields sold it to Joseph P. Kennedy in 1946. Floodlights at night reveal its handsome Art Deco massing. Its adventurous motifs in ceilings, terrazzo, and stonework include triangles, arcs, arrows, and Mayan elements. Murals by Jules Guerin grace the lobby, which was reconfigured in 1991 to include retail stores.*

1938 of Ludwig Mies van der Rohe to head the Architecture School of the Armour Institute (now the Illinois Institute of Technology), the Chicago School continued evolving and soon left Art Deco in the dust.

Forestalling this evolution, in a major way, was Frank Lloyd Wright. Everything he did was Modern, yet he consistently scorned the other Modernists. Wright pioneered architectural innovations that became key elements of Art Deco, such as corner windows, flowing horizontal window bands, cantilevered sunscreen window "eyebrows," and the use of new technology such as glass tubing, cork flooring, and prefabricated cast concrete. He stood alone. In 1910, his work was published in the *Wasmuth Portfolio*, in Berlin. This event had a tremendous impact on European architects like Walter Gropius and Ludwig Mies van der Rohe. After the construction of the Imperial Hotel in Tokyo, Wright's influence truly reached around the world. Marion Mahony, chief renderer in Wright's Oak Park studios, prepared the drawings for the *Wasmuth Portfolio*. She and Walter Burley Griffin, another architect in the office, got married. In some ways, Griffin was ahead of Wright. He had done Mayan and pre-Columbian work as early as 1905, years before Wright's interest in it. In 1912, Griffin won the competition to design a new capital in Canberra, Australia, so he and Marion moved there. Griffin's work in Australia gradually became Art Deco in style. His 1924 Capital Theatre in Melbourne is a prime example. In 1936, they moved to India, and he further spread his style.

Wright's teacher, Louis Sullivan, with his dictum "Form follows function," provided the basis for the Modernism of the Bauhaus and much of the architecture of the 1950s, but in Chicago today, only Sullivan's magnificent Auditorium

Chicago Board of Trade, 141 West Jackson Boulevard, Chicago. ARCHITECT: Holabird & Root, 1928. This view from the lobby mezzanine highlights long sleek expanses of marble. The backlit opaque light panels run across the ceiling and down the walls, in an exciting variation on a common Art Deco banding technique. The new high-rise addition by Helmut Jahn is one of the best examples of integrating new with old. Ceres, the original trading room mural by John Norton, was moved into the new addition and given a prominent position in the atrium.

Theater and the Carson Pirie Scott Department Store on State Street are still standing. Wright's work has been much better preserved, but his delightful 1914 Midway Gardens, done with Alfonso Iannelli, have long since vanished. After serving as one of Chicago's most important entertainment centers, hosting jazz greats like Bix Beiderbecke and Benny Goodman, it was ignominiously converted to a car wash and then demolished in 1929.

Thus, from their Chicago base did Sullivan and Wright shake the architectural world. Soon, however, there came back from Europe a reply, a new wave of architectural thinking. As Gropius and Mies gained in importance, the florid, elegant Art Deco of Paris began to seem seriously excessive. As the rare woods and etched-glass trim became too expensive, they became irrelevant during the Great Depression, and decorative detail disappeared entirely from the cold, hard, glass-and-stainless-steel buildings designed after World War II.

The Chicago Architecture Foundation held an eight-week Art Deco program in 1979, coordinated by civic activist Bunny Selig. After Barbara Capitman's 1981 lecture,

Lynn Abbie, Jean Nerenberg, Bunny Selig, and a few others who had taken the course were inspired to form CADS. Ruth Knack, editor of *Planning* magazine, with offices at the University of Chicago, agreed to edit the new CADS newsletter. With the design assistance of her husband, William, she put together the newsletters that helped spread the word on Art Deco and gain 175 members by the following year. Ruth was a serious architectural historian, having written a 1977 book, *Preservation Illinois*. CADS's most brilliant event ever was held on August 29, 1982: Deco Day on the *Clipper*. The *Clipper* is a 1930s streamlined vessel that was then berthed at Navy Pier. Mayor Jane Byrne declared "Deco Day in Chicago," and seventeen hundred attended the event.

Perhaps, one reason that Barbara was greeted so warmly by Art Deco lovers in Chicago was the extensive preparation they had been given through the consistently outstanding writing of the late *Chicago Tribune* architecture critic, Paul Gapp. He published a manifesto on Chicago Art Deco that was the cover story of the *Tribune*'s Sunday Magazine of June 11, 1978. It was filled with lavish color pictures of the city's greatest and most appealing Art Deco sites. Research assistance was provided by Eleanor Gordon and Jean Nerenberg, the latter also providing the photographs.

The splendor and beauty of Chicago's Art Deco once again regained respectability, and there was abundant reason to celebrate. Barbara lived long enough to see Adrian Smith of Skidmore, Owings & Merrill create in 1989 a new Art Deco tower for Chicago's skyline in the style of New York's Rockefeller Center. The beautiful twenty-nine-story building—the first in an urban complex called Cityfront Center—unreservedly pays tribute to its older New York cousin. The tower has setbacks and massing like the great RCA (now GE) tower in the heart of Rockefeller Center. As in Gotham, the anchor tenant here is none other than NBC, and the network's peacock proudly adorns the façade. This neo-Deco tower also has a series of flying buttresses encircling its midlevel setbacks, in an overt reference to the neighboring Chicago Tribune Tower. The competition to design the Tribune Tower did much to shape Art Deco. The irony is that it was not the winning entry of Hood and Howells in the Gothic style that created the sensation in the competition. It was the second-place entry by Eliel Saarinen—a sleek stripped-down proto–Art Deco tower—that inspired many of the world's top architects finally to abandon the strictures of Beaux Arts Classicism and embark on a revolutionary new architecture. At first this resulted in bold Art Deco towers, but as architectural decoration became obsolete, the result was a glut of glass towers that soon were just as tiresome as the profusion of fake Greek temples had been.

Chicago, like Boston, has a rich architectural heritage, although considerably smaller. From the Windy City's rich and abundant catalog of Art Deco structures, local authorities have recognized as local landmarks only four: Holabird &

Carbide & Carbon Tower, *230 North Michigan Avenue, Chicago.* ARCHITECT: *Burnham Brothers, 1928. This twenty-six-story office tower was built by industrial giant Union Carbide & Carbon, today known as Union Carbide. Gold-glazed terra-cotta trim reflects the brilliance of the sun, maker of coal eons ago. The use of color (green/black) in the façade was unheard-of in a Chicago skyscraper, though not unknown elsewhere. This was Northwestern Terra Cotta Company's largest project in their own home town.*

Root's 1928 Chicago Board of Trade; Graham, Anderson, Probst & White's innovative 1931 Field Building; Burnham Brothers' glistening crystalline green 1928 Carbide & Carbon tower; and finally, William Pereira's 1938 Esquire Theater on the Near North Side. The Carbide & Carbon tower was constructed the year Ernest Graham left D. H. Burnham & Co., after which it became Burnham Brothers. Graham went on to form Graham, Anderson, Probst & White, one of Chicago's premier firms. The first three landmarks listed have been accorded a modicum of respect, but the city designated only the exterior of the Esquire Theater as a landmark. This designation inexplicably allowed a gruesome remodeling of the theater into a multiplex cinema and a renovation of the main foyer that forever wrecked the building as a historic

Bismarck Hotel, *171 West Randolph Street at North LaSalle, Chicago. ARCHITECT: C.W. Rapp & George Rapp, 1926; Interior redesign: Kem Weber, 1941. This hotel lobby, with its brass elevator doors, rich wood panels, and marble ziggurat door frames, is located in Chicago's fabled Loop. Kem Weber, a noted California designer, remodeled the hotel's interiors and furnishings in 1941.*

Office Building, *1 North LaSalle Street, Chicago. ARCHITECT: Vitzthum & Burns, 1930. Brass eagle light sconces flank elevator doors in this lavish lobby, lined with fine marble and punctuated with outstanding metalwork. It is so well maintained that it still looks brand new.*

Daily News *(Riverside Plaza), 400 West Madison Street, Chicago. ARCHITECT: Holabird & Root, 1928. Two views: Architects used different elevator doors in the multiple lobbies of this labyrinthine former newspaper plant. Art Deco detailing was preserved in the adaptive-reuse of this phenomenal structure on the Chicago River, just across from another Art Deco landmark, the Opera House.*

site. Today, a visitor can get only a general idea of the elegance of the original.

Just as Chicago has bustled to build greater towers, so has it routinely shunted aside and razed celebrated masterpieces. Most buildings by "The Master" (as Frank Lloyd Wright always called his mentor, Louis Sullivan) are completely gone. Also gone since 1973 is Holabird & Root's 1929 Michigan Square building and its Diana Court, with Carl Milles's famed central statue of Diana. Only a few artifacts of this outstanding court survive, scattered throughout the Midwest. Diana herself is safely nestled in the University of Illinois's Student Union building, downstate in Champaign-Urbana. Some of the wondrous Edgar Miller etched-glass panels from the Diana Court stayed in Chicago and wound up in Arnie's, one of the earliest restaurants with Art Deco revival decoration in the country, which opened in 1974. The loss of the Diana Court is truly one of the country's greatest Art Deco tragedies.

In Barbara's 1981 visit to Chicago with Leonard—and on the occasion of our return trip a decade later—one brilliant man, Robert Sideman, conducted the most comprehensive Art Deco tour imaginable. Sideman became so engrossed in our tour of downtown Loop buildings that he left his car parked at a bus stop to join us so he could point out a few more features he had forgotten to mention before we went in. When we all emerged from Holabird & Root's

1928 *Daily News* building at 400 West Madison Street, we discovered to our horror that the efficient Chicago Transit Towing fleet had done its job well—no car! When we regained the car from the city pound an hour later, we gingerly resumed our Art Deco adventure.

Barbara knew, and we soon learned, that the real masters of the Chicago Art Deco style were Holabird & Root. Besides the Board of Trade building, their credits include countless Illinois Bell buildings, the Chicago Auto Club, and the 1927 masterpiece Palmolive (now Playboy) Building, at 919 North Michigan Avenue. We visited dozens of Holabird & Root buildings and only scratched the surface. Not only was Holabird & Root Chicago's premier Art Deco architectural firm, but its influence reached far beyond Chicago, for it was responsible for the North Dakota State Capitol at Bismarck; the Jefferson County, Alabama, courthouse; the Remington Rand building in Washington, D.C.; the A. O. Smith Building in Milwaukee; the Rand Tower in Minneapolis; the Racine County Courthouse in Wisconsin; and, in Minnesota, the famed Saint Paul City Hall/Ramsey County Courthouse Building—to name just a few!

A slightly more prestigious Chicago firm was in second place in Art Deco work. Nevertheless, the firm—Graham, Anderson, Probst & White (GAP&W)—was responsible for an impressive list of Chicago's best and many important buildings elsewhere. GAP&W's significant out-of-town work includes the Detroit Federal Building, the Bryant Building in Kansas City, the Philadelphia Post Office, and 20 Pine Street, New York City. GAP&W was the favorite architectural firm of the immensely important Field family and designed many Marshall Field stores in the area. It also did the great Shedd Aquarium and the largest commercial building on earth, the Merchandise Mart—both for the Field family. It designed the famed Chicago Opera House and the main downtown post office at 433 West Van Buren Street. Sometimes the Art Deco detailing is very subdued, as at the opera house. Sideman explained it thus: "Chicago has a lot of cautious Art Deco."

Here are some of the other buildings that were highlights of Sideman's tours both for Capitman and for Kinerk–Wilhelm.

Two of Andrew Rebori's most outstanding efforts are the 1930 Cudahy Library and the 1938 Madonna della Strada Chapel, both on the campus of Loyola University, 6525 North Sheridan Road. The library has a mural by John Norton titled *Travels of Ignatius Loyola*, plus a striking ziggurat tower, sundial, and cross.

Then, there are two fantastic Pueblo Deco high-rise apartment towers near the campus of the University of Chicago—so similar, yet designed by two different architects. The first is the 1929 Powhatan at 1658 East Fiftieth Street, designed by Robert S. De Golyer and Charles L. Morgan. It has native American themes everywhere, a fantastic top-floor ballroom, a large tiled swimming pool, splendid original elevator cabs, and 522 decorative window spandrels. While

standing in the rain admiring this building, we were greeted by past association president Frances Pen, who was responsible for initiating a program of sensitive historic renovations throughout the exclusive residential co-op. She took pity on us and invited us in for a tour from basement to ballroom. The top floor has the best view of Powhatan's immediate neighbor, the Narragansett at 1640 East Fiftieth Street, by Leichenko & Esser.

One of the commonest types of Art Deco buildings nationwide is Sears department stores. Many of these are the product of a single Chicago firm: Nimmons, Carr &

59

Laramie State Bank (Citizens National Bank), *5200 West Chicago Avenue at Laramie Avenue, Chicago.* ARCHITECT: *Meyer & Cook, 1928. Northwestern Terra Cotta Company made this panel. The mint-machine operator, inundated with coins, conveys the frenzied pace at which money was created in 1928, the year before the start of the Great Depression. Architectural-art commissions like this decreased drastically after the stock market crash, finally to be revived by the PWAP (Public Works of Art Project), beginning in 1933.*

Lake Shore Drive Bridge, *47th Street & Lake Shore Drive, Chicago.* ARCHITECT: *Unknown, 1937. Outstanding sculpture and light fixtures like these may be found on famed Lake Shore Drive, along Lake Michigan's shore. These were, until recently, in very sad repair. The city became aware of their importance due to unrelenting preservation pressure from Lynn Abbie and the Chicago Art Deco Society.*

Hyde Park Chevrolet Showroom & Garage (Hyde Park Garage), *5508 South Lake Park Avenue at 55th Street, Chicago.* ARCHITECT: *M. Louis Kroman, 1929. This humorous terra-cotta façade was appropriate for this early automobile dealership. Gears, dashboards, stoplights, and other auto artifacts decorate the "Roaring Twenties" building on the Southside, near the University of Chicago.*

Madonna della Strada Chapel, *Loyola University, 6525 North Sheridan Road, Chicago.* ARCHITECT: *Andrew Rebori, 1938. Suggesting the blades of a huge turbine, or perhaps a stylized toaster, the Madonna della Strada Chapel at Loyola University sits majestically on Lake Michigan's shore. Glass brick integrated into the exterior arches permits dramatic shafts of sunlight to illuminate the altar in the chapel. Rebori was one of Chicago's most individualistic architects.*

Wright. George Nimmons of this firm also did the 1913 Arts-and-Crafts proto-Deco Franklin Publishing Company at 720 South Dearborn Street, with beautiful tile work illustrating the history of printing.

A noted Chicago sculptor did artwork for buildings all over the country. Lorado Taft maintained his studio on South Michigan Avenue near the Art Institute in the old Studebaker Showroom building, which was converted to a celebrated artists' colony shortly before the Art Institute moved from a small adjacent building into its present splendid Classical home across the street. One of Taft's most celebrated works in the area, *Fountains of Time*, is found near the campus of the University of Chicago.

Of all the Chicago firms, Holabird & Root is the one that regularly used distinguished artists to add drama and beauty to its buildings. It employed artisans such as John

Storrs, who did the aluminum Roman goddess Ceres sculpture on top of the Board of Trade. It used John Norton, who did the huge mural of Ceres now in the central atrium of the Board of Trade's new Helmut Jahn annex. Norton also did the mural on the lobby ceiling of the old *Chicago Daily News* building showing the steps necessary to produce a modern daily newspaper. Alvin Meyer, who did the sculpture over the clock and the eagle entrance at the Board of Trade, also headed Holabird & Root's in-house sculpture department and did much of the exterior decoration for which the firm became so renowned.

We have already mentioned Frank Lloyd Wright's influence on the evolution of Art Deco. Wright incorporated in his work the best of his mentor, Louis Sullivan, and then picked up the Cubist-inspired geometry of his collaborator, Alfonso Iannelli, who was in the vanguard of the world's Art

Palmolive (Playboy) Building, 919 North Michigan Avenue at Walton, southeast corner, Chicago. ARCHITECT: Holabird & Root, 1927. One of the earliest and best examples of the Skyscraper Moderne genre is featured in this vintage postcard. The thirty-seven-story masterpiece was topped by the extraordinary two-billion-candlepower Lindbergh Beacon. A gift from Elmer Sperry of Sperry Gyroscope, the beacon was visible for miles and was Chicago's nighttime skyline signature. When Palmolive abandoned it and Playboy magazine moved in, the street-level façade was heavily altered.

Powhatan Apartments, 1658 East 50th Street, Chicago. ARCHITECT: Robert S. DeGolyer and Charles L. Morgan, 1929. These skyscraper-style co-op apartments near the University of Chicago on the Southside are visible from South Lakeshore Drive. The complex includes a beautifully tiled swimming pool and an original rooftop ballroom with views of Lake Michigan and surrounding Chicago.

Powhatan Apartments, 1658 East 50th Street, Chicago. ARCHITECT: Robert S. DeGolyer & Charles L. Morgan, 1929. The Midwest's premier Pueblo Deco edifice contains doors featuring Powhatan braves in the metal grilles, flanked by arrow-in-quiver lamps. Almost as impressive is its neighbor, the Narragansett, designed the following year by a different architect, but maintaining the Indian theme. Powhatan and Narragansett are, of course, Native American tribal names.

Travel & Transportation Building (demolished), Century of Progress Exposition of 1933, Chicago. ARCHITECT: Hubert Burnham and E.H. Bennett, with John A. Holabird, 1930. This vintage postcard touts the fair's most remarkable building. This engineering marvel features a roof suspended from cables. A key building in the 1933 fair's plan, it was designed in 1930. In keeping with World's Fair practice, most pavilions, including this one, were demolished in 1934 at the end of the fair.

Deco designers. As early as 1911, Iannelli created graphics that were decades ahead of their time. Wright himself seemed to pass through three distinct phases in his designs. The middle period was the most Art Deco, as he graduated from his wood-beamed cottages and bungalows in suburban Chicago to the geometric concrete textile-block constructions more often found on the West Coast. His Art Deco output peaked with the Johnson Wax headquarters and research tower in Racine, Wisconsin (see the Milwaukee chapter). In Wright's later years, he abandoned geometry and took inspiration from the warm, round, green-and-brown earth itself.

Chicago's western suburb of Oak Park is blessed with Frank Lloyd Wright's studio-office, many homes that he designed, and his outstanding Unity Temple, completed in 1905 after his return from Japan. While Oak Park is architecturally best known for its Wrightian treasures, it is also an Art Deco paradise: Here we find Thomas Lamb's 1936 Lake Theater at 1020 Lake Street; a 1929 Marshall Field store by GAP&W at Lake and Marion Streets; Wieboldts and Woolworth stores; and the U.S. Post Office.

Many of the most popular Art Deco buildings in Chicago are movie theaters. Also, there are many landmark theaters here that are not Art Deco, such as the great Chicago Theatre on State Street. All the Chicago theaters are superbly cataloged in photographs, newspaper clips, and other memorabilia, such as usher uniforms, blueprints, and posters, at a unique resource in suburban Elmhurst. The material is housed at the Theatre Historical Society (THS) Archives. This resource, directed by retired schoolteacher William Benedict, helps architectural historians and theater buffs every week of the year. The staff, along with THS President Joe DuciBella, provided the authors with a complete list of every Art Deco theater in the THS catalog and helped us discover quite a few around the country hitherto unknown to us.

Probably Chicago's greatest contribution to Art Deco architecture was the 1933 Century of Progress Exposition, where nearly every building was in the Art Deco style. This was a big change from the architecture at the 1893 World's Columbian Exposition in Chicago, where Louis Sullivan was entirely ignored in his attempts to reject Beaux Arts Classicism for the fair design in favor of a more modern style. Sullivan's ideas were flatly rejected, and this rejection nearly sent his career into eclipse.

By 1933, however, Chicago was ready for some modern thinking, and the two most influential designers of the fair were chief designer Raymond Hood and his assistant, Louis Skidmore. And, not surprisingly, the consulting architect at this fair was none other than Paul Philippe Cret. The fair was laid out on a three-and-a-half-mile fill along Lake Michigan. The smashing success of this fair helped Art Deco become the most popular form of architecture in America for the balance of the decade. The exposition was a major planning and aesthetic triumph for Skidmore, who went on to plan

X-183   TRAVEL BUILDING AT NIGHT   PRINTED IN U.S.A.

the New York World's Fair of 1939–1940 before becoming a partner in one of the most successful architectural firms of the century: Skidmore, Owings & Merrill. In 1933, Hood, Skidmore, and Cret worked with many notables: Board of Design Chairman Harvey Wiley Corbett, Hubert Burnham (son of the famed D. H. Burnham), Charles Dawes, Norman Bel Geddes, Holabird & Root, Albert Kahn, George Keck, Walter Dorwin Teague, and Ralph Walker. In addition, Joseph Urban produced a vibrant color scheme for the entire fair. How could it *not* have been a smash success? Many of the country's architects went to see it. Some went right home and began copying the designs immediately; for instance, Clarence Kivett copied his Katz Drug Store in Kansas City, Missouri, directly from Cret's Tower of Science at the fair.

They called the fair A Century of Progress, and indeed it was. It brought Art Deco to a large public and reemphasized its relationship to the new and modern—a break from the past. This fair showed clearly how science and industry could together create a new and better world.

The romantic era of Art Deco both opened and closed in Chicago. What is now termed the Machine Age was replaced by the Nuclear Age in 1942, when in a secret, shielded space under the seats of the University of Chicago's Ellis Street Stadium near Fifty-sixth Street was born the first self-sustaining controlled nuclear reaction in history. The site is now a Chicago Historic Landmark.

Elsewhere

BEVERLY SHORES, INDIANA

There were several single-family demonstration homes at the Chicago fair that eventually found their way to Indiana, still on the shores of Lake Michigan. Kinerk and Wilhelm journeyed to see them with Chicago Art Deco Society charter-member Ruth Knack. The six surviving homes now comprise the Beverly Shores/Century of Progress

Architectural District at the Indiana Dunes National Lakeshore, forty-five miles southeast of Chicago. The names of the homes are Florida Tropical Home, House of Tomorrow, Armco Ferro Mayflower House, Cypress Log Cabin, Cypress Guest House, and Wieboldt-Rostone House. All except one are occupied. When the leases expire, the homes become the property of the National Park Service. Soon after the fair ended, Robert Bartlett moved these homes by barge across Lake Michigan to Indiana as a publicity stunt to lure buyers to his housing development. He named the new neighborhood Beverly Shores, and today it is indeed as lovely as he must have promised.

AURORA, ILLINOIS

Two of the greatest surviving Art Deco movie palaces are in suburban Chicago. The first is the Aurora Paramount Performing Arts Center, an exotic 1931 zigzag delight by C. W. and George Rapp. Built by the Paramount Publix conglomerate on the eve of its bankruptcy, the theater survived for decades as a popular downtown movie house and finally underwent a $3-million restoration by the city when it became an arts center for the community.

PARK RIDGE, ILLINOIS

The second great Art Deco theater, with by far the best Cubistic decoration anywhere, is the 1928 excursion into fantasy called the Pickwick Theater, by R. Harold Zook for Zook & McCaughey.

Paramount Theater (Performing Arts Center; 2,016 seats), 23 East Galena Boulevard, Aurora, Illinois. ARCHITECT: C.W. Rapp and George Rapp, 1929; Restoration architect: ELS Design Group with Conrad Schmitt Studios, 1976. Here is one of Rapp & Rapp's greatest Art Deco movie theaters. Built in the heart of Aurora along the Fox River, it opened in 1931. It has always been very popular with the citizens of Aurora, who formed a downtown redevelopment corporation and saved it after obtaining a $10.3 million grant from the state of Illinois. During 1977, the entire building was updated to the standards of a modern performing-arts center. Conrad Schmitt Studios restored the interior, including this auditorium sidewall section. It reopened to sell-out crowds on April 29, 1978, and has been doing well ever since.

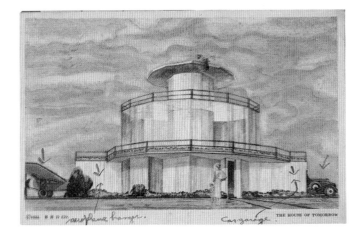

House of Tomorrow, *Chicago Century of Progress Exposition of 1933, Now at Indiana Dunes National Lakeshore Recreation Area, 214 Lake Front Drive, Beverly Shores, Indiana.* ARCHITECT: *George F. Keck for Keck & Keck, with Leland Atwood, 1933. The brothers Keck created this steel-frame and glass "House of Tomorrow" as shown in a souvenir postcard for the 1933 Chicago Exposition. The two garages were for the family car and a plane. After the fair, this and six other model homes were moved across Lake Michigan by barge to this town fifty miles southeast of Chicago. These now are listed as a historic district in the National Register of Historic Places.*

Pickwick Theater (1,500 seats), *5 South Prospect Avenue, Park Ridge, Illinois.* ARCHITECT: *R. Harold Zook for Zook & McCaughey, 1928. This spectacular original fire curtain inspired by the Paris Exposition complements the Futuristic proscenium. An original three-manual, ten-rank Wurlitzer theater pipe organ is visible at the left. The organ console originally was decorated in the same exuberant pattern as the fire curtain.*

Bloom Township High School, *10th Street at Dixie Highway, Chicago Heights, Illinois.* ARCHITECT: *Royer, Danley & Smith, 1931. Sculptural zigzags and geometric trim dress up this entrance. The architect harmoniously blended elements from both German and French styles. The school is in a suburb about thirty miles south of Chicago.*

4

CINCINNATI

THE TRAIN CITY—THE REAL RADIO CITY—
AND SOAP, TOO!

Moon River . . . . lazy stream of dreams.
Where vain desires forget themselves in the
loveliness of sleep. Moon River, enchanted
white ribbon, twined in the hair of night,
where nothing is, but sleep. Dream on, sleep
on, care will not seek for thee. Float on, drift
on, Moon River, to the sea . . .

—WLW Radio Broadcast Transcription, c. 1936, Cincinnati,
Ohio—For a brief period, the most powerful radio station on
earth at 500,000 watts.

CINCINNATI SPREADS ACROSS SEVEN ROLLING HILLS,
sloping down to meet the banks of the Ohio River. This pristine location made it a gateway to the opening frontiers of
the American West early in the last century. After the Civil
War, it saw new growth as waves of German immigrants,
finding it similar to the old country, settled in to make it a
bustling commercial center. They built breweries, meat-
packing plants, and pharmaceutical companies.

To carry on their cultural traditions, the Germans began
a *Sängerfest*, or music festival, in 1873. This was the first such
festival in the U.S.A., and one that continues to this day
under the name The May Fest. So successful was it that an
enormous hall was needed to accommodate it each year.
The newly built Richardsonian-Romanesque Music Hall was
erected in a section of the city called ·Over-the-Rhine.

So conservative were the good burghers of Cincinnati
that they did not build a modern train station, even though
their factories and stores were outpacing most of the nation.
Finally, the railroads joined to build a new Union Terminal,

Coca-Cola Bottling Company (F&W Publications), 1507
Dana Avenue, Cincinnati. ARCHITECT: *John Henri Deeken;*
Muralist: John F. Holmer, 1938; Restoration architect:
Chris & Knoop, 1987. Executed and installed in the main
lobby stairwell after the building opened, this original
mural features River Downs and Coney Island, two popu-
lar Cincinnati recreation areas. Other highlights in the
lobby are the shiny metal railings and futuristic light fix-
tures.

Carew Tower complex, Starrett-Netherland Plaza Hotel
(OMNI), 35 West 5th Street at Vine Street, Cincinnati.
ARCHITECT: Walter Ahlschlager with Delano & Aldrich,
1930; Restortion architect: Richard Rauh, 1982–1992.
Built by the giant Starrett Construction Company on land
owned by the influential and wealthy Emery family, this
impressive three-building urban complex is crowned with
light beams in the moonlit view illustrated in this vintage
postcard. Serving as a prototype for the Rockefeller
Center to come, it included a thirty-one-story hotel, a
forty-nine-story office tower, and a twenty-eight-story
garage (now demolished). It was erected in only thirteen
months. The ten-year restoration of the complex has
been directed by Richard Rauh, an Atlanta architect.

Hall of Mirrors Ballroom, Starrett-Netherland Plaza Hotel
(OMNI), Carew Tower complex, 35 West 5th Street at
Vine Street, Cincinnati. ARCHITECT: Walter Ahlschlager with
Delano & Aldrich; Designers: George Unger and Colonel
Joseph Reichl, 1930; Restoration architect: Richard Rauh,
1982–1983. A mezzanine is de rigueur for seeing and
being seen in a ballroom. Here, the metal railing features
musical themes, including Pan, the god of music. The
hotel was part of the Carew Tower, Cincinnati's most
innovative urban project. It remains a pre-eminent example of 1925 Paris Exposition style. The center chandelier
did not survive a disastrous fire, but most of the other elements are in this original form.

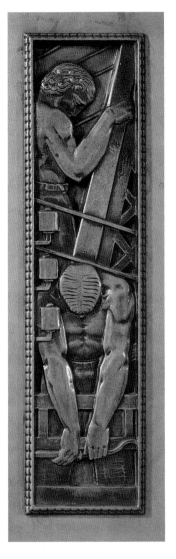

Starrett-Netherland Plaza Hotel (OMNI), Carew Tower complex, *35 West 5th Street at Vine Street, Cincinnati. ARCHITECT: Walter Ahlschlager with Delano & Aldrich; Designers: George Unger and Colonel Joseph Reichl, 1930; Restoration architect: Richard Rauh, 1982–1983. One of a pair of whimsical and beautiful Rookwood ceramic fixtures, this seahorse lamp is typical of pure French Art Deco decor. Stylized animals abound in the architectural carving and artwork found throughout the hotel. Restoration of the entire Carew complex by Rauh & Associates is an ongoing project, for which $28 million was spent on the hotel alone. (Member of National Trust's Historic Hotels of America)*

Cincinnati Bell, *36 East 7th Street at Elm and Plum Streets, Cincinnati. ARCHITECT: Harry Hake for Hake and Kuck; Sculptor/metalwork: Oscar Bach, 1931. Men lay phone cable in these panels in the lobby of one of the best of Bell Telephone's urban towers. Bach contributed his fine telephone-themed metalwork throughout its twelve stories of harmonious massing and setbacks.*

but much later than nearby cities like Chicago and Saint Louis. The railroads agreed to put the station in a valley about a mile west of the Music Hall, down a broad tree-lined boulevard. The Cincinnati Union Terminal was begun in 1930 and completed in 1933. The original plans called for a Victorian-style massive structure with towers and crenelated battlements. At the last minute, the wizard of Art Deco, Paul Philippe Cret, was brought in as a consultant. He suggested smoothing the rough edges and moving the new station toward a new Modern look. The chief designer was Roland A. Wank, who later worked on the TVA dams. The terminal, with its twenty-one associated buildings, bridges, viaducts, and walkways, was indeed built in a coordinated Art Deco style. The project was so massive that it can be compared only to the largest projects of the 1930s—Hoover Dam, Golden Gate Bridge, and Rockefeller Center.

Cincinnati's first successful Art Deco preservation campaign focused on saving the Union Terminal. It was threatened numerous times, until it was finally converted into two museums and was put back into a condition nearly as sparkling and exciting as when it was brand new. When word got out in Cincinnati that the terminal, considered a white elephant for years because of national decline in rail traffic, was being eyed for demolition, the battle to save it began. Nomination papers were quickly researched and completed, and it was listed on the National Register of Historic Places in 1972, the first Streamline Moderne structure so honored. At that time the only other Art Deco projects listed were the Folger Shakespeare Library (1969) in Washington, D.C., and the Paul Rainey Memorial Gates at the Bronx Zoo (1972) in New York City.

At this same time, a "Revive Union Terminal" campaign was begun by Dr. Gabriel Weisberg of the University of Cincinnati Art History Department, along with Mrs. Frances Croty, an M.A. candidate whose thesis was on the terminal. By the fall of 1972, their group had led to the formation of an official city body called the Save the Terminal Task Force. By 1973, the railroads had decided they would definitely demolish the long concourse to the terminal because they wanted to run the new double-decked railcars to transport automobiles through the yards. These "piggybacks," as they are called, were a few inches too tall to pass under the concourse. First, automobiles had put the terminal in decline, now they were killing it.

The task force, fearing the worst, drew up immediate plans to save the fourteen large silhouette mosaics by Winold Reiss that lined the concourse. Each of these mosaics depicted a major Cincinnati industry of the 1930s. Doubters said the mosaics were too large and heavy to be saved. During her thesis research, Mrs. Croty had identified the original manufacturer of the tesserae used in the mosaics: the Ravenna Mosaic Company of Saint Louis. The company was contacted, and it was determined that the murals could be moved. A group of conservators was assembled to create new strategies and techniques for the job. After the task force had received overwhelming civic and corporate support, the huge murals were safely removed, gingerly trucked across the Ohio River, and placed in prominent positions in the new concourses of the Greater Cincinnati Airport in Covington, Kentucky.

This was only the beginning. The most magnificent part of the terminal—the Rotunda with its Newsreel Theater, Rookwood Tea Room, restaurants, lounges, and offices—was still standing. The task force was determined to save it. They produced a poster with a shocking image that commanded immediate attention. The image was a photo of the monumental terminal with sections airbrushed out to make it appear to be in ruins. The poster said simply, "When It's Gone, It's Gone."

Several new uses were tried and failed. By 1980, the terminal had been shuttered once again. The Cincinnati Historical Society, under the leadership of Dr. Gale E. Peterson, initiated talks with the Natural History Museum in an attempt to build a coalition for converting the structure into a civic museum center. Studies were done, and in 1986, the citizens passed a $33.7-million bond issue to fund the conversion.

During the remodeling and conversion to house the two museums in 1990, we asked to see the magical terminal once again. Historical Society President Gale Peterson eagerly agreed, conducting us on a "hard-hat" tour. We were impressed by the meticulous restoration that had already been completed. Exhibition spaces were being carved from the huge parking garages originally under the esplanades and fountains leading to the terminal. As a result, the Rotunda and its original amenities for travelers were left intact for complete restoration. The Rookwood Tea Room became an ice cream parlor; the former ticket office, the museum gift shop; and the entrance to the long-gone concourse, a giant-screen Omni-Max theater.

The decline of the terminal had been totally reversed by 1991, when, after three years of work and a total expenditure of over $56 million, splendid new exhibition spaces were opened in the new Museum Center. The Rotunda, with its Art Deco emphasis on Art (murals, patterned terrazzo, glass, and metalwork) now serves as one of the grandest museum lobbies in the world.

Perhaps the quality of the work in the terminal was an outgrowth of the role that the city played during the Arts-and-Crafts movement earlier in the century. The Shop of the Crafters, a workshop that produced furniture and decorative objects, and the world-famous Rookwood Pottery were both founded on the principle of bringing art and beauty into the life of everyone, thereby making it richer and more rewarding. Art Deco continued this tradition. Although often thought of in connection with mass production and the Machine Age in the U.S.A., it was, after all, an *art décoratif*, or decorative art. Not only the Rookwood Pottery but several centers of the Arts-and-Crafts movement across the country, such as Detroit's Pewabic Pottery, also used the new lan-

Cincinnati Union Terminal (Museum Center), *1301 Western Avenue at west end of Ezzard Charles Drive, Cincinnati.* ARCHITECT: *Roland A. Wank for Fellheimer & Wagner, with Paul Philippe Cret, 1930; Restoration architect: Arthur Hupp II for Glaser Associates, 1988. With its massive fountains and monumental façade, this is America's most majestic Art Deco train terminal. It was saved and restored by the people of Cincinnati, who passed a $33.7-million bond issue in 1986 to provide a site for the historical and natural history museums. A $68-million restoration was conducted from 1988 to 1993. (Photograph by Jack Scally)*

Cincinnati Union Terminal (Museum Center), *1301 Western Avenue at west end of Ezzard Charles Drive, Cincinnati.* ARCHITECT: *Roland A. Wank for Fellheimer & Wagner, with Paul Philippe Cret, 1930; Restoration architect: Arthur Hupp II for Glaser Associates, 1988. Recently reopened to house two museums, the terminal was fully refurbished, including the fountains and spillways running along the long approach to this giant landmark. Much of the exhibition space for the new museums was reclaimed from the original underground garages beneath the fountains and driveways leading to the terminal. This allowed the most impressive portion of the building, the breathtaking, huge rotunda lobby, to be restored and left as is. (Photograph by Michael D. Kinerk)*

Cincinnati Union Terminal (Museum Center), *1301 Western Avenue at west end of Ezzard Charles Drive, Cincinnati.* ARCHITECT: *Roland A. Wank for Fellheimer & Wagner, with Paul Philippe Cret; Sculptor: Maxfield Keck, 1931.*

Cincinnati Union Terminal (Museum Center), 1301 Western Avenue at west end of Ezzard Charles Drive, Cincinnati. ARCHITECT: Roland A. Wank of Fellheimer & Wagner, with Paul Philippe Cret; Muralist: Winold Reiss, 1930. The Buck Rogers–style digital-clock tower over the main information desk is the central element in the terminal's sweeping semicircular rotunda. Bold-colored terrazzo strips flow into the entrance of the now-demolished great concourse. Originally, fourteen giant mosaic frescoes were installed in the concourse. Saved through extraordinary effort as demolition proceeded in 1973, the frescoes are now on view at Greater Cincinnati's airport in Covington, Kentucky.

Cincinnati Union Terminal (Museum Center), 1301 Western Avenue at west end of Ezzard Charles Drive, Cincinnati. ARCHITECT: Roland A. Wank for Fellheimer & Wagner, with Paul Philippe Cret; Muralist: Winold Reiss, 1930. Growth of Cincinnati, one of two unusual lobby mosaic frescoes, recounts life along the Ohio River through the years. Executed by Ravenna Tile Works, each is 105 feet long, forming a continuous band inside the huge rotunda. Many details are expressed in shiny tile, while other parts of the scene are tinted plaster. The figures in the foreground are twelve feet high. Note the depiction of the Carew Tower/Netherland complex. On the south side of the rotunda is a companion work, History of Transportation.

Cincinnati Union Terminal (Museum Center), 1301 Western Avenue at west end of Ezzard Charles Drive, Cincinnati. ARCHITECT: Roland A. Wank for Fellheimer & Wagner, with Paul Philippe Cret; Sculptor: Maxfield Keck, 1931. Providing a kind of artist's signature at the bottom of an artwork, these architect's stones near the Union Terminal's entrance are executed in perfect Art Deco typography. One identifies the architects of record, Alfred Fellheimer and Steward Wagner. With twenty-two separate buildings, the drafting alone would have kept any firm busy for years. But somehow the terminal opened in just one year, as noted by the second marker. Together these serve as a benchmark of Cincinnati history. (Photographs by Michael D. Kinerk)

Cincinnati Union Terminal (Museum Center), 1301 Western Avenue at west end of Ezzard Charles Drive, Cincinnati. ARCHITECT: Roland A. Wank for Fellheimer & Wagner, with Paul Philippe Cret; Linoleum muralist: Pierre Bourdelle, 1930; Restoration architect: Arthur Hupp II for Glaser Associates, 1988. Although Bourdelle was known as a muralist, he retained techniques learned from his father, famed French sculptor Antoine Emil Bourdelle. This project took him away from traditional painting and allowed him to express his skills in sculpture. Here he portrays his favorite subjects, jungle animals, in innovative carved and lacquered linoleum panels. (Photograph by Michael D. Kinerk)

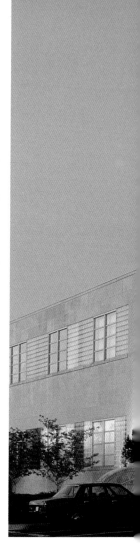

New York, which later built the Empire State Building, hired architect Walter W. Ahlschlager to design the complex. Ahlschlager's assistant, George Unger, became chief designer, working closely with hotel general manager Colonel Joseph Reichl, who seemingly had the last word on everything. The interiors ran the gamut from pure French Art Deco to Streamline Moderne to Surrealism. Construction of the entire complex took just an amazing thirteen months from the demolition of previous structures in August 1929 to the first tenant's moving in on October 1, 1930. Over one thousand workers labored twenty-four hours a day, some workers raising the steel structure above while others were "finishing off" the floors below.

Hotel guests could dine in the high French Deco restaurants, take tea in the resplendent Palm Court, dance in the grand ballroom (a Deco version of the Hall of Mirrors at Versailles), and then see a show in the surrealistic Pavilion Capriccio or shop in one of many shops in the Rookwood-tile-lined arcade. The lucky few could even ensconce themselves in one of the two-story hotel suites, with an Art Deco balcony overlooking their own private salon, complete with a grand piano. For fresh air, they could step out onto the suite's private terrace to admire a commanding view of the Queen City of the Ohio River. Or they could go to the highest point in the city, the forty-fifth-floor observation deck of neighboring Carew Tower.

The lucky visitor could cross the street to the Gibson Hotel (now demolished) and luxuriate in its interiors by Viennese architect and colorist Joseph Urban. Another block away was the newly remodeled Shillito department store, with gleaming copper, brass, and aluminum marquees.

Meanwhile, twenty-four hours a day, the radio station WLW, the Nation's Station, was beaming live music and entertainment that were second to none. Many a career was launched here at Powell Crosley's flagship station, including Fats Waller, the Mills Brothers, and Rosemary Clooney. The de luxe studios had etched mirrors on the walls in an Art Deco sunburst pattern, plus a coffered ceiling with ultra-modern lighting fixtures, parquet floors, and the famous Wurlitzer pipe organ with sunburst organ grilles. This radio station was, as they so often said in those days, "the last word."

Powell Crosley, the inventive brain behind WLW, made the first car radio, the "Roam-E-O." He started out making car accessories and crystal radio sets. Once he had decided he wanted the most powerful radio station ever dreamed of,

guage of Art Deco to modernize their works and ensure their relevance and commercial success.

If train travel did not suit their plans, visitors to 1930s Cincinnati had other terminals to arrive at, including the streamlined Greyhound Station, the more adventurous Lunken Airport with its three Art Deco hangars and Nautical Moderne terminal, or traveling by taxi on one of the Art Deco–styled parkways that cross numerous viaducts spanning the hills of the city. By whatever means, one could arrive downtown via an underground entrance to a world "direct from the Paris Exposition of 1925"—the Netherland Hotel. On entering the hotel, the visitor was surrounded by a virtual Art Deco paradise. Here was a first-of-its-kind city within a city urban complex, completed several years before the famed Rockefeller Center in New York City. (Cincinnati seemed to be New York's architectural New Haven, having also built in the nineteenth century the Cincinnati Suspension Bridge, a tryout for the engineering techniques later used by John A. Roebling in his world-famous Brooklyn Bridge.) The Carew Tower complex was built on a prime square block in the heart of the city, and it comprised three towers sitting on a five-story common base with an upper, lower, and mezzanine arcade linking the thirty-one-story hotel, the forty-five-story Carew Tower Office Building, and the twenty-eight-story futuristic garage, one of the largest ever built.

Cincinnati's civic-minded and wealthy Emery family, in partnership with the Starrett Brothers Construction firm of

he set to work to devise a series of fifty-ton transformers, huge vacuum tubes requiring five hundred gallons of water per minute to cool them, and the most unusual antennae of the time to take his station to the top. He created many stars in the process, including the Williams Brothers and Doris Day (then known as Doris Mae Kapelhof). Crosley wanted the station to play soft, soothing music all night, should he chance to tune in when troubled and sleepless. He had a certain feeling in mind for the nighttime magic spell he wanted on his airwaves. He felt that the proper tone for his Art Deco station was a subdued, dreamy one much like a Gauguin painting from Tahiti or a Maxfield Parish twilight canvas. The poetic announcement in the epigraph at the start of this chapter opened the Moon River Broadcast each night. Millions heard it and never forgot.

The station was also an innovator in other ways. The phrase "soap opera" was coined here to describe the popular daily drama that was sponsored by Cincinnati industrial titan Procter & Gamble. Since the firm was trying to sell soap, the name stuck. The government broke Crosley's heart in 1939 when pressure from competitors forced it to set a maximum limit of fifty thousand watts for radio broadcasters. WLW was no longer "The Nation's Station," and Crosley sold it. The antennae and other equipment are now asleep in the original building in suburban Mason, Ohio. It will never again be equaled.

Cincinnati is still strongly Art Deco. It has treasured buildings from the period, finding new uses for them when necessary. Cincinnati's worst mistake in preserving its past was the loss of every movie palace downtown. Now—too late—Cincinnatians have finally realized that they need some theaters again and, of course, they can *never* replace the great 1920s and 1930s palaces that were destroyed. Two more losses have been the Greyhound Station and Joseph Urban's unique interiors in the Gibson Hotel.

A ten-year process of preserving and restoring the decorative details while updating the technical systems of the aging Netherland Hotel- Carew Tower Office Complex and Arcade is now nearing completion. The hotel restoration, under the direction of Atlanta architect Richard Rauh, was completed first. The hotel's splendor can be matched only by New York's Waldorf-Astoria, and even the Waldorf doesn't have the dramatic spaces of the OMNI Netherland Plaza, as it is now named. Ahlschlager was a theater architect and a master of spaces. He created dramatic rooms and then expanded them through the use of stairs, mezzanines, and balconies. Thus, the room could be seen from many vantage points so that none of the expensive details would be overlooked or wasted. The Emery family continue to show a commitment to the complex, and they were lucky enough to find a first-class restoration architect in Rauh, who was equal to the monumental challenge.

The Cincinnati *Times-Star* newspaper building was vacated when the paper was closed, but it didn't remain empty long before restoration began. Former press rooms were converted into an enormous atrium office space. The restoration supervisor and major tenant, Burke-Marketing, recently moved out when Hamilton County purchased the building for much-needed court and office space.

An excellent streamlined Coca-Cola bottling plant has been recycled as the offices of the F & W Publishing Company. The company is so proud of the building that it printed a brochure about the building's history. Large expanses of glass brick supply ample light to the offices of the editors, artists, and support staff. Especially noteworthy to Cincinnatians are the period murals of two favorite riverside summer attractions: River Downs Racetrack and Coney Island Amusement Park, with its sleek, screaming rides, and the Moonlight Gardens, an outdoor "ballroom," where the sounds of the renowned Big Bands could be heard.

Times-Star *Building (Hamilton County Offices & Courts),* *800 Broadway at 8th Street, Cincinnati.* ARCHITECT: *Samuel Hannaford & Sons, 1931; Restoration architect: Basil H.M. Carter, 1985. Elevator doors in this finely detailed masterwork illustrate why this building was listed in the National Register of Historic Places in 1983. The paper was merged with the* Post *and known for two decades as the* Post Times-Star. *Eventually vacated, in 1985 the building was converted to offices for Burke Marketing, and its lobbies and boardroom were nicely restored. In 1992, it was sold to Hamilton County for use as courts and offices.*

Lunken Airport, *262 Wilmer, Cincinnati. Muralist: William Harry Gothard, 1937. This Federal Art Project mural features a man soaring in flight over the Ohio River and metropolitan Cincinnati, with the Carew Tower complex visible at lower right. The 204-acre site was a bequest to the city by Edmund H. Lunken in 1928, and it contains three original brick hangars with Art Deco aviation decoration. This was originally the site of the Aeronca Aircraft factory that predated the terminal. The Art Deco Eastern Parkway was built to connect this terminal to the center of the city.*

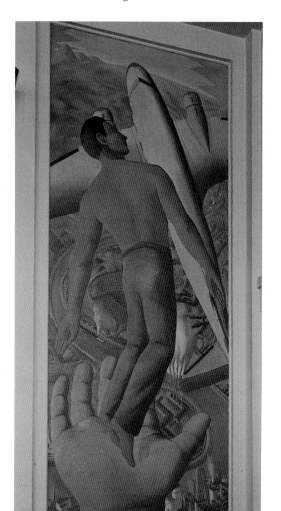

The Columbia and Eastern Parkways have not been widened or altered in any major respect since they were first built. Because of their increasing age, they will soon be experiencing infrastructure problems and may become endangered, as are many roads and bridges across our nation. More than anything else, they give this city an Art Deco ambience all its own. In a city that has fought hard to preserve its treasures, projects like the parkways will surely be on the preservation agenda of the 1990s.

A Cincinnati Art Deco Society has never been formed, but a few collectors and dealers have specialized in the era and were willing to share their knowledge. Alfred Nippert

spent years looking for and preserving every historical document, drawing, photograph, and plan that could be found concerning the Union Terminal. In so doing, he has become an expert on all aspects of rail travel during the period and has even collected a fleet of period railcars that he leases out. When Barbara came to visit, he took her to the cavernous old terminal and performed his imitation of the station master's voice echoing through the terminal: "Track Six, Louisville & Nashville's Pan-American: Louisville, Bowling Green, Nashville, Decatur, Birmingham, Montgomery, Pensacola, Mobile, and New Orleans—booooooarddddd!"

Father and son, Max and Peter Palm are antiques pickers *par excellence*, and Susan Sizemore saved many an Art Deco treasure from the trash heap as she nearly cornered the market in the 1970s on what was then widely viewed as junk. Now Peter and fellow collectors Don Joyce and Grady Richards each have a warehouse of period radios, tubes, advertising materials, neon display signs, antennae, and related memorabilia. They happily shared their collections and memories of the days when Cincinnati's WLW ruled the airwaves and directed us on an excursion to Mason, Ohio. There we saw the original Crosley transmitter and the unique "double" broadcasting tower, one tall tower upside down, resting on its tip, and the other upright, both being bolted together feet-to-feet at the middle. The whole thing sits on giant insulators, so that when it was charged with half a million watts, it wouldn't collapse in a blob of molten steel. A Voice of America shortwave antennae farm is down the road from WLW, and thanks to Don Joyce's advice, we drove to see the original Voice of America Cincinnati headquarters—also Art Deco.

The Cincinnati Historical Society has reprinted the souvenir program from the opening day of the restored Union Terminal and markets reproduction jewelry and Cincinnati Union Terminal–related gifts in its shop in the lobby. But all this activity does not take the place of an Art Deco Society. Barbara announced several times that one had been formed, but then nothing happened. Maybe some day soon her dream will come true.

After all, Art Deco is more than just a style; it's a state of mind. Paul T. Frankl said it best in his 1930 book, *Form and Reform:*

> Style is a unifying principle which integrates all external creations of a period . . . the spirit of the *Zeitgeist* enters into every one of our creations and constructions. Our very gestures, our carriage, our dancing, our pastimes, our way of preparing food, our methods of transportation, our system of banking, our shopping, our advertisements, our restaurants, our manners . . . reveal a fundamental pattern of mind which seeks expression in these disparate activities.

Times-Star *Building (Hamilton County Offices & Courts), 800 Broadway at 8th Street, Cincinnati.* ARCHITECT: *Samuel Hannaford & Sons; Sculptors: Ernst Bruce Haswell and Jules Brys, 1931; Restoration architect: Basil H.M. Carter, 1985. A palatial sixteen-story plant was built by the politically powerful Taft family for its newspaper the Times-Star. On the corners of its tower are allegorical figures representing Truth, Patriotism, Progress, and Speed— the four essential qualities of a newspaper. These figures stand as sentinels at the base of the tower's French "perfume bottle-stopper" top. The luxurious executive offices and boardroom are just below.*

5

DALLAS AND FORT WORTH

WHERE THE ART DECO CLOCK STOPPED
IN 1936

*The past is a work of art, free of
irrelevancies and loose ends.*

—Max Beerbohm in *Comment*

DALLAS AND FORT WORTH ARE SISTER CITIES IN
North Texas. They share an airport, but as is the case with
Minneapolis and Saint Paul, each city wants to maintain its
own identity. In fact, there is a bit of a rivalry between these
sisters and has been for some time. When Father Texas was
planning his centennial in 1936, he decided to celebrate it in
Dallas. Sister Fort Worth was hurt and felt left out.

Luckily, before a sibling war as big as the state itself was
waged, newspaper owner, power broker, and Fort Worth
citizen Amon Carter had a long chat with Father Texas. In
order to maintain peace and harmony at home, Pa suddenly
decided to stage one of the events—one dear to the heart
of all Texans, the rodeo—in Fort Worth. Both cities were
united by the excitement of hosting this important one-
hundredth-birthday celebration. The sisters knew that if they
wanted to "do Pa proud," they must cooperate and put
forth a superhuman effort. After all, both sites, Fair Park and
the Will Rogers Memorial Center, had to be completely finished in just one year.

Today, the cities are fiercely independent and quick to
point out their differences to anyone who will listen. How-

*Texas Centennial Esplanade Fountain, Extending from
Parry Avenue Entrance, Fair Park, Dallas. ARCHITECT:
George Dahl; Sculptor: Laurence Tenney Stevens;
Frescoes: Pierre Bourdelle, 1936. A fountain and pool
run the length of the 1,000-foot esplanade. In the
background is the fair's original Transportation Building
(now the Centennial Building), in front of which is a
statue representing Spain's early dominion over Texas.
Also visible is a Bourdelle fresco of a man and eagle
entitled* Locomotion.

79

Federal Building (State Fair Administration Tower), 3809 Grand Avenue, Fair Park, Dallas. ARCHITECT: Donald S. Nelson with George Dahl and Centennial Staff; Sculptors: Raoul Josset, José Martin, and Julian Garnsey, 1936. This fine building was designed by Nelson, the Dallas-based architect of Fort Worth's Will Rogers Memorial. He also worked on Chicago's 1933 Century of Progress Exposition with Paul Philippe Cret, creator of the famed Science Tower. The eagle at the top of this tower was designed by Raoul Josset and executed by José Martin. The sculptural frieze at the base was by Julian Garnsey. Also visible on the left side of the tower are some light fixtures of the Cotton Bowl stadium, the best-known Art Deco destination in the park.

Hall of Administration (Park Maintenance Building), 1240 Washington Avenue, Fair Park, Dallas. ARCHITECT: George Dahl and Centennial Staff; Sculptor: Raoul Josset, with José Martin; Muralist: Carlo Ciampaglia, 1936. A leaping-dolphin fountain was placed in front of the signature Spirit of Centennial statue. In the aperture behind the statue is a map of the Lone Star state by Ciampaglia. This niche and sculpture were added in a 1936 modernization of the 8,000-seat coliseum built in 1910. Friends of Fair Park currently are trying to raise money for conservation of these works.

ever, they are united by at least one thing—Art Deco—and it is some of the best in the U.S.A. So good, in fact, that if they were to work together as they did in 1936, these cities could make their Art Deco an irresistible attraction.

Fort Worth has a historic city center where many buildings of all styles are combined and preserved. Here, one almost has the feeling of being on the back lot of a Hollywood movie studio. Although it has skyscrapers, this city somehow has maintained a human scale that gives it an intimate, friendly feeling much like that of Miami Beach's Art Deco District.

Of course, not all the buildings here are Art Deco, but they are interesting in that one can see how Art Deco architecture developed. As Judith Cohen has so thoroughly illustrated in her 1988 book *Cowtown Moderne*, many of the diverse elements that were combined to make the U.S.A.'s unique Art Deco style can be seen within blocks of each other in Fort Worth. From the Dutch and German styles of de Klerk and Höger, to the Glasgow school of Charles Rennie Macintosh, to Edgar Brandt and the French Exposition style, to pre-Columbian, Native American, and even Arabic—they are all here. The development of the Art Deco skyscraper can be traced from its timid emergence from the eclectic architecture of the early 1920s to its full maturity a few years later.

If Fort Worth is Art Deco's *ying*, then Dallas is its *yang*. In the Texas Centennial's Fair Park, the later Streamline Moderne style of Art Deco is very well represented. Fair Park is where the clock stopped in 1936. To visit it is to take a step back in time, a time when America was at its creative peak, despite the Depression, a time when world's fairs and expositions captivated the country with their optimistic forecasts of the future. Usually, these fairs were designed to be temporary—everything was demolished at the end of the run. Only Fair Park escaped this fate.

Imagine a grand entrance, an esplanade twenty-one hundred feet long and three hundred feet wide, and a seven-hundred-foot reflecting pool with fountains. Flanking these are courtyards dedicated to the four quadrants of Texas: east, west, north, and south. Along the esplanade are pavilions with arched porticoes, each enclosing a monumental sculpture representing one of the six flags that have flown over Texas: France, Spain, Mexico, Texas, the Confederacy, and the United States. Also on the grounds are an aquarium, a planetarium, museums, an amphitheater, a tall Federal Tower building, and the Texas Hall of State, which in true Texas style dwarfs and outshines the Federal pavilion. The Texas building is so monumental and opulent in its Art Deco detailing that it could be classified as the fifth Art Deco state capitol.

To complete the scene, imagine artwork of every description: murals, frescoes, sculpture, metalwork, glass, ceramics, and lighting. There is also a carnival midway with neon and rides like the awesome Star of Texas ferris wheel. And don't forget a stadium seating seventy-five thousand people. That may not require much imagination because it is

the Cotton Bowl, a famed New Year's Day football venue.

Both Dallas and Fort Worth have their ardent Art Decophiles and leaders in the preservation movement. In Dallas, a group called The Friends of Fair Park is the protector of the historic structures of the Texas Centennial. Philip Collins, the director of education for the Dallas Museum of Art, has done research on many of the Art Deco buildings outside Fair Park and includes some of these boomtime Dallas Art Deco treasures in his museum-sponsored architectural tours.

Fort Worth's Art Deco has, for the most part, been protected through the vigilance of one woman, Judith Singer Cohen. For years, she was Art Deco's lone voice in the Lone Star State. She learned the power of perseverance during the ten-year period in which she battled one publication crisis after another in trying to get her book to press. Thus, one of her greatest triumphs was the publication of her delightful book *Cowtown Moderne*, which captures the feeling of the times better than most architectural books by weaving together the history of the buildings with the social history of the same period. She enlisted her husband, who is an excellent photographer, to document all the Art Deco buildings in Fort Worth.

While Judith Cohen was saving the buildings in Fort Worth, a new group was formed to save the unique buildings in Dallas's Fair Park. The need became apparent when, in 1983, the six museums in the park began thinking of following the move of the Museum of Fine Arts downtown, thus deserting the park. The Dallas Park Board announced it was opposed to the idea of having a survey done to determine the park's historic eligibility. The city had plans to build a wide road up to the Cotton Bowl, which meant demolishing any of the 1936 buildings that were in the way. Activist Mary Ellen Degnan went to Mrs. Stanley Marcus, the chair of the Park Board, to say that a group was being formed to have a historic survey done. Mrs. Marcus planned to hire her own land-development consultants. The fledgling Friends of Fair Park (FFP) hired the former head of the National Trust's preservation programs, Russell Keune, to do the survey. Virginia McAlester was elected the first president of FFP, and the survey was completed. The goal was to preserve the original buildings in the park by its 50th anniversary in 1986, which was also the 150th birthday of Texas. The campaign eventually led to Fair Park's being declared a National Historic Landmark. The only other such landmarks in Texas are the Alamo and the state capitol. One reason the park was given such status is the homogeneity of its collection of Art Deco pavilions, all designed under the supervision of a single visionary architect, George Dahl. Free tours of the park on Thursday evenings, roughly May through September, are given regularly by Deb and Jerry O'Brien, owners of the White Horse Gallery, at 3607 Parry Avenue, across the street from the park's main entrance.

William Lescaze designed the Magnolia Lounge, the only building at the 1936 fair designed by a non-Texan. The

State of Texas Building (Hall of State), *3939 Grand Avenue, Fair Park, Dallas.* ARCHITECT: *Centennial Architects Association; Supervising architect: Donald Barthelme; Sculptor: Allie V. Tennant, 1936. Texas's namesake, a majestic warrior from the native Tejas tribe, stands before the state's pavilion. The eleven-feet-tall gilded-bronze figure, sculpted by one of Texas's leading women artists, is framed by Texas limestone pilasters seventy-six feet tall. This Stripped Classic temple to Texas was created in a single year by a consortium of ten architectural firms, under the supervision of Donald Barthelme of Houston.*

State of Texas Building (Hall of State), *3939 Grand Avenue, Fair Park, Dallas.* ARCHITECT: *Centennial Architects Association; Supervising architect: Donald Barthelme; Interior architect: Adams & Adams, 1936. This unusual Texas-longhorn wall fixture utilizes various metals with glass-rod diffractors. All of the extraordinary fixtures and artwork in this building were commissioned expressly for this shrine to Texas and designed and built by Texans.*

State of Texas Building (Hall of State), 3939 Grand Avenue, Fair Park, Dallas. ARCHITECT: Centennial Architects Association; Supervising architect: Donald Barthelme; Interior architect: Adams & Adams; Muralist: Eugene Savage, 1936. Savage's central State of Texas historical mural is in the most sumptuous building in the park. The mural is on the south wall in the "Great Hall of Six Flags," a giant room measuring ninety-four feet by sixty-eight feet, by forty-six feet high. This memorial hall to the Lone Star State has rich verde-marble floors and San Sabastian–stone columns.

State of Texas Building (Hall of State), 3939 Grand Avenue, Fair Park, Dallas. ARCHITECT: Centennial Architects Association; Supervising architect: Donald Barthelme; Interior architect: Adams & Adams; Muralist: Eugene Savage, 1936. This Stripped Classic Art Deco settee has Mayan-inspired armrests and triple-fin treatments on the leg supports. The opulent all-marble hall still contains its original furniture. The existence of this great collection of original period furniture in such magnificent architecture explains why the entire park is one of Texas's few National Historic Landmarks, in select company with the Alamo and the State Capitol.

Magnolia Lounge was restored in 1985 by the Friends of Fair Park, and retains most of the authentic features and fixtures. The building is done in classic International Style with a Nautical Deco exterior. There had been a plan to raze it, but an unexpected public outcry saved it for the subsequent restoration, to the tune of $800,000. It is now the office of the Friends of Fair Park, which has enormous treasures within its control and yet will not really control the buildings at all should higher government authorities decide to do some developing of their own. But savvy and tough, Dallas's Friends of Fair Park has secured as its executive director Craig Holcomb, an ex-city commissioner to whom doors open wide when he calls anywhere.

Beginning in 1947, Margo Jones popularized the Magnolia Lounge by operating a theater-in-the-round here, with the assistance of people like Tennessee Williams. The little lounge got its name from the original Dallas petroleum firm absorbed by Mobil Oil. It had been called Magnolia Oil Company in the days when Texas was part of the Old South. But Socony Mobil's representation of energy, the mythical winged horse Pegasus, soon replaced the lovely but staid magnolia blossom.

The existence on the fairground of a slick, sophisticated building by Lescaze is a tribute to this mother lode of authentic and extraordinarily well-preserved Art Deco buildings, which is a historic district that rivals Miami Beach's.

Much of the restoration in the park has been funded by the generosity of the Meadows Foundation, which gave the first grant to restore the Magnolia Lounge. It also gave a seed grant for the restoration of Carlo Alberto Ciampaglia's *Rocket* mural, plus grants to restore the aquarium, the planetarium, the music hall, and some of the museums so they would stay in the park. In 1991, the foundation gave $58,000 for the National Park Service to survey eleven additional structures.

Most magnificent is the Texas Hall of State Building, designed by the Texas Centennial Architects Association Incorporated, which included Ralph Bryan, DeWitt & Washburn, Flint & Broad, Fooshee & Cheek, T. J. Galbraith, Anton F. Korn, Mark Lemon, Walter Sharp, Arthur E. Thomas, and H. B. Thompson. The final design was by Donald Barthelme of Houston, and Adams & Adams of San Antonio, associate architects, were responsible for details and interior finishes. Within the hall are rooms, once again, for the four quadrants of the state. The West Texas Room is not exactly Art Deco, but a combination of Arts-and-Crafts and Pueblo designs. The North Texas Room features a mural: Fort Worth is represented on the left, Dallas on the right, and Old Man Texas in the middle. The artists got some subtle jabs in at Fort Worth by portraying Dallas in a more favorable light. The East Texas Room has rich wood paneling in Texas gum, and the South Texas Room walls are silver-leafed, with murals featuring cowboys, women picking cotton, oil workers, and a farmer plowing. This mural is by James Owen Mahoney. In an unexpectedly un-Texan twist, the

most opulent and lavish of all the rooms is Memorial Hall, a large room designed by three Yale professors. Giant Eugene Savage murals cover two walls, which are finished in marble and other sumptuous materials.

The Federal Tower building is by Donald S. Nelson, who also worked on Fort Worth's Will Rogers Memorial Center. Its interior remains intact, with an appropriate red-white-and-blue color scheme and original Gilbert Rohde–style furnishings made by the Herman Miller Company. Nelson was from Chicago, where he worked on the 1933 exposition with Paul Philippe Cret. It was Cret who recommended Nelson to George Dahl for the Texas fair, and also for work on the Will Rogers Memorial Center. On the strength of this recommendation, Nelson was hired for both projects.

The fair is so extensive that a day can easily be spent wandering about from building to building. Since time was not a luxury we could enjoy, Craig Holcomb conducted a quick golf-cart tour for us that included the following structures: the 1948 automobile building, on the south side of the esplanade (it replaced the Varied Industries Building, destroyed by fire in 1942); the Hall of Administration with the *Spirit of the Centennial* sculpture by Raoul Josset with José Martin, and the Centennial Building, an Art Deco remodeling of a 1905 building.

Other notable buildings at the fair include the Food and Fiber Building; the Embarcadero; the Poultry Building; the Hall of Horticulture (now the Garden Center); the Museum of Natural History; the Museum of Fine Arts (now the Science Place); the Aquarium, with sculpture by Allie Victoria Tennant; and finally, the 1936 "model home." And there is also a 1958 Garden Center built in Deco-Echo style.

Leaving the fair, we found that Dallas is very spread out and that its other Art Deco assets are scattered. One needs a car to see them all. Most interesting is a huge Pegasus neon sign downtown. Pegasus was the popular symbol of the Socony Mobil brand of gas distributed by the Standard Oil Company of New York, owners of the local Magnolia Oil franchise.

Other significant downtown Dallas buildings include the 1931 Tower Petroleum building, by Mark Lemon, at 1907 Elm Street, and the 1927 Bell Telephone tower, by Irvin Ray Timlin, at 4100 Bryan Avenue (he also did the small ones in Fort Worth). Otto Henry and Frank Witchell did two of the largest buildings, both erected in 1931: the Dallas Power & Light Company (T.U. Electric) at 1506 Commerce and the Lone Star Gas Company at 301 South Harwood.

Gordon Conway, one of the premier illustrators working in the Art Deco style, lived in Dallas, but the site of her house is now occupied by a large Trammell Crow building. The Art Deco connection has not been lost, however, for on this site is a sculpture garden with works by Antoine Emil Bourdelle, father of Pierre Bourdelle, who worked both at the Cincinnati Union Terminal and at Fair Park.

Dallas's greatest surviving movie palace is the suburban

Gropius design, with corner windows, glass-brick walls, thin tubular-steel columns, window eyebrows, a spiral staircase, a two-car garage, and an upper deck. There are two similar homes around the corner.

After touring the residential neighborhoods, one can cross over from Dallas to Fort Worth and barely notice any difference until one reaches the very different downtown of the cowboy city of Fort Worth. We took a walking tour, recommended and published by Downtown Fort Worth Incorporated and printed by the City of Fort Worth. It does include several of Fort Worth's finest buildings, which just happen to be Art Deco.

The history of the stockyards and the cattle trade is illustrated downtown in a very prominent *trompe l'oeil* mural entitled *Chisholm Trail*, in the 400 block of Main Street, by famed contemporary artist Richard Haas. The real stockyards are a few miles away from the Art Deco towers of downtown. One of the finest office towers (and also a great restoration job) is downtown Fort Worth's 1930 Sinclair Building, by Wiley G. Clarkson, at 106 West Fifth Street. It was built by Richard Otto Dulaney, who announced in 1927 that he would construct the town's first million-dollar skyscraper. The building is named for Sinclair Oil, the original main tenant. Judith Cohen was instrumental in gathering the documentation needed to complete the authentic restoration of the building.

Two very unusual railway buildings are the Texas & Pacific Passenger Terminal and Warehouse, on Lancaster Street at Main. Herman Koeppe designed them for the firm of Wyatt C. Hedrick in 1928. The passenger station was closed in 1967. In 1978, the complex was placed on the National Register. In that same year, the terminal was converted into a commercial office tower in an adaptive-reuse project. After little success, its owners in 1985 proposed the erection of a shopping-center complex on the site. This ill-advised plan was halted in 1986. The terminal's windowless end walls have a distinct and unusual Arabesque suggestion,

Lakewood Theater (1825 Abrams Road) by H. F. Pettigrew, with interior design by Eugene Gilboe for Franklin & Gilboe. It was built by Karl Hoblitzelle, the president of Texas-based Interstate Theatres, and it opened October 27, 1938. A great series of extraordinary mint-condition murals in its lobbies was created by Perry Nichols, Victor Lallier, and Harry Carnohan. The murals feature popular late-1930s Disney figures like Mickey Mouse, plus Max Fleischer originals like Popeye. In 1984, the theater was purchased by B. B. Barr, a local entrepreneur who ordered a rehab by Barbara Young. They revamped and polished up this gem to play first-run features once again. The exterior features an original big tower and a newer little tower, both decked out in splendid blue and red neon with yellow and white letters. The most unusual things about it (so far) are that it still has a single big screen and shows only one movie. At the time of the restoration, a rare vintage theater organ was moved into the theater's long-empty pipe chambers from the Old Mill Theatre in downtown Dallas.

The Lakewood has been a landmark in its upscale northeast Dallas neighborhood ever since it was erected to anchor a 1930s shopping center. This was an early transfer of commerce to an outer residential area. The Lakewood Shopping Center was developed to serve the new Machine Age chariot—the automobile.

There are several fine streamlined and Art Deco private residences around the city. We visited a few near 6900 Gaston Avenue. One by an unknown architect looks like a

Lakewood Theater (1,101 seats), 1825 Abrams Road, Lakewood Section, Dallas. ARCHITECT: H.F. Pettigrew; Interior designer: Eugene Gilboe for Franklin & Gilboe; Muralist: Perry Nichols, Victor Lallier and Harry Carnohan; Sculptor: José Martin, 1937. This futuristic 60-foot-high lighthouse sign tower, illuminated by red and blue neon and cases of light bulbs, draws 7,000 watts of power. This east-side Dallas landmark is hard to miss. Restored in 1984 by Barbara Young, the interior contains original murals inhabited by popular childrens' cartoon characters of the day, including many Disney figures. (Photograph by Michael D. Kinerk)

with two crown-shaped structures on each end and intricate designs in the brick. It rises thirteen stories right beside the main railway tracks. The adjacent freight station is brick with a limestone veneer. Both narrowly survived a recent expressway widening, which after public outcry was forced to detour around the two landmarks. Such fine architecture is sure to find a viable use eventually.

The principal Art Deco architects in Fort Worth were the firms of Wyatt C. Hedrick and Elmer G. Withers. Herman Koeppe did most of the design work for Hedrick's firm. These two firms worked together on many projects, so most of the design credit should go to Koeppe.

Among Koeppe's more interesting projects were the 1930 Central Fire Station and Alarm Signal Station at 1000 Cherry Street, the previously mentioned Texas & Pacific Passenger Terminal, and Fort Worth's Old City Hall (now the police station) at Throckmorton and Tenth Street, a WPA project.

Koeppe also worked on the interiors of the huge Will Rogers Memorial Center's coliseum and tower. The auditorium was designed by Donald S. Nelson. The most outstanding exterior feature here is a continuous band of mosaics along the roofline by Mosaic Tile Company of Zanesville, Ohio. Koeppe designed this massive artwork in two parts, entitled: *Romance of Range* (on the Coliseum) and *Settlement and Industrial Development of West* (on the Auditorium).

The ubiquitous Paul Philippe Cret did a building in Fort Worth with a local architect, Wiley G. Clarkson. The 1933 U.S. Courthouse at 501 West Tenth Street is a five-story building having the only WPA murals in the city.

Saint Louis architect Irvin Ray Timlin was engaged by Southwest Bell to create several medium-size district exchange buildings. These outstanding Art Deco buildings are tucked away in quiet suburban residential neighborhoods and are not easy to find.

Very easy to find, however, is the 1936 S. H. Kress store in downtown Fort Worth at 604 Main Street, by the master of all the Kress buildings, Edward F. Sibbert of New York. Another nearby Art Deco landmark is the now-abandoned 1929 Blackstone Hotel (601 Main Street) by Mauran, Russell and Crowell of Saint Louis, working with local architect Elmer G. Withers. This very important social hub was the first Art Deco–style skyscraper in Fort Worth.

Downtown's most splendid terra-cotta façade is on the 1930 Western Union Telegraph Building by James B. Davies, at 314–316 Main Street.

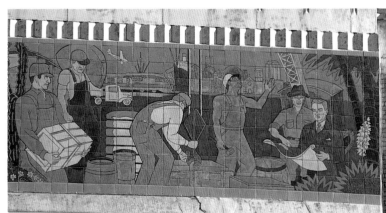

Will Rogers Memorial Center, *3301 West Lancaster Street, Fort Worth.* ARCHITECT: *Coliseum and Tower: Herman P. Koeppe for Wyatt C. Hedrick; Auditorium: Donald S. Nelson for Elmer G. Withers, 1936.* This civic-improvement project, spearheaded by Fort Worth Star-Telegram publisher Amon Carter, was his city's contribution to the Texas Centennial celebration. Ever competing with Dallas, Fort Worth felt obliged to build this jumbo auditorium and coliseum. These are tied together by a Saarinen-style "Pioneer Tower."

Will Rogers Memorial Center, *3301 West Lancaster Street, Fort Worth.* ARCHITECT: *Coliseum and Tower: Herman P. Koeppe for Wyatt C. Hedrick; Auditorium: Donald S. Nelson for Elmer G. Withers, 1936.* Koeppe created the brilliantly colored tile friezes based on Texas history. The work runs along the roofline of both the auditorium and coliseum. This detail is from the auditorium frieze entitled Industrial Development of the West. Each of the two friezes is ten feet tall and two hundred feet long. Koeppe's designs were executed by the Mosaic Tile Company of Zanesville, Ohio.

Texas & Pacific Railroad Passenger Terminal, *1600 Throckmorton Street, Fort Worth.* ARCHITECT: *Herman P. Koeppe for Wyatt C. Hedrick, 1929.* Texas & Pacific created this traditional two-story train station with an unusual ten-story office tower above. Construction was not assured until civic fathers pushed through a $3 million bond issue for surrounding roads and bridges. The façade design is an unusual mixture of Arabesque and Zigzag, while the passenger lobby is splendid French Art Deco. Opened in 1931, it was abandoned by the railroad in 1967, but was saved and refurbished for office use in 1978. In 1992, it was once again being considered for a role as a regional transportation hub linking buses and high-speed rail.

GUARDIAN
BUILDING

GUARDI
BUILDI

6

DETROIT

THE MOTOR CITY

We are the first nation in the history of the world to go to the poor house in an automobile.

—Will Rogers

LIKE SO MANY GREAT CITIES, DETROIT ROSE ON THE banks of a strategic river. The Detroit River runs to the sea through a chain of lakes, emptying into the Saint Lawrence River. This waterway was charted by the French shortly after English rival Henry Hudson had charted the great bay to the north that was named for him. The French explorers landed eventually at a spot that would become the center of Detroit.

Fort Pontchartrain was established here in 1701 by Antoine de la Monthe Cadillac. As early French explorer Adrian Joliet traveled upriver, he encountered rocky rapids and a narrow passage. It was necessary to cross over the land, and at this site on the bank, a settlement was established. In French, "city on the straits" is *ville d'etroit*. It was definitely in the right place, straddling two great lakes and sitting in the heartland of the richly forested and fur-laden Northwest Territory.

The English claimed the territory in 1760, but Ottawa chief Pontiac didn't care for the British and started a war in 1763. The natives were subdued in 1794 by General "Mad" Anthony Wayne. By 1800, it had become a bustling town of mostly wood-frame construction. In 1805, Michigan territorial Chief Justice Augustus B. Woodward arrived with a big vision for this small settlement. He proposed a plan for redevelopment based on the work of Pierre L'Enfant, whose celebrated design for Washington, D.C., had been inspired by Paris. Woodward's design incorporated L'Enfant's formal streets radiating from a central point—the river landing—as

Union Trust (Guardian Building), 500 Griswold Street, Detroit. ARCHITECT: Wirt Rowland for Smith, Hinchman & Grylls, 1928. These Dahlstrom elevator doors are made of the new Machine Age metal, Monel. Adding vibrant color are exquisite Tiffany Favrile glass insets forming the initials "U.T." Rookwood "reverse ziggurat" ceiling notches add a Mayan flavor. The building is now home to the Michigan Consolidated Gas Company, which restored the interior in 1985.

Union Trust (Guardian Building), 500 Griswold Street, Detroit. ARCHITECT: Wirt Rowland for Smith, Hinchman & Grylls; Sculptor: Joe Parducci, 1928. Guarding this entrance cupola is a Cubist-winged aviator. Mary Chase Stratton, founder of the nearby Pewabic Pottery, executed the tiles used in the stepped-notch ziggurats. Flanking the door are relief sculptures entitled Safety and Security. The exterior was restored in 1977.

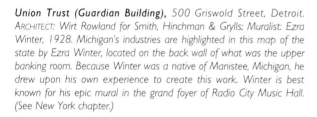

Union Trust (Guardian Building), 500 Griswold Street, Detroit. ARCHITECT: Wirt Rowland for Smith, Hinchman & Grylls; Muralist: Ezra Winter, 1928. Michigan's industries are highlighted in this map of the state by Ezra Winter, located on the back wall of what was the upper banking room. Because Winter was a native of Manistee, Michigan, he drew upon his own experience to create this work. Winter is best known for his epic mural in the grand foyer of Radio City Music Hall. (See New York chapter.)

Union Trust (Guardian Building), 500 Griswold Street, Detroit. ARCHITECT: Wirt Rowland for Smith, Hinchman & Grylls, 1928. One of the finest of the late 1920s office towers, this tan-orange brick and terra-cotta building was conceived as a high-rise cathedral of finance, complete with a symbolic thirty-six-story spire, where the bell tower would be. This configuration is atypical for an Art Deco skyscraper; most have a tall section in the center between two symmetrical lower wings. Soon after it opened, the building changed hands, owing to financial failures arising from the Great Depression. In this vintage postcard it is referred to by its second name, Union Guardian Trust Building.

Union Trust (Guardian Building), 500 Griswold Street, Detroit. ARCHITECT: Wirt Rowland for Smith, Hinchman & Grylls; Mosaic Design: Ezra Winter, 1928. A Michigan pine tree rises from a base that encapsulates the banking firm's original credo. Also by Winter, this glass tile mosaic is the centerpiece of the lobby.

in other early cities like Boston, Cincinnati, Charleston, or Saint Louis, where cargo, after shipment over water, could be unloaded, traded, and reloaded.

While Woodward expected economic development to spring from the river, little did he know that the real driving force of Detroit's development would come a century later in the motor car. Unfortunately, his wish to establish a major city on the bank of the river was given tragic impetus by a terrible fire in 1805. After the conflagration, Judge Woodward assumed the powers of governor and was to able to change Detroit from a simple wilderness fort settlement into a well-planned modern city, crossed by wide boulevards. A hundred years later, his wish had been fulfilled beyond his dreams. The Machine Age arrived right on cue in Detroit, as giant commercial enterprises sprang up, attracted by the fine roads and facilities that Woodward had established. Because it was booming throughout the early twentieth century, Detroit is blessed now with some of the greatest Art Deco treasures in the country.

Detroit was growing at the same time that the United States was preparing to become the industrial titan of the world. It was on the existing nineteenth-century industrial bases that the great corporations grew, earning enough money to pay for the lavish cathedrals of commerce in the Art Deco style. Many of the tenants of Art Deco skyscrapers were occupying their second or third home by 1929.

Here, as nowhere else, we see the pervasive and profound influence of the automobile. A style evolved in Detroit that we may call Industrial Deco, promulgated by Albert Kahn, who did the early Ford plants, plus factories and offices for Chrysler and General Motors (GM). He designed the city airport, both Detroit newspaper buildings, an early television studio, assorted offices, and hundreds of other buildings of every description. He was responsible for the huge headquarters of General Motors at 3044 West Grand Avenue, across the street from the lavish Fisher "New Center" building. And he designed several world's fair pavilions, for he was the favored architect of the auto industry, which always built prominent structures at these expositions. Kahn introduced reinforced concrete into American factory design, which made possible windows and expanded open space. He also designed homes for the auto barons.

GM's Fisher Brothers wished to make a positive mark on their burgeoning hometown. In 1928, they commissioned Kahn to design the New Center at 3011 Grand Boulevard, close to the Detroit Institute of Arts, on the northern edge of downtown. This urban complex—predating Cincinnati's Carew and New York's Rockefeller Center—was to be a

Penobscot Building, 645 Griswold Street, Detroit. Architect: Wirt Rowland for Smith, Hinchman & Grylls, 1927. A Penobscot tribal chieftain presides over the five-story limestone entrance of this monument to Michigan's native culture. The façade and interior art work present an encyclopedia of Native American Art Deco–style motifs. Directly across the street is the more colorful Union Trust (Guardian Building) by the same designer.

tower of great beauty and utility rising above the city around it, housing thousands of workers and their cars, and containing shops, theaters, restaurants—indeed, every amenity of modern city life. And above all else, the brothers wanted the New Center to make a statement, to be a supremely desirable place to work or visit. Kahn was very successful, and the Fisher Building, as it is now called, is a wonderful twenty-six-story monument to planning and design, comparing favorably with all others. Kahn commissioned Hungarian sculptor Geza Maroti, a member of the new Cranbrook Academy faculty (more on this later), to shape the center's overall textures. The results were splendid, if somewhat exuberant. As was expected from all great late Roaring Twenties projects, the building was filled with frescoes, murals, granite-relief sculptures, marble, and lots of brass and other fine metalwork.

In Detroit, as in so many other cities, we again see the hand of Paul Philippe Cret, who designed the 1927 Stripped Classic addition to the older Italianate Detroit Institute of Arts. He worked on this project with his frequent collaborators, Zantzinger, Borie & Medary. At the same time, the institute commissioned twenty-seven frescoes by Diego Rivera on the theme of Detroit's industries and sciences. By the end of the first Art Deco era, this neighborhood at the corner of Grand and Cass Avenues had become very significant: It hosted the 1922 GM Headquarters; the Institute of Arts with its new 1927 addition; the adjacent 1941 Horace Rackham

Memorial Auditorium; and, of course, the luxurious 1928 Fisher New Center building with its theater and shopping arcade—precursor to today's suburban malls.

One remarkable designer, Wirt Rowland, was responsible for Detroit's two most magnificent Art Deco towers. (He also designed several Michigan Bell buildings.) The 1928 Penobscot and the adjacent 1929 Union Trust Buildings, at 645 and 500 Griswold, respectively, are a testament to Rowland's talent. Rowland worked in the distinguished Detroit firm of Smith, Hinchman & Grylls. These buildings should be classified as Pueblo Deco, because of the pervasive Native American motifs found in both. The Penobscot, with its tribal name, has an edge in this regard. However, the Union Trust Building was finished more lavishly. The Union Trust project was so massive that the architect specified entire rooms full of tile from both of the Midwest's leading tile firms, Rookwood and Pewabic. The results are striking, with an entrance in Pewabic tile, and the lower lobby and elevator vestibules lined with Rookwood tile. The vaulted upper banking-room ceiling appears to be tile but actually is stenciled and painted in sixteen colors on cloth to absorb

noise in the big room. There also are several works in the building by celebrated Michigan artist Ezra Winter. After a Great Depression bankruptcy, the thirty-six-story Union Trust changed hands and was renamed the Guardian Trust Building. The present owner, Michigan Consolidated Gas, commissioned a two-year restoration in 1975. Further restoration was carried out between 1983 and 1985, some of it being done by the sons and grandsons of an original artisan, Anthony Eugenio.

The even-taller forty-seven-story Penobscot Building is a matching tribute to its designer. Both buildings are crammed with great glass, murals, sculpture, and craftsmanship. Detroit would not be the same without these great towers.

Horace H. Rackham Educational Memorial, 100 *Farnsworth Street, Detroit. ARCHITECT: Harley, Ellington and Day; Sculptor: Marshall Fredericks, 1941. White Georgia marble frames the auditorium entrance in this superb Stripped Classic façade. When the building opened, the west wing served the University of Michigan and the east wing housed the Engineering Society of Detroit. At the entrance are tall smooth piers, capped by Fredericks's four sculptural reliefs evoking the building's dual functions: Engineering and Education. Fredericks was associated with Cranbrook Academy in Bloomfield Hills, Michigan, and still maintains a studio nearby.*

Elwood Bar (Elwood Grill), 2100 *Woodward Avenue at Elizabeth Street, Detroit. ARCHITECT: Unknown, 1936. A regular dining spot for members of the Detroit Art Deco Society since its restoration in 1988 by Detroit preservationist/businessman Chuck Forbes, this diner is in a resurgent neighborhood north of downtown. One block away is the Music Hall, which has an Art Deco façade. Across the street is the fabulous 5,000-seat Fox Theater, once owned by Forbes, then sold to Little Caesar's Pizza owner Michael Ilitch, who gave it an $8-million restoration, giving the neighborhood a really big boost. (Photograph by Michael D. Kinerk)*

Detroit naturally pioneered the creation of superhighways. Davison and Henry Cabot Lodge freeways, among the nation's earliest, were built in 1942. Only the 1936 Arroyo Seco (now Pasadena) Freeway came earlier, linking Los Angeles and Pasadena.

There have been some major successes in Art Deco preservation projects in Detroit, led by people like preservationist-businessman Michael Ilitch, who owns the Little Caesar's Pizza empire. Another is Chuck Forbes, who in 1984 bought the legendary five-thousand-seat Fox Theater, holding it until 1987, when Ilitch bought it and began an $8-million restoration. Now renamed the Fox Center, it is a first-class facility, booked much of the time. Forbes still owns the wonderful Art Deco Elwood Diner across the street from the Fox. He reworked this 1936 bar into a streamlined paradise for Art Deco lovers and hungry passers-by.

Other preservation successes are the result of dedicated work by the small but ambitious Detroit Art Deco Society (DADS), founded June 1986 by Ann Duke. She and her top officers, Chuck Zuccarini, Janine Menlove, and Chuck Cirgenski, have arranged tours and parties to gain new members and win publicity for preservation. Recently, the society merged with the leading preservation organization in the county, Preservation Wayne, which is headed by William S. Colburn, himself an avid Decophile. Colburn frequently leads Art Deco tours himself, and the two groups hope to reinvigorate and stimulate each other. One of their most successful recent ventures was "Lobbying for Preservation," a progressive affair organized to highlight downtown's great little-seen and little-appreciated lobbies. This enthusiastic group rallied its key members to conduct us on a day-long tour of the city and its sprawling suburbs, with stops at the Elwood Diner for lunch and late-night dinner in the former bank that is now an Art Deco–theme restaurant in the resplendent Fisher Building arcade.

Elsewhere
Cranbrook Academy, Bloomfield Hills, Michigan

One of the major impacts on the artistic and design community in Detroit—and, indeed, on the whole nation—was the founding of Cranbrook Academy in 1925 by art lover and newspaper mogul George Booth, owner of the *Detroit News* and a chain of smaller Michigan newspapers. He was phenomenally successful in achieving the kind of institution he wished for. One of the earliest proto-Deco architects in the world was Eliel Saarinen, who set standards in his native Finland that would prove to influence architects for decades. Booth invited Saarinen to become president of his new Cranbrook Academy, and the offer was accepted. The influx of great talent had begun.

In 1929, sculptor Carl Milles came to visit Cranbrook and never left, joining the faculty at Saarinen's invitation. Charles Eames led the design department, Harry Bertoia headed the metal department, and Saarinen's wife, Loja, created a textile-weaving department. Booth founded Cranbrook because of his long interest in the Arts-and-Crafts movement, but Saarinen gently moved the school toward Modernism. The comparisons to the Bauhaus are inevitable.

One of Saarinen's favorite designs is telescoping squares. At Cranbrook, he used the design pattern in a cubic, three-to-five-part column, rising in sections. He used it for support columns and tower designs. His building bases were often square. The top of his entry for the Chicago *Tribune* competition, with its sectioned-off, stepped-up, vertical-ribbed fenestration, resembles the flared-fluted decoration of Cranbrook's loggia columns and entrance-gate pylons.

While still in Finland, Saarinen had designed the pivotal 1910 Helsinki Rail Station, with its giant arched entry portal and handsome, sleek tower. His stepped-back polyplanar geometric massing was exactly the type favored by famed renderer Hugh Ferris and extolled by Paul T. Frankl. Both praised Saarinen's work in their 1930s architectural texts. Saarinen further advanced his career by submitting his thoughtful and creative designs for many major American projects, competing with such giants as Raymond Hood, George Howells, D. H. Burnham, and Walter Burley Griffin. He was responsible for a room in a 1929 industrial-art exhibition at New York's Metropolitan Museum of Art entitled "The Architect and Industrial Art."

Cranbrook's outstanding campus eventually included a cornucopia of Saarinen's buildings. His early buildings here are notable for their use of tan brick and copper roofs. His commission extended until the campus was complete, and his designs were continually updated so that they were ever-more modern and less decorative. To this day, the academy

Cranbrook Academy, 500 Long Pine Road, Bloomfield Hills, Michigan. ARCHITECT: *Eliel Saarinen, 1925; Restoration architects: Schervish/Vogel/Merz, 1986. Cranbrook Academy's loggia has tripartite, square support columns in a fluted sheaf-of-wheat design, which is reminiscent of Lalique but instilled with Saarinen's geometric simplicity. To fulfill newspaper baron George Booth's vision in creating this renowned institution, Saarinen called upon Oscar Bach to design the metalwork, and he commissioned pieces by master sculptors Géza Maróti, Carl Milles, and Paul Manship. (Photograph by Michael D. Kinerk)*

influences some of the world's finest designers as they study here. It is worth a visit to the campus to view Saarinen's buildings, as well as to see the many fine sculptures and other artwork on display. Among the more impressive Art Deco masterpieces are metal works by Oscar Bach and the 1933 sculpture *Triton* by Carl Milles in the reflecting pool at the school's Institute of Science.

Detroit's other notable Arts-and-Crafts establishment is the Pewabic Pottery Works, established in 1907 by Mary Chase Perry Stratton, in a studio just off Woodward Avenue and close to downtown. In order to remain viable and up-to-date, Pewabic produced Art Deco designs like its primary competitor, Cincinnati's Rookwood Pottery. In its earliest days, just like Cranbrook, it began as an Arts-and-Crafts community. After Stratton died in 1960, the company was closed. It was revived in 1982, and in 1985, it helped with the restoration of its early work in the Union Trust (Guardian) Building.

Royal Oak, Michigan

In suburban Royal Oak, we find one of the nation's great Art Deco churches, the Shrine of the Little Flower, 2123 Roseland Avenue at North Woodward and Twelve Mile Road. In the early days of radio, there developed a new phenomenon: the radio minister. Father Charles Coughlin, a very successful preacher, yet reportedly a sinister Nazi sympathizer, achieved great success preaching on the radio. He collected so much money he felt the need to build a great church for his ministry. In 1927, a modernistic tower was designed by Henry J. McGill, who also designed the outstanding Church of the Most Precious Blood in Queens, New York. By 1929, the tower of the Little Flower had been erected. It is covered with beautiful sculptures of biblical figures. Oddly, on the Archangel Michael we see the visage of Father Coughlin himself. It's no miracle, for Coughlin's face and other references to him appear throughout the lovely church in excellent sculptures by the renowned René Paul Chambellan. The Great Depression slowed Coughlin down, but he raised enough money to complete the church in 1933.

We leave Detroit by noting Henry Ford's own passion for historic preservation. In the midst of the Art Deco era, Ford began thinking about preserving his own recent past. He created Greenfield Village in 1929 to "preserve the history of the past." In 1986, this museum mounted an impor-

tant exhibition on Ford's own times entitled "Streamlining America." Millions have visited this fascinating preservation laboratory and have not only enjoyed themselves but learned from the lessons only history can teach us.

Kalamazoo, Michigan

There is a notable 1937 work, *Fountain of the Pioneers*, by sculptor Alfonso Iannelli in Bronson Park, across from City Hall in Kalamazoo. Iannelli, an early collaborator of Frank Lloyd Wright and a brilliant Art Deco graphics designer in his own right, won a competition to design this fountain, located at 241 West South Street.

Ford-Wyoming Drive-In Theater, 9633 Joseph Campau, Hamtramck, Michigan. ARCHITECT: Unknown, c. 1946. Following the Art Deco "rule of threes," this drive-in movie screen's superstructure features attractive Moderne massing. This is an example of Delayed Deco—projects of 1940s design built after World War II and into the 1950s. (Photograph by Janine Menlove)

Transcontinental Highway across Boulder Dam

© DESERT SOUVENIR SUPPLY

1B-H2433

96

7

HOOVER DAM

EIGHTH WONDER OF THE WORLD

*Driving away from Hoover Dam via Las Vegas,
the route lay not far from an officially
sequestered area where is being generated
power of a different order, designed for a different purpose. . . . Modern science, which
knows no national boundaries, has thrust into
man's fallible hands unprecedented power:
power in building, power in destroying.*

—Hugh Ferris
Power in Building, 1953

U.S. HIGHWAY 93 ARCS ACROSS THE TOP OF
majestic Hoover Dam like a delicate ribbon above the shimmering water of Lake Mead and over a canyon that ends far
below in an awesome battery of turbines, transmission lines,
and surging electrical energy. The roadway links Arizona and
Nevada while spanning the chasm of the Colorado River
through the valley of the Black Mountains. This steel and
concrete highway is the apotheosis of Art Deco.

   Engineered carefully and made to be beautiful, Hoover
Dam is without question one of Art Deco's finest monuments. It is an attempt to harness the earth's energy and
rechannel it. The dam's main form slopes sharply, rising five
hundred feet, punctuated by four towers above the paved
roadway. The original plans called for crenelation of the
structure, but the only visible examples of that ancient
fortress form are in the stone retaining walls zipping through
the hills and flanking the walkways. There was no need for
such embattlements, except against the water. But astutely
anticipating a steady stream of visitors, the designers included
large elevators and handsome public facilities within the
monumental structure, a veritable oasis of water, cool con-

*Hoover Dam, U.S. Route 93, crossing Colorado River,
Nevada-Arizona border, Boulder City, Nevada. ARCHITECT:
Gordon B. Kaufmann, with U.S. Bureau of Reclamation
engineers, 1931. Constructed of poured concrete and
steel, the beauty of this great forty-four-story dam was
determined partly by engineers' structural equations and
partly by the gifted Los Angeles architect Gordon
Kaufmann. The shape allows the dam to hold back bil-
lions of gallons of water. The restrained energy is
unleashed in the magnificent dynamos 700 feet below.*

*Hoover Dam, U.S. Route 93, crossing Colorado River,
Nevada-Arizona border, Boulder City, Nevada. ARCHITECT:
Gordon B. Kaufmann, with U.S. Bureau of Reclamation
engineers, 1931. This vintage postcard served to promote
Hoover Dam, with its four streamlined Stripped Classic
water intake towers rising out of Lake Mead. Four other
service towers jut above the roadbed to house high-speed
elevators and utilities. Over the service tower entrances
are massive sculptural panels by Oskar Hansen.*

Hoover Dam, **Winged Figure of the Republic,** *U.S. Route 93, crossing Colorado River, Nevada-Arizona border, Boulder City, Nevada.* ARCHITECT: *Gordon B. Kaufmann, with U.S. Bureau of Reclamation engineers; Sculptor: Oskar J.W. Hansen, 1931. Near the dam is a large terrazzo plaza that pinpoints the dam's location in a celestial map of the universe, providing a time-line of the earth's great engineering achievements, such as the pyramids. Poised above the map, as if ready to ascend to the heavens, is this great thirty-foot-high bronze cosmic figure, one of an identical pair by Hansen. A 142-foot flagpole (shadow at right) rises between them.*

Hoover Dam, U.S. Route 93, crossing Colorado River, Nevada-Arizona border, Boulder City, Nevada. ARCHITECT: *Gordon B. Kaufmann, with U.S. Bureau of Reclamation engineers; Artist: Allan True, 1931. Intricate Native American designs enhance the durable and beautiful terrazzo floors in the dam's labyrinth of corridors. Great care was taken in designing the dam to marry art and engineering in every aspect of the project. (Photograph by Michael D. Kinerk)*

crete, and vast electrical power in the center of the ancient, parched Sonoran Desert. As one steadily descends into the valley, the red walls of five-thousand-year-old cliffs etch the blue sky. The massive dam comes into sight. Above the two main entrance towers are large, allegorical cast-concrete panels by Norwegian sculptor Oskar Hansen. One depicts the fivefold purpose of the dam; the other traces the area's history. Just off the highway approaching the dam are more works by Hansen, including a brilliant celestial map in the plaza and two 30-foot-tall mythical bronze-winged statues resting on four-ton Diorite bases. Between the statues is a 142-foot flagpole for Old Glory as well. It took amateur astronomer and mathematician Hansen five years to work out the exact placement of all the stars in the universe throughout the time line described in the celestial map. He charted a cycle of history called a *Platonic Year* and pegged it to 25,694.8 ordinary earth years. Hansen traced history across this period, right up to the exact moment the dam would be dedicated to serve the public. He named the complex map in the terrazzo the *Processional Diagram of a Platonic Year.*

Professor Richard Guy Wilson of the University of Virginia has studied and written extensively on the dam. He views it as one of the country's major Art Deco projects of all time and has urged his students to study it as he has. His papers and lectures illuminate the complexity of its engineering and describe its design. First, he describes the four towers: Two outer towers provide utilities and restrooms, and two inner towers house elevators to the concrete labyrinth below. The outer vestibule walls are lined floor to ceiling with Vitrolite structural-glass panels: the women's side is black, the men's, dark green. The massive doors are bronze. The interior terrazzo corridors are distinguished by authentic Native American motifs, making this a Pueblo Deco enclave, designed by Denver artist Allan True. Wilson explains, "They show the indebtedness to Native American geometrical patterns."

The only architect involved in the dam was a singularly influential one: Gordon B. Kaufmann of Los Angeles, who was listed as a "consultant" to the staff of engineers. He had come from England to California in 1914 and had designed many buildings there. He viewed the dam project strictly as an exercise in "Form follows function." Kaufmann said that the dam was viewed by all its designers as being complementary to the landscape rather than dominating it. The concrete was poured for weeks and weeks, never ceasingly. A network of pipes carried cool water to help the concrete harden properly. Kaufmann made studies of the exact shading in concrete surfaces to be achieved. The result is that the face of the dam on the bottom and along the powerhouse walls is shaded noticeably darker, while the dam's upper face is lighter. Even the massive water-overflow, spillway-outlet gates were consciously moved further downstream so that they would merge better into the background of the canyon.

Now that the Art Deco significance of the dam's original design has been brought to the attention of the U.S.

Bureau of Reclamation, which administers the dam, it has decreed that all new construction, such as the just-completed Visitor Center, must be compatible with the original design.

Elsewhere
Phoenix, Arizona

This is the location of the fabulous Arizona Biltmore Resort Hotel designed in 1929 by Frank Lloyd Wright, although one of his estranged understudies was the architect of record, and there was a nasty contretemps over who deserved what fee. Nevertheless, the hotel's entire façade is a brilliant expanse of Wright's "textile block" construction. Here also are a few of the famed 1914 Wright-Iannelli "Sprites," rescued from the demolished Midway Gardens in Chicago. The interior of this hotel has been audaciously modified so many times that it is impossible to tell who designed what. Some is good; some is bad. The outstanding features are the enormous dining room and the splendid tiled pool area, surrounded by Wrightian fountains, arcades, and irresistible private bungalows.

We visited the Arizona Biltmore many times with our Phoenix tour guides, Walter Strony and Thomas Lind, both collectors of Art Deco who live in a fine Spanish Mission Pueblo Deco house. Both Strony and Lind—on separate days—assisted us on our tours of Art Deco Indianapolis because we happened all to be there at the same time.

Yosemite Village, California

In the rugged California mountains near the Nevada border is the Ahwahnee Hotel, a 1927 lodge by noted architect Gilbert Stanley Underwood, better known for his handsome train stations, libraries, and large commercial buildings. The Ahwahnee has unusual interior appointments, including murals by Jeannette Dyer Spencer. It is operated for guests at the famed Yosemite National Park.

Bisbee, Arizona

A distinct Pueblo Deco treasure in this secluded little town is the 1931 Cochise County Courthouse by Roy Place, with sculptures of prospecting miners. The term Pueblo Deco is believed to have been originated by architectural historian Marcus Wiffen, who wrote a book by the same name.

Cochise County Courthouse, *Quality Hill, Bisbee, Arizona.* ARCHITECT: *Roy Place; Sculptor: Lew Place, 1931. Copper miners carved in stone sit astride the main entrance to the courthouse. The architect originally was from the Boston firm of Shepley, Rutan & Coolidge. His seventeen-year-old son was the sculptor on this project. (Photograph by Richard Byrd)*

Cochise County Courthouse, *Quality Hill, Bisbee, Arizona.* ARCHITECT: *Roy Place, 1931. This Art Deco courthouse was built in an old Arizona copper boom town. It has splendid metalwork including brass entrance doors, each of which has a figure holding a sword of justice. Mining and survival in the hardscrabble desert are themes developed in the decoration throughout the building.*

Cochise County Courthouse, *Quality Hill, Bisbee, Arizona.* ARCHITECT: *Roy Place; Sculptor: R. Phillips Sanderson, 1931. This wood-relief panel by Sanderson is from a series in the lobby illustrating frontier life. Themes include mining, prospecting for ore, dance-hall girls, poker, gunslingers, lynchings, and stagecoach travel. The county was named for Cochise, a great Apache chief.*

8

INDIANAPOLIS

THE CIRCLE CITY

Indianapolis shaped my point of view for life. Tree-lined vistas, broad boulevards and solid buildings with granite, marble and stone, bronze and copper, confirmed from birth my instinct for permanence and a predilection for style.

—*Nathaniel Alexander Owings*, founding partner of Skidmore, Owings & Merrill, quoted in *Indianapolis Architecture*, 1975.

INDIANAPOLIS, LIKE WASHINGTON, D.C., IS A CITY of monuments and war memorials. Several mostly classical monuments and public buildings are here, including the national headquarters of the American Legion. These are situated on a very European central mall called Veterans Plaza, which stretches through the heart of the city. The mall was laid out near the turn of the century. Buildings along the mall that were erected in the 1930s and 1940s, while blending in with the earlier Beaux Arts look, have Art Deco fixtures, lights, and other decorative touches. The mall stretches north for blocks from Monument Circle, a center-city hub from which major streets emanate like the spokes of a wheel. At the center of the circle is a great monument to veterans of the nation's wars, with heroic sculpture, huge fountains, rushing waterfalls, and an observation deck at its summit.

It is from this central hub that the city gets its nickname: the Circle City. On Monument Circle, at 5 East Market Street, is one of the great Art Deco office buildings in America. One of several Egyptian Art Deco structures in the city, Circle Tower shows how Indianapolis was influenced more than any other city by the King Tut craze that swept the world after 1922. The multi-setback building is a 1930 masterpiece by Indianapolis's most important Art Deco architectural firm, Rubush & Hunter. The designers paid

Circle Tower, 5 East Market Street, Monument Circle (southeast side), Indianapolis. ARCHITECT: Rubush & Hunter; Metalwork: Oscar Bach, 1930. Stainless-steel elevator doors in this unique building were "bronzed," by using Bach's proprietary technique. Identical doors were featured in a 1930s display in the Procurement Division of the Treasury Department, Washington, D.C., promoting new uses of maintenance-free stainless steel.

Circle Tower, Second-Floor Barbershop (Studio 2000 Hair Salon), 5 East Market Street, Monument Circle (southeast side), Indianapolis. ARCHITECT: Rubush & Hunter, 1930. This barbershop interior is a fascinating artistic creation featuring numerous black and silver glazed-tile representations of the barber's art, including this electric "sunburst" exhaust fan, flanked by scissors and combs. When it was "updated" from a barbershop to a hair salon, the proprietors took care to preserve the original decor.

undisguised homage to the tombs of ancient Egyptian pharaohs.

This Egypto-Deco tower, with its stepped-ziggurat parapets and splendid brasswork, compares favorably with any Holabird & Root or Ely Jacques Kahn edifice. It features polished stainless-steel elevator doors specially treated to look like brass; they are illustrated in a 1929 Oscar Bach architectural-metal brochure. On the second floor is the former Circle Tower Barbershop (more recently, Studio 2000 Hair Salon), which is surely the most impressive Art Deco hair emporium ever designed. Barbara Capitman's voyage took her here, and she never forgot that wonderful barbershop. "No Deco buff would want to be remotely near Indianapolis without visiting the second floor Circle Barbershop," Barbara wrote in her journal.

In our follow-up tour of Indianapolis's Art Deco hot spots, we met with our longtime friend Tim Needler. After we explained our book to him and told him Barbara's passion for the Circle Tower and its barbershop, he immediately put us in touch with his friend Jim Rogers, former president of the Indianapolis Historic Preservation Commission. Rogers, in turn, put us in touch with Bill Selm, author of the historic site designation report for the building. He wrote:

It [the Circle Tower] remains today the city's finest high-style Art Deco building, and it also represents the creativity and sophistication of the firm [Rubush & Hunter] in using the popular style to conform to the height limitations of the day. It is not merely a perfunctory setback, but a dramatic, stepped, modernist pyramid.

Indianapolis has another Egyptian-influenced skyscraper within walking distance of the Circle Tower: the 1929 Architects & Builders Building at 333 North Pennsylvania, also by Rubush & Hunter. This 1929 remodeling of an earlier building served as practice for the even more splendid Circle Tower. These two outstanding structures place Indianapolis at the forefront of cities with Egyptian-inspired Art Deco towers. The city also had an Egyptian movie theater, Zarings, which was demolished in the 1960s. The giant World War Memorial in the mall (not to be confused with the earlier-mentioned Revolutionary and Civil War memorial in the Circle) is adjacent to the Architects & Builders Building. On its uppermost floors, it has an Egyptian-style memorial temple to the dead. In this beautiful, huge, tomblike room, one almost expects to encounter incense and hieroglyphics. The memorial was designed in 1929 by the Cleveland firm Walker & Weeks. In the main entrance foyers are large lighting fixtures that are its most Art Deco feature.

A few blocks out from the Circle, along the central mall, is a great fountain by Sterling Calder and a pre-Deco classic Greek public library of 1917, one of the earliest buildings by the distinguished Paul Philippe Cret. Working with Cret was Milton B. Medary of the Philadelphia firm Zantzinger, Borie & Medary. Cret and Medary later did projects together in Washington, D.C., and Detroit. (In 1927, Medary designed the exquisite Bok Singing Tower in Lake Wales, Florida. See the Miami chapter.)

As in all big American cities, apartment houses are the commonest Art Deco building type. The 1929 Admiral Apartments, at 3025 North Meridian Street, is undoubtedly the finest example here. This judgment is confirmed by the gregarious Glory June, Indianapolis's most eminent Art Deco historian and author of *Art Deco Indianapolis,* a 1980 book funded and published mainly thanks to Ms. June's personal determination. (She won funding from the Indiana Architectural Foundation, the National Endowment for the Arts, and the Indiana Arts Commission.)

The next most numerous Art Deco building type here is banks. While many cities have one or two downtown bank towers, Indianapolis has seven suburban banks designed in 1947 by Dietrich A. Bohlen. Bohlen's firm is said to be the oldest architectural firm in the U.S.A., having evolved from Bohlen & Sons, established in 1850. Bohlen also designed the 1949 Crown Hill Mausoleum at 700 West Thirty-eighth Street.

Four surviving WPA fire stations were built here in 1935. Two are in imminent danger of demolition by the city. Also, there are several Art Deco pavilions within the precincts of the Indiana State Fairgounds that are of a rather pre-Deco Germanic-Dutch inspiration. A great Indiana Bell skyscraper at 240 North Meridian Street was designed by Vonnegut Bohn & Mueller in 1939. Kurt Vonnegut, Sr., a partner in the firm, is the father of famed novelist Kurt Vonnegut, Jr.

One of the most brilliant of Indianapolis's Art Deco

masterpieces is Rubush & Hunter's 1931 Coca-Cola Bottling Plant, now a motor-vehicle pool and administrative center for the Indianapolis public school system. This building, at 801 North Carrollton, features superb metal rails and grilles, together with wonderful terrazzo floors, lights, and an excellent glazed white terra-cotta façade, boasting outstanding renditions of Edgar Brandt's frozen fountains and floral motifs. The splendid metalwork was by Joseph Willenborg of the William Herman & Son Decorating Co. He was also responsible for the Egyptian metalwork at the Circle Tower. Most of the terra-cotta work on the Coke building, as well as the best terra-cotta throughout the city, is credited to Alexander Sangernebo, who worked from 1892 to 1931 for the Indianapolis Terra Cotta Company.

Another wonderful adaptive reuse project can be seen in the conversion of the 1928 School No. 80 into private residential apartments, now appropriately called the School 80 Apartments. A wise old owl carved in stone over the entrance sets the stage for this delightful reuse of the low-rise Germanic Deco suburban schoolhouse at 920 East Sixty-second Street near North Guilford Avenue. The firm of McGuire & Shook designed the original school. An adjacent 1948 school library is part of the project and was saved through the efforts of Glory June and her Art Deco–loving friends. The Art Deco annex to the schoolhouse apartments is still used for functions by the Marion County Public Library system.

Other great Indianapolis buildings include the 1934 State Library at 140 North Senate Avenue by Pierre & Wright; a 1928 Pueblo Deco design also by Pierre & Wright; the Old Trail Building next to the state capitol at 301 West Washington Street; an original Sears, Roebuck & Co. (now a supermarket) at 333 North Alabama Street; the 1937 former H. P. Wasson Department Store downtown at 2 West Washington Avenue, again by the ubiquitous Rubush & Hunter; and the 1936 WPA Naval Armory, 1560 West Thirtieth Street on White River Parkway, with its four murals by Charles Baverley.

Indianapolis established the nation's first Union depot in 1853. In 1913, the Union Railway Company built elevated tracks and a two-story structure over them. The elevated main lines running into the heart of the city were incorporated into a splendid 1925 Romanesque pile, which was so successful that it was done over in 1930 to add new entrance canopies, concourses, and an overall upgrade. This new construction was Art Deco and was very skillfully and unobtrusively integrated into the lovely older architecture. After the passenger trains had long left the old station to rot, it was wisely saved and restored, and it is now a festival market center development, sensitively done, incorporating a unique Holiday Inn hotel. In addition to its normal rooms, the Union Terminal Holiday Inn has Pullman cars permanently parked upstairs along the old platforms to provide additional suites for the hotel. Each car has its own identity and is named for a famous person, such as Winston Churchill, Louis Armstrong, Charlie Chaplin, Greta Garbo, Rudolph Valentino, Cole Porter, and Amelia Earhart. One car, the Jean Harlow, is totally fitted out in Art Deco style. This wonderful and adaptive reuse project may be found at 39 West Jackson Place, at South Capitol and Louisiana Streets.

Nestled in the wooded hills surrounding the city are several more treasures. Indianapolis is blessed with many fine

Art Deco schools, university dormitories, and classrooms. The first is the small campus of Marian College. It was made possible when an unusual group of splendid 1920s Arts-and-Crafts mansions was donated to establish a college. This pristine neighborhood was created by some automobile tycoons who had joined in 1909 as investors in the Indianapolis Motor Speedway racetrack. Prime among them was Miami Beach's founder, Carl Fisher. Of his three partners, two, James Allison and Franklin Wheeler, also built great houses here. Allison's was a monument to Beaux Arts elegance, but Wheeler's was filled with beautiful Rookwood tile appointments. (Allison was also a Miami Beach pioneer with Fisher before its Art Deco development began.) With the later addition of several Art Deco buildings, this campus became a real Art Deco treasureland. The college's main entrance gate is at 3200 North Coldspring Road. The gate was designed by the distinguished Dietrich A. Bohlen, who also did the newer Delayed Deco buildings on campus: the gymnasium and Clare Hall (1948) and Marian Hall (1954). Another excellent Delayed Deco school is the 1951 Emmerich Manual Training High School at 2405 Madison Avenue, again by Bohlen. (Glory June takes credit, by the way, for coining the term *Delayed Deco* in her book.)

A splendid Art Deco classroom building may be found in architect Tom Hibbons's 1928 Butler Hall at 4550 Clarendon Road on the beautiful campus of Butler University. This streamlined building has notable Aztec influences.

The Indianapolis area has not one, but two diners. One of these streamlined dreamboats is on East Thirty-eighth Street at Shadeland Avenue. The other is a few miles west of town in Hendricks County, at 9784 Highway 40 West. Glory June insisted we make the drive to this diner so we could experience "the best tenderloin sandwich in Indiana."

Elsewhere in the wooded outer hills of Indianapolis is the estate of pharmaceutical mogul Eli Lilly. On these grounds was built in the 1960s the new Indianapolis Museum of Art. Barbara Capitman's mentor and friend Carl Weinhardt, Jr., became its first director. Later, he went to Miami as director of the Vizcaya Museum, Charles Deering's former villa on Biscayne Bay, the greatest residence in Miami and host to presidents, popes, and lovers. Weinhardt was Barbara's first and most respected ally in the drive to identify and preserve Art Deco. While still in Indianapolis, he hired a bright young scholar and administrator named Peggy Loar to help him lead the Indianapolis Museum. Loar, after serving at the Smithsonian Institution in Washington, later came to Miami Beach to establish the Wolfsonian Foundation's museum, which houses the enormous collection of Mitchell Wolfson, Jr., another early Capitman supporter and friend. With the intertwining histories of Fisher, Allison, Weinhardt, and Loar, it seems Indianapolis and Miami Beach are inextricably linked.

Lilly had many interests outside his business, including historic preservation. He and his wife restored the home of the famed Hoosier pioneer settler William Conner. In 1934, Lilly commissioned several murals for his third-floor ballroom in the "PWAP" (Public Works of Art Project) style, now called *Social Realism*.

Hoosier historian J. Kent Calder wrote a book on the art in the Lilly mansion, and he discovered that artist Grant Wood had turned down the commission because he was too busy but had suggested a student, John D. Pusey. Lilly and Pusey agreed on the theme "Aspects of Personality." Pusey painted eleven panels on religion, music, the courage of agricultural and industrial workers, athletics, and social-mindedness. He worked from cartoons on brown paper that are now in the Indiana University Art Museum in Bloomington. Pusey moved to Hollywood in 1931 to work as a set designer and art director, further feeding the film machine with Art Deco artistic fervor. At his death in 1977, Eli Lilly left his house to Indiana University.

Elsewhere in the Hoosier State
Auburn, Indiana

In Auburn, there is a one-of-a-kind museum in the original 1930 French Art Deco administrative offices and showroom for the Auburn Automobile Company. With its wonderful patterned floors, ceilings, and chandeliers from Italy, it is truly memorable. Indiana was responsible for many of the world's Art Deco–era automobiles, including the Studebaker, the Duesenberg, and the Stutz Bearcat. The competing car-manufacturing concerns merged in 1926 to form a single company. They made the Cord and the Auburn, many examples of which are on display in this Art Deco showplace. The museum is on State Road 8, off I-69, twenty miles north of Fort Wayne.

Bloomington, Indiana

The hilly southern Indiana town of Bloomington is home to Indiana University. Co-author Michael Kinerk went to school here, studying journalism and computer science. The journalism lectures were conducted in Robert Frost Daggett's 1940 Art Deco Woodburn Hall on East Seventh Street. In the main lecture hall are two of a series of twenty-two murals by Thomas Hart Benton. Because of the wisdom of IU President Herman B Wells, the murals were acquired and placed in various campus buildings including the great IU Auditorium, designed in 1940 by Eggers & Higgins with A. M. Strauss of Fort Wayne.

The murals were commissioned for the Indiana Pavilion at the 1933 Chicago Century of Progress Exposition. Benton's friend Thomas Hibbon, an Indianapolis architect, recommended Benton to Colonel Richard Lieber, the director of the Indiana Department of Conservation, who headed the commission to supervise Indiana's pavilion. Hibbon was the architect, so Benton got the commission and was asked to complete murals that were twelve feet high and two hundred feet wide to ring the exhibition hall. The only catch: they had to be ready in only five months for the opening of the Chicago exposition. Benton immersed himself in Indiana history (not very much different from the history of his native Kansas). With the painting assistance of students from Indianapolis's Herron School of Art, Benton completed the egg tempera brilliantly—and on time. The continuous progression of stories and the elongated romantic figures are very similar to Benton's better-known series based on the history of the U.S.A. that is now on permanent display in the lobby of New York's Equitable Life Insurance headquarters. After the Chicago exposition, the Indiana murals were ignominiously trucked to a rural storage depot. Wells had only to ask the governor for them and the university got them for nothing. When they were reinstalled in Bloomington in October 1940, Benton personally supervised.

In our travels retracing Barbara's steps, we spoke with Nanette Esseck Brewer, a curator at the IU Museum of Art. She showed us Benton's eighty-eight original sketches and studies for the murals, which the university now owns. Much of the available information on the murals comes from scholarly research by Brewer and Kathleen A. Foster, curator of nineteenth-and twentieth-century art at the museum. These now are among IU's richest treasures, although perhaps not as valuable as the original Gutenberg Bible also on campus in the Lilly Library. Our trip to Bloomington was brilliantly choreographed by an IU administrator, Dr. Don McMasters, who pulled strings and worked miracles to make it possible for us to see every Art Deco building and every Thomas Hart Benton mural and, in addition, to interview museum curators—in a six-hour period during summer break when all the buildings were closed!

9

KANSAS CITY

THEY'VE GONE ABOUT AS FAR AS THEY CAN GO

What is most clearly and heartbreakingly revealed in any presentation is that the buildings . . . represent the last great period of decorative art. We are struck with the poignant reality that it will never be possible to do this kind of work again.

Art Deco . . . is primarily the art of the skyscraper age. As such it is extraordinary that these structures have been systematically excluded from the modern architecture textbooks, or relegated to footnotes.

Ada Louise Huxtable
"The Skyscraper Style" column in *The New York Times*
November 17, 1974

PEOPLE WHO ARE FAMILIAR WITH BROADWAY musicals almost certainly have seen or heard the song about Kansas City from Rogers and Hammerstein's hit musical *Oklahoma*. In it, a traveling Oklahoma cowboy, having returned home, tells his neighbors how dumbfounded he was by the level of modernity to be found in Kansas City.

This song was based upon fact.

During the 1920s and 1930s, Kansas City was booming. The farming, aircraft, and automobile industries had many workers and supported many banks. Local business built more and more buildings, and the city got thoroughly up-to-date in no time. Jackson County political boss Tom Pendergast was one big reason. He wheedled and waggled and paid off his way to get to the top, and he kept the construction industry going strong right through the Depression.

Power & Light, 1330 Baltimore Avenue, Kansas City, Missouri. ARCHITECT: Edwin M. Price for Hoit, Price & Barnes, 1930. Beams of radiant energy issue from dynamos and then mesh with palm fronds and other Paris Exposition motifs. Most of the imagery on this thirty-story tower alludes to the generation of power. Water and the sun, two natural sources of power on earth, are themes found throughout the building. The power company is reportedly searching for a new home and may soon abandon this splendid downtown landmark.

Power & Light, 1330 Baltimore Avenue, Kansas City, Missouri. ARCHITECT: Edwin M. Price for Hoit, Price & Barnes, 1930. This closeup of the thirty-story tower, topped by a prismatic glass beacon of varying colors, shows its nighttime brilliance. The top setbacks contain concealed floods to light the sections above. The building quickly became Kansas City's leading landmark. (Photograph by Bob Barrett, copyright © 1987. Used by permission.)

44 NEW CITY HALL, KANSAS CITY, MO.

All the Los Angeles and New York big shots knew this because they had to stop over in Kansas City when flying cross-country on the old DC-3's. Many of the planes were made in Kansas City, and the airport here was a stopping off and reembarkation point for the stars, the executives, and the adventurous who were flying when trains still ruled the land and cabins were *not* pressurized.

Everybody knew Kansas City was a great modern city because everybody could see those Art Deco downtown towers when flying into the main airport. The metropolitan area of Kansas City covers five counties in two states and was a center of aviation manufacturing and engineering. The Missouri portion of Kansas City was where Pendergast had his machine and ran his county as did Boss Tweed in New York before him and Mayor Richard Daley in Chicago after him. An authoritative and autocratic style of government was the trademark of these big-city bosses—and the trains ran on time.

Pendergast left two extraordinary Art Deco complexes here. The first is the 1933 PWA Municipal Auditorium (211 West Thirteenth Street) by Joseph Murphy for Gentry, Voskamp & Neville, with Hoit, Price & Barnes. The second is the 1936 Civic Center at Twelfth and Oak Streets. Both are great monuments to the people of Kansas City. To help us tour these complexes, we were greeted in downtown Kansas City by photographer Bob Barrett, local pundit and commentator Shifra Stein, and scholarly local architect and Art Deco expert Richard Farnan. They were responsible for a feature layout in

City Hall, 414 East 12th Street at Oak Street, Kansas City, Missouri. ARCHITECT: Wight & Wight, 1936. A vintage postcard celebrates the massive thirty-two-story city hall, one of many projects launched by notorious Jackson County Democratic Party boss Tom J. Pendergast. Pendergast had interests in many interrelated money-making endeavors like local liquor outlets and the Ready Mix Concrete Company.

Apartments, 3027–29 Troost Avenue, Kansas City, Missouri. ARCHITECT: Unknown, 1929. An Art Deco pastel palette is used in this façade. Kansas City has outstanding glazed terra-cotta scattered throughout the city.

Bryant Building, 1102 Grand Avenue, Kansas City, Missouri. ARCHITECT: Graham, Anderson, Probst & White, 1930. This downtown landmark was the work of an esteemed Chicago firm. Here are details of the window treatments. The building's carved granite and white glazed brick express the French geometric fleur-de-lis style. Even after having been restored in 1984, the building is still endangered. In 1991, empty and forlorn, it had reverted to the mortgage holder, Bankers Trust.

the July 1986 *Historic Preservation* magazine of the National Trust. The layout was filled with some of Bob's best shots of Kansas City Art Deco. Shifra and Richard did research, and Shifra reviewed the city's history. Their article also explored the fantastic world of Boss Pendergast, as he used his position of patronage to enrich himself and his friends while building a much bigger and richer city.

Before this article was published, Farnan had interviewed two of the major architects in Kansas City's history: Clarence Kivett and Robert Bloomgarten. Their firm, Kivett, Frowerk and Bloomgarten, was responsible for the colorful futuristic 1934 Katz Drug Store (now Osco Drugs) at 3948 Main Street, with its bold tower and corner striping. Kivett told Farnan of his own visit to the 1933 Chicago fair, where everything was really up-to-date, and he said he had done this

store with a flair because of his appreciation of Paul Philippe Cret's Tower of Science at the fair. Here is another tribute to Cret's influence, but this is not Cret's usual classic sternness. Rather, it is a bold, colorful image like the pre-Deco Dutch sensation *De Stijl*.

All over the city, and especially in the neighborhood of the Osco Drugs tower, there are excellent examples of Art Deco terra-cotta façades in brilliant glazed colors. Most of this work was executed by the workers who had left the Saint Louis Terra Cotta Company and founded Kansas City Terra Cotta and Faience Company.

Bob Barrett arranged for us a tour of the magnificent municipal auditorium, coliseum, and little theater—backstage, upstairs, and downstairs. It is a massive structure, all created by Joseph Murphy, chief designer for Gentry, Voskamp & Neville. The auditorium has many wonderful murals in the public spaces, most being 1936 works by Walter Alexander Bailey.

Barrett drove us around the city to see the tall streamlined apartment buildings and the splendid terra-cotta façades. We saw the abandoned 1928 Auburn Motor Car Showroom and Garage at 1401 Baltimore, attributed to architects McKechnie & Trask. The city also has a rare 1936 Kem Weber–designed residence, the Bixby House at 6505 State Line Road. We saw the 1936 Public Works Administration (PWA) municipal complex at 414 East Twelfth Street, by Wight & Wight, There are three different buildings in the government center: the great city hall, the tall

Jackson County offices, and a police administration–municipal-court building. The project got rolling after Pendergast pushed through a public-financed $48-million bond issue to pay for the new city and county offices. The complex is comparable to many state capitols—except they usually have only one main building, not three. Over the entrance to the Jackson County courthouse are carved these words: "The Strength of the Republic Is Not in Its Material Wealth, but in the Loyalty of Its Citizens, Who Believe Their Government Is Just." Also decorating the building are idealized symbols of the people's sovereign power: the scales of justice and the lamp of wisdom.

Boss Pendergast propelled the city's native son Harry S Truman to the U.S. Senate in 1935, after showing him how to use public money to get works projects off the ground during the Depression. Pendergast also selected Truman to become a county judge. Soon, before his departure for Washington, Truman assumed county administrative duties, overseeing the construction of much of Pendergast's ambitious civic complex. Truman was never touched by Pendergast's graft and corruption. He became a U.S. Senator and later became Franklin Roosevelt's Vice President. The New Deal's public-relief programs, which lifted the country out of the Great Depression, copied Pendergast's formula of massive public-works programs and widespread employment for legions of voters. Virtually every dime of federal money sent to Missouri went to Boss Tom's coffers. Everything really *was* up-to-date here by 1936.

The 1930 tower built by Kansas City Power & Light (1330 Baltimore Avenue) designed by Edwin M. Price, is an especially outstanding example of Zigzag Modern, with its illuminated crown, elaborate carving, and stylized façade. Recently, the power company abandoned its longtime home, and the building's future is in jeopardy. Perhaps the city will recognize that this tower, like several other imperiled Art Deco towers downtown, is a great treasure for the city and should be proudly maintained. Also empty and in danger are the 1930 Bryant Building (1102 Grand Avenue) by the famed Chicago firm Graham, Anderson, Probst & White, and the 1929 Professional Building by Smith & McIntyre. The old Fidelity Bank, now used as federal offices at 911 Walnut, is sadly crumbling and is slated for abandonment even by the government. The loss of any of these buildings will only add to an already abundant supply of downtown vacant lots

paved over for parking, as is painfully evident when one visits City Hall's twenty-sixth-floor observation deck, where parking lots are the dominant feature of the landscape below.

Perhaps because of its role as a convenient air hub, Kansas City is host to many regional offices for the film studios (as are Minneapolis and Cincinnati). We found attractive, compact little studio office buildings near downtown, always located close together: Fox, Paramount, RKO, and others.

Finally, we ended our tour at the earliest-known Art Deco monument. The Liberty Memorial, near downtown, was designed by H. Van Buren Magonigle. It sits on a great raised stone terrace atop a hill overlooking the city. The entry is flanked by two shrouded sphinxes. The memorial was dedicated in a notable ceremony on November 1, 1921. In attendance were Vice President Calvin Coolidge, French Field Marshal Ferdinand Foch, Admiral David Beatty, and Generals John Joseph Pershing, Armando Díaz, and Jules Jacques. The slender and beautiful column of carved stone has excellent relief figures carved at its top by sculptor Robert Aitken. A large park surrounds this Kansas City landmark.

10

LOS ANGELES

HOLLYWOODLAND AND MORE

In an era of breadlines, Depression and wars, I tried to help people get away from all the misery . . . to turn their minds to something else. I wanted to make people happy, if only for an hour.

—Busby Berkeley
Statement on his film work
in a prologue to a 1973 book about him.

HERE IN THE LAND OF MOVIE MAGIC IS THE SECOND largest collection of Art Deco buildings in the country. But here also are hundreds of Art Deco interiors, plazas, and cityscapes that don't even exist in reality. Los Angeles, home of Hollywood, is the only city that can lay claim to those wonderful black-and-silver make-believe locales where Fred Astaire and Ginger Rogers danced their nights away.

Los Angeles is strictly a twentieth century city, truly a product of the Machine Age, having risen from the arid California desert. Earlier, it contained only lovely old Spanish missions and unborn dreams. The clear blue rainless skies were perfect for making films, where perception is more important than reality. But not only did Hollywood have to manufacture America's dreams and fantasies, it also had to be exciting, always to have something new for the insatiable public. When the drama was thin, the producers relied on magical streamlined sets and chic costumes. Hollywood lured top talent to design sets for the movies, people like Van Nest Polglase (*Flying Down to Rio, Top Hat*), Cedric Gibbons (*Grand Hotel, Our Blushing Bride, Dinner at Eight*), Charles D. Hall (*Modern Times, Broadway*), William Cameron Menzies (*Things to Come*), and Anton Grot (*Gold Diggers of 1933* and *Gold Diggers of 1935*).

Bullocks Wilshire Department Store (I. Magnin), 3050 *Wilshire Boulevard at Westmoreland Avenue, Los Angeles.* ARCHITECT: *John & Donald Parkinson, 1928. Upon returning from the Paris Exposition in 1925, Bullocks vice president P.G. Winnett provided the owner John G. Bullock with a totally new kind of retail store. Incorporating in its decor much of what he had seen in Paris, he designed it to comprise a series of discrete international boutiques, each with a distinctive theme and finely crafted appointments. Revolutionary and decades ahead of its time, Bullocks introduced the concept of locating a major store in the suburbs, sited so as to attract automobile traffic.*

Bullocks Wilshire Department Store (I. Magnin), 3050 *Wilshire Boulevard at Westmoreland Avenue, Los Angeles.* ARCHITECT: *John & Donald Parkinson; Sculptor: George Stanley, 1928. Fine detailing in terra-cotta and copper is a hallmark of the exterior of Bullocks Wilshire. The Gladding, McBean Company created amazing stone-like terra-cotta for the façade of this landmark. It was the most beautiful and sophisticated store in Los Angeles. Over the front entrance is emblazoned the store's original policy: "To Build A Business That Will Never Know Competition."*

The importance of the movie theater in Art Deco–era American culture cannot be underestimated. It was in her Midwestern heart that Art Deco was embraced, beloved, and made a permanent part of the scene. If people didn't know its name (it had no name then), they still knew what it was. It was the Hollywood look. They learned all about it from the movies. The popularity of the Hollywood Art Deco dramas and musicals ensured a stream of money back to the bottom-line boys in New York, like oil gushing from a well. And that stream ensured that the Hollywood designers and producers could build more buildings and make more movies—even in the worst days of the Depression.

In downtown Los Angeles, mostly along Broadway, is the largest movie-theater district remaining in the U.S.A. The fight to save these now-rare giant movie palaces is a constant one. Preservationists Tom B'hend and Preston Kaufman

maintain a West Coast archive, publish articles and books on the old theaters, and recently helped start the Los Angeles Historic Theater Foundation. Cybil Shepherd is a charter member. They have been battling for years to have a local and national theater historic district declared. The district would have twelve movie and legitimate theaters. It would be unique because in no comparable area in the country can one even find twelve theaters. Art Deco theaters will be represented in this proposed district by the Roxie Theater (1932, John M. Cooper) and the Spanish-Deco Tower Theater (1927, S. Charles Lee). Plus, most of the non-Deco theaters have Art Deco marquees dating from the 1940s. If all goes well, this area will soon be enhanced by the work of master theater-renovation experts such as Conrad Schmitt and Rambusch Studios.

Many of the best Art Deco landmarks in Los Angeles were built to serve the entertainment business. Primary among them are the theaters. Some California theater architects had so much work that they worked nowhere else; other major theater architects designed theaters in most major cities. Some of the best Art Deco theaters include B. Marcus Priteca's 1929 Pantages Theater at 6233 Hollywood Boulevard; G. Albert Lansburgh's 1930 Wiltern Theater at 3790 Wilshire Boulevard; S. Charles Lee's 1939 Academy Theater in Inglewood; and Rowland Crawford's 1928 masterpiece, the Avalon Theater, in the casino on Santa Catalina Island.

Of these, the most celebrated preservation case study is the original Warner Brothers Western Theater, now known as the Wiltern. This 1930 project was unusually lavish for the Great Depression, but Warner Brothers still had money at this point, thanks to their daring gambit in talkies known as Vitaphone. As is now well known, this was an amazing but primitive process by which the actors actually spoke right from the screen. The public loved it and Warners prospered, while Fox and Paramount floundered. In 1985, after years of pressure from the Los Angeles Conservancy, the building was renovated by developers Walter, Ratkovich, Bowers, Inc., with advice from A. T. Heinsbergen & Co., a company run by the son of the original muralist, Anthony B. Heinsbergen, who had done murals in many West Coast buildings and also did the Wiltern's splendid Cubist fire curtain, *Vision of the Heavens.*

Coca-Cola Bottling Plant, 1334 South Central at 14th Street, Los Angeles. ARCHITECT: Robert Vincent Derrah, 1936. When Coca-Cola commissioned Derrah to do a simple remodeling and consolidation of several existing buildings on this site, he instead created this Nautical Moderne masterpiece, which has a clever Hollywood-style wraparound façade with matching Nautical Moderne interiors. Derrah, trained in engineering at M.I.T., also worked for Charlie Chaplin and designed the first sound stage at RKO Pictures. Unfortunately, the Derrah interiors for this building are now destroyed.

Eastern-Columbia Building, 849 South Broadway at 9th Street, Los Angeles. ARCHITECT: Claude Beelman, 1929. With its imposing clock and gleaming blue-green Gladding, McBean terracotta façade, this tower is one of the most distinctive landmarks in downtown Los Angeles. The brilliance derives from pulverized gold particles under the glaze. Established as a clock company, Eastern moved into clothing. When it bought the Columbia Outfitting Company, a major competitor, it relocated both stores to the capacious ground floor of this building.

Hollyhock House, Aline Barnsdall Art Park, 4800 Hollywood Boulevard west of Vermont Avenue, Los Angeles. ARCHITECT: Frank Lloyd Wright, 1917. Mayan details combined with stylized hollyhock blossoms, very evocative of Art Deco style, make this home one of Wright's more interesting achievements. Located on top of a hill overlooking Hollywood, it is now a splendid museum operated by the city. Its original owner, Aline Barnsdall, never liked the house and gave it to the city in 1926 after having lived in it for only one year. She also deeded thirty-six acres of prime real estate for the park. (Photograph by Michael D. Kinerk)

117

Los Angeles Stock Exchange (Pacific Coast Stock Exchange), 618 South Spring Street, Los Angeles. ARCHITECT: Samuel Lunden with John and Donald Parkinson; Sculptor: Salvatore C. Scarpitta, 1929. The Stripped Classic slightly-Egyptian main façade is windowless but enlivened by relief panels between piers entitled: Research & Discovery, Finance and Production. The bronze doors were the largest on the West Coast.

May Company, 6067 Wilshire Boulevard at Fairfax Avenue (northeast corner), Los Angeles. ARCHITECT: Albert C. Martin, with Samuel A. Marx, 1939. Reflecting the afternoon sun off its brilliant cylindrical gold-glazed corner, this is the most striking Art Deco store ever erected by the May Company, which has now abandoned it. The massive golden expanse is flanked by futuristic black granite name pylons. Directing customer traffic through such corner entrances has long been a basic tenet of modern commercial architecture. The Art Deco Society of Los Angeles is working with the Los Angeles Conservancy to preserve this landmark and find a new use for it.

Oviatt Building (Rex Restaurant), 617 South Olive near 6th Street, Los Angeles. ARCHITECT: Albert Walker & Percy Eisen; Glasswork: René Lalique, 1927. Conversion to restaurant: Brenda Levin & Associates, 1976. Famed French artist René Lalique created these molded-glass "oranges" for the elevator-door panels of this former haberdashery to the stars. French craftsmen were used exclusively in the creation of this architectural confection. This was Lalique's largest single commission in the U.S.A. More recently, it has been a chic restaurant, often used for movie shots.

Many other buildings were erected to serve the needs of the entertainment industry. Some of the best examples are the legendary Hollywood Bowl (third version), built in 1929 at 2301 North Highland Avenue; William Lescaze's 1939 CBS Studios at 6121 Sunset Boulevard; Samuel Tilden Norton's 1930 William Fox Office Building at 608 South Hill Street; Claude Beelman's 1937 Goldwyn Studios (later MGM) on Washington Boulevard at Overland Avenue; S. Charles Lee's 1928 Motion Picture Arts Building, 5504 Hollywood Boulevard (former home of the Hays office, which administered the motion pictures' "moral code"); and Howard Hughes's 1927 Multi-Color Labs (Producers Film Center), 7000 Romaine Street.

It should be obvious from the above lists that S. Charles Lee was a major player in Southern California theater architecture. He left Chicago in 1921 after working for the great firm of C. W. & George Rapp. After his death on February 5, 1990, the S. Charles Lee archives were bequeathed to the Special Collections Department of the University Research Library at UCLA. Lee designed hundreds of theaters and many of his finest works were exciting Art Deco caprices. Two other notable theaters are the Bruin in Los Angeles and the Fox Florence.

The Los Angeles Conservancy is probably the most active and far-reaching local preservation organization in the United States. Its programs touch everything from Spanish missions to Art Deco, and it publishes new brochures yearly featuring popular walking tours all over its giant territory. It is best known for saving the Wiltern Theater/Pellissier building which is indeed a beloved landmark in Southern California. One of the conservancy's early leaders, Daniel Hoye, was responsible for the inclusion of Art Deco examples in each of the conservancy brochures, no matter what the general topic, from business offices to churches. The conservancy persuaded respected scholar David Gebhard to write a brochure for it entitled *Streamline Los Angeles.* Other brochures have treated such varied topics as "Palaces of Finance," "Old San Pedro," "Terra Cotta," "Miracle Mile," "Hollywood Boulevard," and many more. This well-established group is often able to help its poor cousins at the

Public Library, *630 West 5th Street at South Flower Street (southeast corner), Los Angeles.* ARCHITECT: *Bertram Goodhue, with Carleton M. Winslow, 1922. Goodhue, a pioneer in the Stripped Classic style, had already won acclaim for his design of the Nebraska State Capitol when he was commissioned to design this library. He again engaged Lee Lawrie to do ornamental sculpture. On April 29, 1986, the building was gutted by fire and has been undergoing restoration ever since. Notable in its design are the pyramidal top, recessed vertical strips in the tower, and pilasters with no capitals. (Photograph by Michael D. Kinerk)*

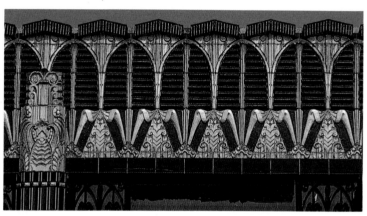

Selig Building, *269 South Western Avenue, Los Angeles.* ARCHITECT: *Arthur E. Harvey, 1931. This parapet detail is taken from a small but memorable commercial building named for Alvin C. Selig, a real-estate developer (not for William N. Selig, Hollywood's 1909 film-studio chief). It features black-and-gold glazed terra-cotta. The demolished thirty-six-story Richfield Oil skyscraper downtown had similar terra-cotta, and there is a hint of its greatness in this façade.*

The Times (Times-Mirror), *202 West First Street at Spring Street, Los Angeles.* ARCHITECT: *Gordon B. Kaufmann; Muralist: Hugo Ballin, 1931. Sources of the News is by Los Angeles's most prolific muralist, Hugo Ballin. A central figure adjusts a large bellows camera, once an essential fixture at any news event. In the background are fanciful renditions of City Hall, a locomotive steaming alongside a super-streamlined train, an airplane, and some of California's rugged landscape. Along with others, this work completely encircles the lobby rotunda. They had been covered up for years, but the Times restored the works to public view again in March 1990.*

Warner Western Theater (Wiltern Theater), *3790 Wilshire Boulevard, Los Angeles.* ARCHITECTS: *G. Albert Lansburgh (theater); Stiles O. Clements for Morgan, Walls & Clements (office tower); Muralist: Anthony B. Heinsbergen, 1930. The inner lobby leading to the auditorium has ceiling murals by L.A.'s most popular movie-palace muralist, Heinsbergen. The theater was part of a larger commercial complex called the Pellissier Tower and was San Francisco architect Lansburgh's only Art Deco theater. It was saved largely through the efforts of the Los Angeles Conservancy.*

121

Art Deco Society of Los Angeles (ADSLA), founded in 1983. Together, these groups have worked to save landmarks such as the May Company. Recently, the fledgling Art Deco Society of Los Angeles has issued two of its own Art Deco brochures: "Santa Monica's Art Deco Architecture" and the "Hollywood Cemetery Walking Tour."

Of course, not every building was made to serve entertainment in Los Angeles. One in particular was designed to get people in and out of town—Union Station, which is a lovely Pueblo Deco monument. Essentially Spanish Colonial, it nevertheless has a profusion of true Art Deco elements, such as the entry doors, lighting fixtures, the original Harvey House restaurant, and various decorative elements. This 1939 combination of Old West designs with the Moderne is not atypical, and it can be quite intriguing. The station, located at 800 North Alameda, was created on the site of an old tribal village, and it now sits at the edge of Chinatown. It was built to serve the passengers of the Southern Pacific, Santa Fe, and Union Pacific railroads. It has been declared Los Angeles Cultural Monument #101 by the Cultural Heritage Board of the Municipal Arts Department, City of Los Angeles. This terminal is unique, being the only train station in the country that is part Spanish Mission and part Aztec Airways.

Southern California has an enormous treasure trove of modern and Art Deco residences, including several by the incomparable Frank Lloyd Wright, from his middle and most Art Deco period. However, other masters also worked here, such as Irving Gill, Kem Weber, and Richard Neutra. We vis-

ited our friend Gaylord Carter, a veteran theater organist from the days of silent movies. We were there to talk about the Hollywood studios and his friends in show business, and to see his house designed by Richard Neutra. Carter was "organist to the stars," friend and confidant of Sid Grauman, Harold Lloyd, Lillian Gish, and many others. His Neutra home, Beach Cliff, is in San Pedro built on a cliff overlooking the Pacific Ocean. On a clear day the view through a great wall of windows is of Santa Catalina Island and the channel. Carter told us how he used to take his boat across the channel to the island, then journey up the hill to the Wrigley family's Art Deco fantasy playground, the Avalon Casino, a 1928 Nautical Moderne masterpiece by Rowland Crawford.

Carter was tapped for fame by Harold Lloyd, because the star said to him, "I like what you do with my pictures, kid." Lloyd traveled regularly from theater to theater (his pictures were very popular), surreptitiously checking head counts against his studio's figures to compute royalty payments. He heard Carter often and took notice of him. Lloyd recommended Carter to his friend Sid Grauman, who also liked Gaylord's musicianship and promoted him to play downtown at the flagship Million Dollar Theater at Broadway and Third Street. This 1917 Spanish Baroque auditorium by William L. Woollett was built at the right time to divert millions of nickels, dimes, and quarters into Grauman's box office. The fantastic profits made possible the much more famous Grauman's Chinese and Egyptian theaters in Hollywood. Gaylord Carter got in

Crossroads of the World Shopping Center, 6671 Sunset Boulevard, Hollywood. ARCHITECT: Robert Vincent Derrah, 1936. Crossroads of the World's central tower is similar to a ship with a conning tower, a contrived blue-tile water line around its base, porthole windows, and upper decks with ship railings. The 150-foot-long structure has six stores on the ground floor, offices above, and is surrounded by small buildings representing architecture from ports around the world.

Warner Beverly Hills Theater (Beverly Theater); demolished, 9404 Wilshire Boulevard at Cañon Drive, Beverly Hills. ARCHITECT: B. Marcus Priteca, 1930. Lost forever is this tower from a demolished movie palace built after the onset of the Great Depression. Priteca may have looked back for inspiration to the splendid design of the entrance gate at the Paris Exposition or Saarinen's similar entry pylons at Detroit's Cranbrook Academy. Priteca designed several other theaters for Warner Brothers in the same year. One notable surviving example is the Warner Theater in nearby San Pedro.

Hollywood Bowl, 2301 North Highland Avenue, Hollywood. ARCHITECT: Allied Architects; Sculptor: George Stanley, 1940. This vintage postcard features Euterpe, Greek muse of music and poetry, who presides over the splendid lighted fountains and pools at the entrance to the Hollywood Bowl. These were dedicated on July 8, 1940, a delightful addition to the world-famous landmark bowl. Restoration was begun for the fountain's fiftieth birthday in 1990. Frank Lloyd Wright's son, Lloyd, designed the concentric radiating circular-waveform shell for the stage. First executed in 1928 in wood, it was rebuilt the following year in concrete. Although much remodeled and expanded through the years, the initial design still remains as the hallmark of this celebrated concert stage.

Wilshire Tower, 5514 Wilshire Boulevard, Los Angeles. ARCHITECT: Gilbert Stanley Underwood, 1928. For years known as Desmonds, a landmark department store on Wilshire, this building has wonderful terrazzo and relief stonework in its entrance. In the lobby the decor is nautical, while the façade features griffins and mythical figures among triangles and swirls. Above the two-level store is a nine-story office tower. Architect Underwood also did the Ahwahnee Hotel at Yosemite National Park and the Omaha Union Terminal, which is illustrated in the U.S.A. chapter.

861—Entrance to Hollywood Bowl, Hollywood, California

NEW STUDIOS OF CBS AND NBC

CBS Studios, *6121 Sunset Boulevard, Hollywood. ARCHITECTS: William Lescaze and Earl T. Heitschmidt, 1939.* **NBC Studios,** *Sunset Boulevard at Vine Street, ARCHITECT: Robert Smith, Jr., for the Austin Company, 1938. Perhaps intended to lure tourists, Hollywood briefly billed itself as an alternative "Radio City" in this 1940 souvenir postcard. Lescaze's superb International-style CBS studios remain, but NBC's streamlined building was razed.*

on all this while Hollywood was still just vacant lots and developers' dreams. Downtown Los Angeles was where the action was and where people came to see the latest and greatest stars.

Eventually, Carter became featured organist at the Egyptian and United Artists theaters before going into radio. He became staff organist for the number-one hit program of the airwaves, "Amos and Andy," but he never forgot those great movie palaces. The 1927 United Artists Theater, with an interior by C. Howard Crane, was the flagship theater for the studio founded by Mary Pickford, Douglas Fairbanks, and Charles Chaplin. Their portraits are painted inside. Outside, it is a most unlikely combination of High Gothic and Paris-style Art Deco. The stonework rivals many a cathedral, but the window spandrels are a frenzy of aluminum zigzags. Carter understood the design of the building where he had played, for living in a Neutra house had given him a keen sense of design. He knew what Art Deco was and sent us back downtown to see the United Artists Theater. "It's Deco, you know," he assured us. All we could remember was the Gothic stone filigree, but we returned to discover that Art Deco is indeed a part of the design scheme.

While on one of our many visits to Los Angeles, we chanced to be there while an exhibit at the Los Angeles County Museum of Art (LACMA) was showing the so-called degenerate art banned by the Nazis. Of course, it is laughable that the Nazis banned some of the most celebrated art of the century, but what is more revealing, once again, is the profound impact on the U.S.A. when these "degenerate" luminaries from every discipline took refuge in this country and helped define here the direction of Art Deco as well as so much more. Among the immigrants, listed with their destinations, were Walter Gropius, who went to Harvard; Eric Mendelsohn to New York; Albert Einstein to Princeton; and Laszlo Moholy-Nagy and Mies van der Rohe to Chicago. Some adventurous souls made their way directly to Hollywood, however: Fritz Lang, Billy Wilder, and Thomas Mann. All of this merely confirms Thomas Mann's 1938 observation: "For the duration of the present European dark age, the center of Western Culture will shift to North America."

Many of Los Angeles's best treasures have been lost forever. Among these were the 1935 Pan Pacific Auditorium

at 7600 Beverly Boulevard, by Walter Wurdeman and Welton Becket, now only a charred shell of the building destroyed by fire in May 1989; the 1928 Richfield Oil Company Building, by Morgan, Walls & Clements, at 610 South Broadway, demolished by its owners, Atlantic Richfield (ARCO) in 1968 to make way for a new high rise; and B. Marcus Priteca's 1930 Beverly Wilshire Warner Theater on Wilshire Boulevard at Cañon Drive in Beverly Hills.

In some sense, the losses of original Art Deco monuments have been offset or slightly mitigated by other works that are clearly intended to be Art Deco, such as Charles Moore's 1990 Beverly Hills Civic Center complex, the 1989 Wells Fargo tower downtown on Figueroa Street, and the new Home Savings building right across from it.

Southern California already had a rich architectural heritage before Art Deco came to the fore. We can find many works by giants like Greene & Greene and Julia Morgan, William Randolph Hearst's noted architect of San Simeon. One of the most important early buildings in the area is the downtown Los Angeles Public Library, 630 West Fifth Street at South Flower Street. Its architect was the distinguished Bertram Goodhue, and the supervising architect was Carleton M. Winslow. In this 1922 work, Goodhue, a pioneer in the Stripped Classic style, commissioned Lee Lawrie to provide rich sculptural detailing throughout the building. Goodhue had already won great acclaim for his design of the Nebraska State Capitol (see the U.S.A. chapter) at the time he began this library. On April 29, 1986, the building was gutted by fire and has been undergoing restoration ever since.

The library is diagonally across from another Art Deco landmark, the former Southern California Edison downtown office, now known as First Business Bank at One Bunker Hill. There is interesting relief carving over the corner entrance and several fine murals inside, including one by Hugo Ballin entitled *Apotheosis of Power.*

There are so many buildings in Los Angeles that it is impossible even to name them all in this book. We surveyed over 396 buildings there. One interesting fact is the very large number of Art Deco theaters there. In most cities, the number of apartments—the most common Art Deco building type—is three or four times higher than the number of any other building type. In Los Angeles, we visited twenty-

nine apartment buildings and twenty-seven theaters. Considering that Los Angeles is a company town for Hollywood, this probably should not surprise us.

A unique feature in front of Clifton's Silver Spoon Cafeteria, near the corner of Broadway and Sixth Street, is its terrazzo sidewalk with scenes of Hollywood history. The images show oil derricks, dancers, and directors making films, as well as a symphony orchestra jazzing it up at the Hollywood Bowl. This is some of the best terrazzo to be found anywhere.

Undoubtedly, the finest building in the French Art Deco style in California is the 1927 Oviatt Building at 617 South Olive Street. Featuring original glasswork by the great French craftsman René Lalique, the place has acquired a reputation for elegance in its current role as the Rex Restaurant. Originally the Oviatt was home to a haberdashery for Hollywood's male stars and others who could afford it. The architects of the building were Albert Walker and Percy Eisen. The 1976 conversion to a restaurant was handled by Brenda Levin & Associates.

Although no longer known by its famous name—Bullocks Wilshire—the store at 3050 Wilshire Boulevard is one of the great American store buildings. Until recently, the building was occupied by the I. Magnin company, but it is now closed. It was brilliantly innovative and exceedingly beautiful when it was created, and it remains so today. Among its splendid features are handsome interior appointments and an immense fresco by Herman Sachs celebrating all forms of transportation. The carriage trade that this store

Pantages Theater (2,812 seats), 6233 Hollywood Boulevard, Hollywood. ARCHITECT: B. Marcus Priteca, 1929. Alexander Pantages erected this shrine to the art of film in the heart of Hollywood. Combining zigzags with elements from France, Germany, Egypt, and Asia, the interior is much like the backlot of a film studio, where sets from wholly different worlds coexist back to back.

Pantages Theater, 6233 Hollywood Boulevard, Hollywood. ARCHITECT: B. Marcus Priteca, 1929. This theater is considered Priteca's masterpiece. In the main lobby a camera crew flanks one of the twin staircases that ascend through a Romanesque arch on each side of the Expressionistic lobby.

catered to came by car, of course, and it had a parking lot with the main entrance to the store at the back, under the transportation mural. It should be noted that Sachs did a lot of other fine work, including murals at the City Hall and the color scheme for the wonderful Union Terminal Train Station. The store's *raison d'être* was carved in stone over the Wilshire Boulevard entrance: "To Build a Business That Will Never Know Competition." It is anyone's guess what the fate of this landmark will be.

Students attending Hollywood High School have an opportunity to see fine Streamline Moderne architecture every day at their own school. Their handsome campus on Sunset Boulevard is decorated with fine sculptural panels inscribed with inspiring topics and mottoes.

Southern California. In 1861, the building became the office of a U.S. Army quartermaster from Fort Tejon and remained in government service when the Los Angeles City Hall was built in 1884. In 1930, construction began on a new Art Deco City Hall a block up the street, at which time the old site was snapped up by newspaper publisher Otis Chandler. He built a splendid Art Deco news building here with the standard "News of the World" giant revolving globe in the lobby (no Art Deco metropolitan daily would be complete without one). The upper walls of the rotunda host murals by Hugo Ballin, painted in 1934. Accompanying the murals is an inscription that reads: "The newspaper is a greater treasure to the people than uncounted millions."

Los Angeles is a town of heavy Mayan and Asian influences. Some of Frank Lloyd Wright's local houses have a clear Mayan motif, such as the Hollyhock House and several more in Hollywood. The Egyptian, Mayan, and Asian influences are most pronounced in many of the theaters, but they may also be found in residences. When he built the Hollyhock House in 1917 for Aline Barnsdall, Wright used a stylized hollyhock motif as the predominant decorative element throughout the house. Wright might well have known the special importance of this plant in Japan, where there has been an annual spring hollyhock festival for over one thousand years, for he had visited Japan before 1905.

One of the most powerful forces in Southern California is the *Los Angeles Times*. This well-respected and very successful newspaper is housed in an outstanding 1931 Art Deco building by Gordon B. Kaufmann, who is also known for his work on the Hoover Dam. The building, at 202 West First Street, is across the street from Los Angeles's Art Deco City Hall. A plaque on the wall near the entrance to the newspaper's 1948 annex notes that on the site from 1854 to 1855 was School No. 1, the first brick schoolhouse in the city. Then the site was taken by the Butterfield Overland Mail Company. It had a corral for camels, which saw service in the deserts of pre-water-aqueduct

A National Register landmark building stands at 8358 Sunset Boulevard: The original Sunset Tower apartments has now become the trendy Saint James Club. The beautiful fourteen-story tower, designed by Leland A. Bryant in 1929, features plaster friezes of plants, animals, zeppelins, and mythical creatures. High above the entrance are Adam and Eve. A garage at the rear has a frieze of radiator grilles. David Becker renovated the building in 1988 to create the present elegant interior.

In 1934, Robert Vincent Derrah designed a remodeling project to combine several old buildings for the Coca-Cola plant on the south side of downtown Los Angeles, located at 1334 South Central Avenue. This became the nation's most celebrated Nautical Art Deco edifice, for the building appears much like a ship soon to be launched into the deep

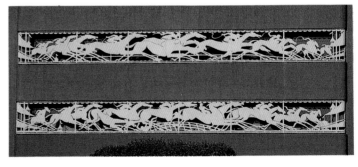

blue sea. In 1975, Coca-Cola made this building its headquarters, and the Nautical Moderne interiors were destroyed during a $3-million conversion by Stanley Gould & Associates. At the same time, the exterior was restored and the bottom portion of the façade was painted black, with a red "water-line" stripe.

Another Derrah tour de force is the 1936 Crossroads of the World Shopping Center at 6671 Sunset Boulevard in Hollywood. With its architectural theme of ports from around the globe, it may well have been an inspiration for Walt Disney's later Epcot Center in Florida. An exact replica of the streamlined ship at the center of the Crossroads stands at the entrance to the Disney–MGM Florida theme park—right behind the replica of the façade of the great Pan Pacific Auditorium mentioned earlier. The Disney–MGM park is nearly all replica Art Deco, and quite outstanding replications, at that. We went on a whirlwind tour of central Hollywood and nearby neighborhoods with our friend Dan Grant, a veteran film-studio professional. He had worked a few years in Miami Beach on the show "Miami Vice," and after moving back to Southern California, he offered to help us with our Los Angeles chapter.

Here are a few more Los Angeles buildings that must be mentioned: Church of Jesus Christ of Latter Day Saints Wilshire Ward, 10741 Santa Monica Boulevard; Eastern-Columbia Building, 849 South Broadway; Frederick's of Hollywood (a former S. H. Kress store), 6606 Hollywood Boulevard; Garfield Building, 403 West Eighth Street; Griffith Park Observatory on Western Canyon Road; Lane-Wells Company (now the Winnie & Sutch Building), 5610 South

Avalon Casino, 1 Casino Way, on Casino Point, northeast shore Santa Catalina Bay, Avalon, Santa Catalina Island, in Pacific Ocean west of Los Angeles. ARCHITECT: Rowland Crawford for Walter Webber & Sumner A. Spaulding; Muralist: John Gabriel Beckman, 1928. A superb example of Nautical Moderne, this is one of nine murals by Beckman. His casino murals tower over the outside walkways and cannot fail to impress any pedestrian passing by the gleaming white casino. William Wrigley, Jr., selected the site after scouting the island in his Pierce Arrow. To lure visitors to his island paradise, he advertised: "In all the world, no trip like this!" The island is accessible by ferry or plane.

Sunset Tower (Saint James Club), 8358 Sunset Boulevard at Kings Road, West Hollywood. ARCHITECT: Leland A. Bryant, 1929; Restoration consultant: David Becker, 1988. This exclusive fourteen-story private club and residence on legendary Sunset Boulevard once was an apartment house for stars working at nearby studios. Its residents have included Howard Hughes, Billie Burke, Paulette Goddard, and John Wayne. Outstanding sculptural friezes grace the façade of this National Register Landmark. It enjoyed a $40-million restoration in 1988, and is now one of the National Trust's Historic Hotels of America. (Photograph by Michael D. Kinerk)

Santa Anita Race Track, 285 West Huntington Drive, Arcadia, California. ARCHITECT: Gordon B. Kaufmann, 1934. Horse-racing, the sport of kings, is well represented here in these silhouette, cutout panels. Today the design is used as the logo for Santa Anita's national promotions and advertising. Kaufmann, corporate architect for the Los Angeles Times, Long Beach Federal Building, ALCOA, and Hoover Dam, is seen here in his most playful and fanciful mode.

Soto Street, Huntington Park; Max Factor, 1666 Highland Avenue, a splendid classical French Art Deco by S. Charles Lee; Santa Anita Race Track, 285 West Huntington Drive, Arcadia; Title Guarantee Trust, 411 West Fifth Street; Pacific Coast Stock Exchange, 618 South Spring; Selig Retail Store Building, 269 South Western Avenue, with its shimmering black-and-gold-glazed terra-cotta façade; U.S. Post Office, Beacon at Ninth Street, San Pedro; and Wilshire Center, 5514 Wilshire Boulevard, the urban shopping center by Gilbert Stanley Underwood.

And there are hundreds more.

During a 1979 trip to Los Angeles Kinerk and Wilhelm met the late Paul Tiberio, one of the first and also one of the best Art Deco dealers in the U.S.A. He was thrilled to meet fellow collectors and promptly invited us to his stunning Paul Laszlo home in the Hollywood Hills. We rode from the store to the house in his classic white Bentley. He was a favored purveyor of Art Deco to superstar Barbra Streisand. "It's too bad you weren't here a bit earlier today. Barbra Streisand was here picking up a few things," he mused, waving her check in front of us. He told us that he had grown up loving Art Deco and had always been waiting for people to get rid of it so he could buy it up before anybody got wise to its true timeless value.

Elsewhere

San Diego

There are many Art Deco treasures in the Southern California metropolis of San Diego. Helen Hobbs Halmay founded the Art Deco Society of San Diego in 1987 and wrote a book on the subject in 1989. There is a special abundance here of Egyptian Revival architecture with Art Deco overtones, and there are several rare surviving buildings from the 1935 California Pacific International Exposition (CPIE).

Avalon Theater (1,154 seats), 1 Casino Way, on Casino Point, northeast shore Santa Catalina Bay, Avalon, Santa Catalina Island, in Pacific Ocean west of Los Angeles. ARCHITECT: Rowland Crawford for Walter Webber & Sumner A. Spaulding; Muralist: John Gabriel Beckman, 1928. The murals in the theater auditorium were painted on jute, then stretched on frames attached to the dome and walls. This theater was one of the first equipped for sound pictures. Beckman, the designer and muralist, later took over art direction at Universal Studios, and also designed the interior of the legendary Grauman's Chinese Theater. Working on movie and TV set designs until his death in 1989, he left a splendid legacy. Among his screen credits for set design are Casablanca, Lost Horizon, The Maltese Falcon, and Chaplin's Monsieur Verdoux.

Avalon Casino Ballroom, 1 Casino Way, on Casino Point, northeast shore Santa Catalina Bay, Avalon, Santa Catalina Island, in Pacific Ocean west of Los Angeles. ARCHITECT: Rowland Crawford for Walter Webber & Sumner A. Spaulding; Designer: John Gabriel Beckman, 1928. Perfectly formed and colorful, but yielding no clue that it's nearly sixty feet in diameter, this massive illuminated centerpiece reigns over the ballroom of the fabulous casino at Catalina, the Wrigley family's private island. This huge round room can hold thousands of dancing couples. The little fish swimming around the fixture's circumference hint at its location on an island in the Pacific Ocean.

Lane-Wells Building (Winnie & Sutch), 5610 South Soto Street, Huntington Park, California. ARCHITECT: William E. Meyer, 1938. A free-flowing waterfall effect dominates this façade, creating a part-Deco, part-International-style whimsical office building.

11

MIAMI BEACH

TROPICAL ART DECO PARADISE

*They [architects] were determined not to use
any older style, like the Spanish. . . . They didn't
quite know where they were headed, but they
wanted something modern, so they smoothed
the balconies, they smoothed everything until
you got the feeling that life was smooth. The
buildings made you feel all clean and new and
excited and happy to be here.*

—Leicester Hemingway (brother of Ernest)
At the first meeting of the Miami Design Preservation League
(MDPL), 1976.
Reported in *Time Present, Time Past,* a monograph published by the
MDPL, 1979.

FOLLOWING BELOW IS BARBARA BAER CAPITMAN'S
account, dated June 15, 1981, of the early history of Miami
Beach's Art Deco District, as well as her thoughts on her
upcoming trip with Leonard Horowitz, written just before
their departure.

Among our acquaintances, Hugo Zamorano first
bought property in the district. He befriended my son
Andrew early on, encouraging him to buy some of
these precious little Miami Beach Art Deco *pastelitos.*
Zamorano owned a great Henry Hohauser building at
735 Fourteenth Place, Miami Beach. He sold it to
Laurinda Spear and Bernardo Fort-Brescia, the acclaimed architectural duo known as Arquitectonica,
which bought the building and rehabbed it. The rehab
of this Henry Hohauser building on Fourteenth Place
was the first rehab in the district—after it became a
district. It had sat dormant for twenty years. Shortly
thereafter, Laurinda and Bernardo had the first party in
the Art Deco District in this building. Andrew and his

*Helen Mar Apartments, 2421 Lake Pancoast Drive,
Miami Beach. ARCHITECT: Robert E. Collins, 1936;
Restoration architect: J.P. Friedman, 1988. This very
handsome apartment building with a view of the Atlantic
Ocean is stylistically reminiscent of the splendid Deco
apartment buildings on New York's Central Park West.
Perhaps for that reason this tower has drawn many
New Yorkers as tenants.*

Breakwater Hotel, 940 Ocean Drive, Miami Beach. ARCHITECT: Anton Skislewicz, 1939; Restoration architect: Les Beilinson, 1987. One of Ocean Drive's crown jewels is the Breakwater Hotel, site of photographer Bruce Weber's revolutionary ads for Calvin Klein's fragrance, Obsession, which featured nude male models on the roof with the bold finial as backdrop. The resulting flood of models and other photographers initiated the renaissance of the Art Deco District as an international fashion hot spot.

Hotel Cardozo, 1300 Ocean Drive, Miami Beach. ARCHITECT: Henry Hohauser, 1939. One of the sleekest and most appealing of Miami Beach's Deco delights, the Hotel Cardozo was one of a group purchased in 1979 by Andrew Capitman, thereby launching the fledgling Art Deco Hotels. In the former card room, just off the lobby, Margaret Doyle opened the Café Cardozo, the first and only Ocean Drive café to exist in the year the Art Deco District was listed in the National Register. In 1992, with over thirty restaurants, bars, and cafés on the street, famed singer Gloria Estefan and her husband Emilio bought the hotel and plan to make it the brightest star on Ocean Drive.

new bride, Margaret Doyle, had many dinner parties in their restored Art Deco apartment there. Robert Venturi; his wife, Denise Scott Brown; Andres Duany; and Elizabeth Plater-Zyberk all came many times. Michael Kinerk and Dennis Wilhelm came here many times. And so did I. It was a place of great memories in the development of our Art Deco District.

I was to have many happy times in Henry Hohauser locations in Miami Beach. I subsequently moved into one at 1211 Pennsylvania Avenue. It was from here that I began making preparations for my big Art Deco U.S.A. tour. I had been brought up on books about Arctic exploration and then found new worlds reading with small sons, exploring in the American frontier. Still later came stories of archaeological expeditions—Schliemann's search for Troy. When we lived on Martha's Vineyard, we became sailors, cruising our wooden sloop from Maine and Nova Scotia harbors. Our consciousness was filled with tales of circumnavigators—Joshua Slocum and the *Spray* out of New Bedford. For me, in the roles of housewife, record keeper, navigator, and ship's chandler, the preparation for journeys was always essential to the legend.

There are new possibilities occurring now, new allies and challenges in the sudden explosion of interest in my Miami Beach Art Deco District. The new wave of support is unparalleled—even by the days when it was placed on the National Register of Historic Places and became national news as the first Art Deco district anywhere, and the largest and youngest twentieth-century district. This groundswell of support has been largely due to two events.

The first was tragic: the delayed, unexpected demolition of the beautiful New Yorker Hotel by selfish, short-sighted local would-be developers. [The

New Yorker site has remained vacant for ten years.]

Last May, in London I met with Dan Cruikshank, scholarly young editor of the noted *Architectural Review*. He considered the New Yorker loss "inconceivable," like losing one of the buildings at Bath, the bastion of Britain's Roman ruins and Regency architecture.

The second event has been a source of such pleasure that we almost hate to leave. It is the opening of the twenty-seat Café Cardozo, along Ocean Drive. (The Cardozo was the site of the first Art Deco Week Festival in 1978 and was featured in *A Hole in the Head*, a 1959 Frank Capra movie starring Frank Sinatra and Edward G. Robinson.) The café is a relatively modest, delightful brasserie. It makes clear what no amount of planning reports, hypothesis, or research ever could. It's clear there is a ready audience

Marlin Hotel, *1200 Collins Avenue, Miami Beach.* ARCHITECT: *L. Murray Dixon, 1939; Exterior restoration: Jess Bickelhaupf, 1991. This became the first Miami Beach hotel to be refurbished without cutting financial corners, thanks to Chris Blackwell, the founder of Island Records, and Miami Beach developers Craig and Scott Robins. Art Deco façade details are highlighted in polychrome paints, with new cobalt blue neon tracing added to all four sides. Neon highlighting, while not original to this building, was nevertheless found on many other buildings in the District.*

for the charms of the district. Three weeks old, the café has regulars who return to experience this revived 1930s way of life in many moods. At breakfast, grateful shadows of morning are reflected in a freshly hosed terrazzo view of tropic-green ocean, and in the evening, the porch tables are taken by young people gazing at the moon and palms, saying "This is the way we always expected Miami to be."

We are looking for ways to get out additional copies of the Anderson, Notter Finegold plan for development of the district that has arrived after more than a year's intense work by many of us. I meet this week with the new Miami Beach Development Corporation Executive Director, Richard Hoberman. He has the grave responsibility of using the $100,000 grant from the state for revitalization of our decayed neighborhood. A major part of our program is a cottage industry for the aged needleworkers who have retired here and whose incomes are pitiful. Part of our trip will feed distribution outlets, technical help, and fresh ideas back to the district for this program.

Leonard has been working at Charles Pawley's architectural office for two weeks now. Wednesday he will submit a design to the county review board. This study must be accepted before Leonard will be free to go off! The colors are controversial gay pastels. Theoretical battles have been waged behind the scenes about this palette!

Basically, we are designers. I've been writing about architecture, interior design, and fine arts and crafts all my sixty-one years, most of that time in New York. My husband, Bill Capitman, taught business and social responsibility here at Florida International University for two rich years before he died of cancer in 1975. He was known among designers as *the* visual marketing expert. Together, we examined the American public at the request of big corporations and big government. We worked with industrial designers who served Madison Avenue. It had been our hope right along that people's organizations and government can and should use the skills of big business to sell good ideas and causes. We think the little Café Cardozo illustrates that this can be done. We want to find out on our trip how it is being done in other cities.

Miami Beach citizens have been conned and hyped so much by so many quick-buck artists that there is a good deal of cynicism down here on our isolated peninsula. Because Miami is getting a new

New Yorker Hotel (demolished), 1611 Collins Avenue, Miami Beach. ARCHITECT: Henry Hohauser, 1940. This was the greatest loss the Art Deco District ever suffered. Owner Abe Resnick and his partners publicly promised to preserve the hotel, but they demolished it April 4, 1981. It has been a weed-strewn empty lot ever since. The Miami Design Preservation League subsequently adopted the hotel's façade in its corporate logo. A decade later, after the District had achieved worldwide fame, Resnick's son James helped the new owner get a demolition permit for the adjoining Sands Hotel, and it too was demolished, leaving an even greater void. (Photograph courtesy the Capitman Archives)

Park Central Hotel, 640 Ocean Drive, Miami Beach. ARCHITECT: Henry Hohauser, 1937. Strong design elements combine to make this the centerpiece of Ocean Drive. The three octagonal windows over the entrance, the recessed vertical spandrels, and the hotel's name stylized in neon serve to introduce the visitor to the grandest lobby in the Art Deco District. The façade, awash in brilliant white and periwinkle blue as designed by the late colorist and designer Leonard Horowitz, has a vibrancy visible from a mile out in the Atlantic Ocean. Flamboyant owner Tony Goldman, after refurbishing the hotel and opening a restaurant in its lobby, turned his attention to tireless promotion of his beloved Ocean Drive, and becoming its honorary mayor.

shot at world tourism, it might just be the right time to drop that cynicism. We are going to see how less cynical people succeed, and we hope our trip can provide some new directions and some support for new ideas in the Miami Beach District.

Finally, we are preparing in the usual way. We are having my four-door, four-cylinder, one-year-old Chevette overhauled. I called Detroit, and the public-relations director of Chevrolet said the cheapest car in the line would hold up for our ten thousand miles of mountain and desert travel. I asked Chevrolet to sponsor our Art Deco tour project, since we would be using their product. They weren't interested. Another lost marketing opportunity! We are taking the hopes of a lot of people whose fortunes still rise and fall on the success of the Art Deco District. We are keeping our fingers crossed that it will be here next September.

In 1992, more than a decade later, Barbara's friend Michael Kinerk reflects on what has happened in Miami Beach and what it means.

Now, at the end of the century in which the Art Deco movement began, in this adolescent age of a new machine— video—we begin to look back circumspectly on Art Deco. It was the arresting video imagery of Miami Beach (and the hip stereo music to go with the flashing pastel colors) that made Michael Mann's TV show "Miami Vice" a hit, beginning in 1984. The success of that TV show brought the fashion photographers and models here. Each event leapfrogged over the previous one to make the Art Deco District even more desirable than before. When Miami Beach was built, it was the age of the machine, but more than that it was the age of a vibrant futurism that is especially evident in the spaceship finials topping Miami Beach's oceanside late–Art Deco hotels. There are many similarities between today's video age and the distinctly earlier age of radio. Art Deco is about the age of radio, the emanation through space of energy, the transmission of information. It is about an adulation of pure form, of efficient yet beautiful functionality.

This design-oriented approach, coupled with mass-marketing theories, merged in Barbara's head with her love for art and architecture. This combination caused her to settle on her adopted city of Miami Beach as a starting point for a worldwide quest to find and protect the architecture of this exciting and easily identifiable style from her own lifetime. She found, after the death of her husband, a unique South Florida home bursting with tiny Art Deco delights, spread evenly along a subtropical sandbar overrun with elderly New York City retirees. She found what then only she could see: the Miami Beach Art Deco District, with its whimsy and lush palm fronds framing buildings that had a very curious relationship to the elegant, towering, and truly awesome structures of her Chicago and New York Art Deco childhood.

Plymouth Hotel, *336 21st Street, Miami Beach. ARCHITECT: Anton Skislewicz, 1940; Restoration architect: Juan Lezcano, 1992. This striking night view shows why this hotel's image was used in 1977 on the first poster to promote the emerging Art Deco District. Since January 1988, it's been the living quarters for members of the New World Symphony, a student-training orchestra conducted by Michael Tilson Thomas. They perform nearby in the Lincoln Theater, another Art Deco landmark. Both the theater and this hotel were restored with support from the National Foundation for Advancement in the Arts, an organization founded by cruise-ship magnate Ted Arison and his wife Lin.*

She found she could recognize the essentials of Art Deco everywhere in her Miami Beach world. It was so easy to spot those characteristic patterns of three parallel straight lines, the ninety-degree corner curves, the soaring finials, and the expanses of glass brick. She especially loved the most remarkable theater in Miami Beach, the Cinema Theater (1235 Washington Avenue, 1938). It was a late design by the giant of theater architecture Thomas Lamb. When this building was threatened with demolition in 1978, it was the only thing that had stirred me in Barbara's wacky and seemingly hopeless campaign to create a historic district here. But I rallied to her side, consulting with her daily to plot a course

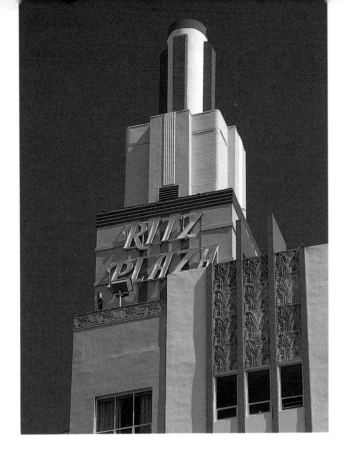

for saving the wonderful streamlined picture palace. She immediately "elected" me to the board of her nascent organization, the Miami Design Preservation League (MDPL). I never left the board, and today I serve as the longest-surviving member from this era. The Cinema Theater did not do badly, although it is now stripped of almost all of its original fixtures and a priceless mural. It survives in its fifth incarnation as a nightclub—having actually started as a nightclub in 1931 before becoming a theater, then taking a long holiday with the movies, and then going back to being a nightclub. Barbara never forgot my early support and friendship. I never forgot her strength and vision.

Our third partner in this enterprise, Dennis Wilhelm, who has been a collector of Deco artifacts since 1974, had already met this remarkable woman in 1977, joining her at a dozen Art Deco meetings that were a cross between a 1920s-style Parisian salon and a midwestern family get-together. At these meetings—which I missed—those present were treated to talks by noted designers, slides of great buildings, and lively discussions. Most of the programs focused on the vision of this astonishing place as it began to emerge, phoenix-like, from its sad role as "God's waiting room"—a decaying retirement retreat by the sea, largely untouched or cared for since its phenomenal creation during America's Great Depression. It was and still is a potent antidote for depression.

Randy Juster, like Barbara, was born in Chicago and eventually emigrated to a coastal city (San Mateo, California). Though he did not yet know Barbara, he was already scouring the nation for photographic records of these incredible Art Deco American monuments that he too loved so much.

This was the genesis of our team, and this is how this book came to be written.

When Barbara's son Andrew took over the management of seven oceanside Art Deco hotels, I joined with Margaret Doyle and Dennis Wilhelm to refurbish and restore to glory the lobby of the 1937 Victor Hotel, 1144 Ocean Drive, by L. Murray Dixon, the most cerebral of the group of architects who created the Art Deco District. Dixon was the one who worked in the office of Schultze and Weaver, designers of New York's Waldorf-Astoria and of Miami Beach's famed Roney Plaza Hotel. The Roney was special, one of the best we had. At the time of the Victor restoration, there was absolutely nothing glamorous or desirable about Miami Beach as far as any of my friends was concerned. Even I, who wanted to share Barbara's dreams, doubted they could actually come true. But here we were, sweating and struggling to restore this magnificent lobby. It was a suitable set, on which the dream could be sketched out clearly. Now Ocean Drive is awash with sidewalk cafés and late-night jazz clubs. If it is not like its original halcyon days, it is at least an agreeable re-creation. And for all I know, it's better.

In the early days, the MDPL's office was run by Barbara Capitman and her two associates, Lynn Bernstein and Diane Camber, now director of the Bass Museum. Architect

Andres Fabregas was Barbara's top adviser. When he retired, Karalyn Robinson Kana took over as chair. Much of the administration was done by attorney Denis Russ, who eventually helped Barbara establish the Miami Beach Development Corporation (MBDC), which he now heads. At this time, the board of the MDPL had co-chairs: the late Carl Weinhardt, Jr., director of the Vizcaya Museum, and Mitchell Wolfson, Jr., a millionaire friend of Barbara's who was amassing such a large collection of important early-twentieth-century "decorative and propaganda arts" that he was obliged to establish museums in Miami Beach and Genoa, Italy, just to keep track of it. He has since turned it over to The Wolfsonian Foundation, directed by Weinhardt's brilliant former assistant from Indianapolis, Peggy Loar.

Early Art Deco District rehabilitation efforts were spurred on by programs nurtured by the tremendously successful Metro-Dade County Department of Community and Economic Development, led by Ernest Martin, Ph.D. Eventually, Dr. Martin was persuaded to chair the MDPL board of directors from 1985 to 1988. But before that, he instituted a vital program to enhance the new Historic District. The way it worked was simple: The government would pay for part of the cost if an owner or commercial business leaseholder would simply repaint the façade of their building. The program targeted Washington Avenue. Under the direction of Bernstein (now associate director of the MBDC), Washington Avenue began to look great. The journey from slum to paradise for the District was to take only ten years, and it essentially started with nothing more than fresh paint and a big dream.

In 1982, Art Deco restoration materials were nearly nonexistent. It was necessary and desirable to salvage and reuse the hotels' original assets. New parts usually meant a special fabrication. The Victor Hotel lobby was a supreme example of the Miami Beach Art Deco lobby. It was larger than most and more glamorous. "Miami Vice" came to film its TV-goes-MTV series in September 1984, and the Emmy-award-winning set designers quickly discovered that the lobby spaces of the shuttered Victor Hotel were an ideal location for everything from cafés to department-store sales floors. The beautiful lights, pastel colors, and matching terrazzo floors gave a look to the scenes that was dynamite for the unblinking TV camera lens. A prime feature in that front lobby was the large Earl LaPan mural. It was overhead on the mezzanine level, at the end of the long two-story lobby. The favorite LaPan subjects, flamingoes and watery Everglades grasslands, were here in abundance.

After Andrew Capitman's venture ran out of money, he was forced to sell out at a loss. He, like his mother, was ahead of his time, and not trusted by the establishment. He retreated to New York and then to London to do business elsewhere. It was left to others to pick up the challenge and become Art Deco developers. Among the earlier people to attempt this were Gerry Sánchez, the first true restoration expert, and Donald Meginley, the first true Art Deco hotelier. They are gone now, but part-time New Yorker Tony Goldman has emerged to lead his fellow developers with élan and pizzazz. Goldman has invested in many Art Deco District properties but is best known for running the Park Central Hotel, 640 Ocean Drive, designed by Henry Hohauser in 1937. By frequently entertaining writers from Japan, Sweden, Germany, France, and Italy, Goldman has ensured a

steady flow of favorable stories about Miami Beach, just as Barbara Capitman had done a decade earlier. It was she who first understood that the key to success in promoting the Art Deco District was articles in every newspaper and magazine. But it was the camera's eye, finally, that ensured the fame of her beloved District.

Goldman and his fellow developers have now organized an Ocean Drive Association that unambiguously allies itself with the preservation community. Goldman was a patron of designer Leonard Horowitz, and in Leonard's last days, as he lay dying of AIDS, Tony made sure that Leonard had a comfortable apartment and free utilities. Tony never talks about that. He also provides support to district artists. He leads the effort to keep the Art Deco District in the international spotlight, giving interviews and appearing on television in many countries. He works to improve the quality of the Historic District, and he knows how to do it. But he has a lot of help. There are several other leading Art Deco developers who have allied themselves squarely on the side of historic preservation, including Mel and Marilyn Schlesser, Mark Soyka, Clark Reynolds, Saul Gross, and José Fernandez. The city administration now listens carefully to any discussion about improving the Art Deco District. A strict ban on demolition throughout the National Register District passed the Miami Beach City Commission unanimously in October 1992. The message about not tearing down the building is now being heard loud and clear throughout the city.

In the past few years, the MDPL has convinced the City of Miami Beach to name streets in the Art Deco District for both Barbara Capitman and Leonard Horowitz. Tenth Street

at Ocean Drive is now Barbara Capitman Way, and Eleventh Street is now Leonard Horowitz Place. The names are very fitting, but they scarcely give these two the full tribute they deserve. We have recently elected a new group of city commissioners to run the city, and we hope that, led by Neisen Kasdin, an attorney who previously led the Miami Beach Development Corporation as chairman, the city administration will move ever closer to the idea of commercial development through the enhancement of our historic properties.

Since Barbara's death on March 29, 1990, the MDPL has come a long way. Nancy Liebman ran the organization with the same iron hand as did Barbara and got many city department heads to listen seriously when construction or renovation was not going according to code or to the Historic Preservation Board's wishes. The board of the MDPL continues to enjoy the service of some longtime members who worked for years with Barbara—people such as Janet Aptaker, Alan Baseman, Matti Bower, Aristides Millas, Thorn Grafton, Betty Gutierrez, Coman Leonard, and Keith Root. Attorneys I. Stanley Levine and Joseph Z. Fleming have also assisted the MDPL board since Barbara's early days.

Saint Charles Hotel (Avalon Hotel), 700 Ocean Drive, Miami Beach. ARCHITECT: Albert Anis, 1941. A splendid corner tower illustrates how the architect, Anis, eschewed the rounded corners of the 1930s and moved toward the bold square geometry of the 1940s. Now called the Avalon, it's one of Ocean Drive's many highlights.

The restorations continue apace, and one architect stands out for having done far and away more successful projects in the Art Deco District than any other individual: Les Beilinson, a former MDPL board member, with over fifty projects to his credit and still counting. Another individual who has a record of persistence and longevity is Richard Hoberman, former chairman of the MDPL board. Long before he was elected to the board, he was a volunteer conducting weekly Saturday tours of the Art Deco District. For almost eight years, he conducted thousands of important visitors around the District, helping them rediscover the joys of Art Deco in the process.

The Malvern group has recently restored the 1940 Ritz Plaza Hotel, 1701 Collins Avenue, by L. Murray Dixon. This is one of the most outstanding renovation projects in the Art Deco District, and the hotel is constantly booked with guests from Latin America and Europe. It was the site for the highly successful First World Congress on Art Deco in January 1991, which was Barbara Capitman's final project.

The arrival of Michael Tilson Thomas with his student-training orchestra, the New World Symphony, gave the Art Deco District a real boost. With money provided by the founder of Carnival Cruise Lines, Ted Arison, the orchestra's parent foundation purchased the 1940 Plymouth Hotel, 2100 Park Avenue, by Anton Skislewicz, as a home for the students, and the 1940 Lincoln Theater, 1600 Meridian at Lincoln Road Mall, by L. Murray Dixon, as its performance home.

Preservation efforts in the District have been constantly bolstered by Barbara's cadre of personal friends and supporters—hundreds strong—including such stalwarts as Emily Beech, Thelma Chavin, Stuart Grant, Sylvia Hooper, Alex Nott, Rhoda Oppenheimer, Evelyn Perlman, Linda Polansky, Octavio Robles, Jeannie Stockheim, and Bernard Zyscovich (recently elected chairman of the MDPL).

One of the most important development companies to take up operations within the Art Deco District is the DACRA companies, led by brothers Craig and Scott Robins. They have done first-class restorations on scores of buildings and recently acquired the historic Cardozo, Carlyle, and Victor hotels, as well as a handful of other prime Ocean Drive properties. They have already negotiated a deal to sell the Cardozo to local singing superstar Gloria Estefan and her husband, Emilio. The Robins brothers have joined with former owner of Island Records, millionaire entertainment mogul Chris Blackwell, to restore the Marlin, Tides, and Netherland hotels. And unrelated to these events, Italian designer Gianni Versace has come into the District and bought the unique Mediterranean Revival Amsterdam Palace apartments for $3 million to transform it into his private residence on Ocean Drive. In short, there are some really big-money people now interested in the District.

Victor Hotel, 1144 Ocean Drive, Miami Beach. ARCHITECT: *L. Murray Dixon; Muralist: Earl LaPan, 1937. LaPan's original lobby mural features Everglades flamingoes. The outstanding original light fixtures of chrome-plated spun copper were refurbished by the authors in 1980 as part of the restoration of the public areas directed by Andrew Capitman and Margaret Doyle. After the Royale Group took control of the hotel and closed it, the mural was vandalized and most of the original fixtures were stolen. In 1992, a restoration was planned by its new owners, DACRA and Chris Blackwell.*

So far, it seems they are interested for the very reason that it is a unique and beautiful historic district. Everyone seems inclined to work together with the City of Miami Beach to ensure that it stays that way.

This is a happy place to wind down this story of the lively teenage years of Barbara Capitman's Art Deco District. May the next twenty years be even better.

As for the hundreds of Miami Beach Art Deco buildings that have not been mentioned here, we pray that our readers will buy MDPL's *Art Deco Guide* by Keith Root, or Barbara's previous book, *Deco Delights*, which deals exclusively with that subject and is filled with absolutely stunning photographs taken by our friend Steven Brooke.

ELSEWHERE
Miami

Across Biscayne Bay from Art Deco Miami Beach is the much larger city of Miami. Here are a few extraordinary examples of Art Deco architecture that we should mention:

The earliest Art Deco building in Miami is a fraternal lodge, the Scottish Rite Temple at 471 Northwest Third

Pan American Seaplane Base and Passenger Terminal at Dinner Key (Miami City Hall), 3500 Pan American Way, Coconut Grove, Miami. ARCHITECT: Delano & Aldrich, 1932. The late, great Pan American Airways began mail service to Havana, Cuba, from Key West, Florida, in 1927. A year later operations moved to Coconut Grove (just after the bayside village was annexed by Miami). This terminal opened in 1934, becoming an integral part of Pan Am's worldwide Clipper seaplane network. It was supposedly the embarkation point for Fred Astaire and Ginger Rogers's famed adventure Flying Down to Rio, their first film together made in 1936. But seaplane service became obsolete as airlines moved to dry land. In 1945, the city of Miami took over the building for their City Hall. Pan Am used the same architect for its Marine Air Terminal at La Guardia Airport (see New York chapter). (Photograph by Steven Brooke, copyright © 1991. Used by permission.)

Mahi Shrine Temple (Boulevard Shops), 1401 Biscayne Boulevard, Miami. ARCHITECT: Robert Law Weed, 1930; Restoration architect: Andres Fabregas for Bouterse, Perez & Fabregas, 1979. Built by one of Miami's finest Art Deco architects, this commercial landmark on Miami's main thoroughfare, Biscayne Boulevard, has seen many uses. Art Deco decoration often incorporates local folklore, flora, and fauna. Here the architect has had Seminole figures carved on the corners of the limestone façade. Now owned by Knight-Ridder, the newspaper and communications corporation, the building's future is uncertain, as the county wants to put a new Performing Arts Center on the site. (Photograph by Andres Fabregas, courtesy the Capitman Archives)

Street, by Kiehnel & Elliott, which was built in 1922 at the start of the King Tut Egyptian Revival craze. It is a classical Egypto-Deco building with great stonework and carving outside, as well as outstanding carved woodwork inside.

The second important fraternal lodge building is the Mahi Shrine Temple (last called the Boulevard Shops) at 1401 Biscayne Boulevard, designed in 1930 by Robert Law Weed. This building was restored by Andres Fabregas as a historic project because it was a leading building in the development of Biscayne Boulevard's upper extension in the early 1930s. Currently, it is awaiting its fate, for a county performing-arts center is proposed for the site, and demolition is a continuing possibility. Also endangered by the same arts-center plan is the Sears store directly across the street at 1400 Biscayne Boulevard, by Nimmons, Carr & Wright, 1929. Sears donated the store to Dade County to help it assemble the site for the proposed arts center. Deco District preservationists are lobbying the county to preserve the building as an integral part of the new complex.

whitewashing of the house. The whitewash did not diminish its Art Deco splendor, however. Throughout the house, in every conceivable application, Shoumate observed the unwritten "Rule of Threes." He also introduced a musical theme in the house, with such motifs as treble clefs in the metalwork. The musical interest was serendipitous because Ignace Jan Paderewski lived in this house during his exile from Poland during World War II. Kooluris has gone to great pains to restore the house as closely as possible to Shoumate's original drawings, and he interviewed the architect many times to ascertain his exact intentions in the original execution of the house.

Palm Beach, Florida

There are only a few Art Deco buildings in Palm Beach and a few more in West Palm Beach, but so great was Barbara Capitman's influence that a healthy Art Deco Society was nevertheless founded here in 1987. The guiding light of this organization is its founder, designer Sharon Koskoff, who was a friend of both Leonard and Barbara.

Worthy of special mention is Kirby Kooluris's splendid 1936 waterfront residence at 1221 North Lake Way, by Belford Shoumate, an associate of the great architectural colorist Joseph Urban. Perhaps because of Urban's influence, Shoumate dictated that the original exterior color of this home be a brilliant blue. Palm Beach just wasn't ready for that, and pressure from the neighbors soon forced the

Steckler (Kooluris) residence, 1221 North Lake Way, Palm Beach. ARCHITECT: Belford Shoumate, 1936. In a city known for its Mediterranean Revival architecture, Shoumate boldly created a rare Nautical Moderne residence. A member of the famed T-Square architectural club of the 1930s, he designed a handful of strictly modern homes and finished them in bright colors that caused panic and loathing among neighbors. He credited the flashy colors to his friend Joseph Urban, with whom he collaborated on the recently destroyed Palm Beach Paramount Theatre. Although the house is no longer bright blue, it is carefully preserved and maintained by the present owner, Kirby Kooluris. Celebrated pianist (and one-time premier of Poland) Ignace Jan Paderewski made this his wartime refuge. (Photograph by Kirby Kooluris)

12

MILWAUKEE

CITY OF MACHINE AESTHETIC

If I were suffered to apply the word genius to only one living American, I would save it for Frank Lloyd Wright.

—Alexander Woollcott, 1931

CENTURIES AGO THE POTOWATOMI TRIBE RULED this land. Around 1818, three families of European descent settled at the confluence of the Milwaukee and Menominee Rivers. By 1839, the Germans had begun arriving in Milwaukee, and by 1880 they had practically taken over the city. Their influence is still felt today, from the names on the businesses—Schroeder, Pfister, Sprecher, Edelweis, Germania—to the heavily Germanic turn-of-the-century-style architecture, to the aromas of beer, sausage, and chocolate that waft from the downtown breweries and factories of Pabst, Miller, Usinger and Ambrosia, permeating the air and invoking memories of the Old World.

Milwaukee is fortunate to have two Art Deco towers downtown, and each is topped by a beacon. Most spectacular is the tower of the Milwaukee Gas Light Company, 626 East Wisconsin Avenue, designed by the local firm of Eschweiler & Eschweiler in 1930. It has the archetypical Hugh Ferris Art Deco massing with sculpted planes set in threes (again, the "Rule of Threes"). This massing of rectangular slabs of varying heights and widths often represents the mathematical proportion 1:2:4, which is another variation of the "Rule of Threes." Even if the proportions change, the groups of threes are ubiquitous.

The illuminated mock gas flame that tops the building looks big enough to have been lit by King Kong, and it embodies the credo of the Machine Age: technology in ser-

Milwaukee Gas Light Company (Wisconsin Gas Company), 626 East Wisconsin, Milwaukee. ARCHITECT: Eschweiler & Eschweiler, 1930. This famed Milwaukee landmark serves as a public weather-forecasting beacon. The twenty-one-foot flame on top changes color to announce the next front passing through: cold or hot, dry or rainy. The weather flame was added in 1956 to this twenty-story symmetrical stepped-back skyscraper. (Photograph courtesy the Capitman Archives)

vice to mankind. The decorative details at street level are worth a close inspection, as are the elevator lobbies.

The second beacon-topped building is the Mariner Tower, 606 West Wisconsin Avenue, today called the Wisconsin Tower. It was built in 1929 and is crowned by a tall illuminated sign that served for years as a beacon to the mariners on Lake Michigan. Today the tower is obscured by a taller building. The lobby and entrance are faced in red granite and the metalwork at the entrance is exquisite.

Milwaukee's real success story in preservation is what is called the Grand Mall. Instead of giving up on the downtown when many of the stores and businesses deserted it for the suburbs, the city connected the vacant buildings by a series of covered walkways, and shops and restaurants were carved out of the cavernous interiors. The mall is enormously successful, the buildings have been preserved, and in the winter it is possible to walk for miles without going outside, or getting cold!

Not far from the end of the mall is the former Warner (now Grand) Theater, 212 West Wisconsin Avenue, by C. W. and George Rapp, 1930. It is an exceedingly rare

example of a quasi–Art Deco transitional theater that combines the new French Moderne style with older French decorative styles. Although the auditorium has been "twinned," one can still appreciate the unblemished splendor of the main lobby and box office. The lobby is finished completely in silver-leaf and mirrors. From the mezzanine above the grand staircase one gains a breathtaking view of soaring silvery French Deco. Mirrors over the main entry amplify and extend the smooth arches and silver argyle-patterned ceiling nearly to infinity. This was an early effort by Rapp & Rapp, but it was merely a precursor to later theater work that is totally Art Deco, such as the Aurora (Illinois) Paramount.

Across from the theater is an equally striking Kresge's store, an example of Art Deco uniformity not unlike Henry Ford's Model-T—a familiar sight in a cluttered and busy twentieth-century landscape.

The Chicago firm of Holabird & Root did several projects in Milwaukee and the surrounding area. The Schroeder Hotel (now Mark Plaza) was underway in 1927 just as the firm was making a transition from one generation to another. The venerable firm of Holabird & Roche had been responsi-

Warner Theater (Centre Grand Theater), 212 West Wisconsin Avenue, Milwaukee. ARCHITECT: C.W. Rapp & George Rapp, 1930. This lobby stairwell mural features an ethereal young lady with doves in flight in the shimmering clouds overhead. Rapp & Rapp were lavish in their use of fine materials, capturing the authentic French Moderne style that was every bit as opulent as the periods that preceded it. Faithfulness to lavish French standards soon was abandoned, however, as less became more in the ensuing Great Depression.

Warner Theater (Centre Grand Theater; 2,431 seats), 212 West Wisconsin Avenue, Milwaukee. ARCHITECT: C.W. Rapp & George Rapp, 1930. Brothers C.W. and George Rapp designed many theaters with French Baroque auditoriums, but only a few with avant-garde French Moderne lobbies like this one. It is finished in silver leaf and mirrors. Warner Brothers were able to build many Art Deco theaters in 1930–1931, when every other studio was nearly broke, because they had the sensationally successful Vitaphone "talkies." (Photograph by Michael D. Kinerk)

ble for some of Chicago's finest buildings. Martin Roche died in 1927. John Wellborn Root, Jr., and John Holabird were both sons of famous and successful Chicago architects, and both were recent graduates of the famed French architectural school, L'École des Beaux Arts. They renamed the firm Holabird & Root and set off with fresh new ideas. In the Schroeder Hotel they introduced hints of Art Deco in the lobbies.

Their design for the A. O. Smith Company Research Building, 3533 North 27th Street, was done two years later in 1929. Although leaning more toward the International Style on the exterior, the interiors are legendary because of the machine aesthetics used in their design. A glass-topped table with a cogwheel base from the lobby was included in the Brooklyn Museum's 1986 exhibition "The Machine Age in America."

A local architect is responsible for two of Milwaukee's best Art Deco buildings. Herbert W. Tullgren worked in his father's firm, Tullgren and Sons, and had a definite flair for Art Deco design. The small-scale 1934 Northwestern Hanna Fuel Company, 2150 North Prospect Avenue, has half-round terra-cotta piers between the windows and half-round canopies above the doors, giving a very streamlined look to what is really a square box. Relief panels above each of the windows show workers in the fuel industry. Color plays a very important role in the work of Tullgren, giving it a personality all its own. In the Hanna Fuel building he chose a shade of orange for the piers and canopies that completely harmonizes with the browns of the brick, yet there is enough contrast to make the rounded elements jump out from the flat surfaces behind them.

Another of Tullgren's great works is a 1937 apartment building near the Lake at 1260 North Prospect Avenue. The eye-catching features here are corner wraparound windows and the two semicircular towers protruding from the façade, giving it a vertical emphasis. The color is green, that perfect shade of Art Deco green that inspired the old phrase "pretty as green paint." This green is used on the frames of all the casement windows and gives the apartment building a distinct identity.

Initially, we had planned to cover Milwaukee simply by inserting the headquarters of the Milwaukee Gas Light Company in the "Elsewhere" section of the Chicago chapter. Barbara had told us this building *must* be in the book because of its bold symmetrical massing, perfectly proportioned setbacks, and a flame twenty-one feet high that constantly monitors Milwaukee's exasperating weather as it changes from red to blue to gold. In her visit Barbara had learned from the president of the company that the flame was added in 1956. But that was okay, because it was Delayed Deco and still perfect. (We have learned that quite a few cities had similar Art Deco weather beacons during the 1930s.) So we decided to go to Milwaukee to see this building and also stop in Racine to study Frank Lloyd Wright's Johnson Wax buildings. Before leaving, we spoke to

Daniel Morris and Denis Gallion, pioneer purveyors of Art Deco. They knew Milwaukee quite well and suggested several other subjects for us. "Don't miss the terra-cotta coal company building and the apartment on the lake along North Prospect," they urged. As this chapter attests, it was advice well taken.

Elsewhere
RACINE, WISCONSIN

The Machine Age called for a purer architecture, a style that would eliminate distractions and add to efficiency. Through the principles of Art Deco design, the architect could "elevate" the factory or office to a higher plateau. Nowhere is this more clearly seen than in Racine, a few miles south of Milwaukee. This is where Frank Lloyd Wright built the famous Administration Building (1936) and Research Tower (1944) for the S. C. Johnson Wax Company, 1525 Howe Street.

Although Barbara Capitman was laughed at in Chicago in 1981 when she mentioned Frank Lloyd Wright in connection with Art Deco, the Johnson Wax Administration Building is now considered the purest example of the Streamline Moderne. The tall Research Tower also owes something to the style. Historian Jonathan Lipman says Wright decided finally to design a streamlined building one day as he and Mr. Johnson were mutually admiring their Lincoln Zephyr automobiles.

Inside, Wright's celebrated "dendriform" columns take the form of slender, tapered lotus stems with wide round tops to hold up the roof. When local building inspectors claimed these columns could not support the building, Wright staged a series of tests amid great publicity, piling tons of sandbags on top of the proposed columns. When they withstood six times their rated capacity, Wright halted the test in triumph. The Johnson Wax Administration Center went up exactly as Wright designed it. In both these buildings there are no windows but miles of Pyrex glass tubes laid together to cover large expanses in both the ceiling and sidewalls. The result: no distracting view, lots of light—eliminate distraction, add to efficiency.

The embellishments Wright used inside are a pure joy to behold. The now-famous interior concrete columns support a glass-cylinder skylight two stories over the workers' heads. The desk, chairs, file cabinets, and lights have been photographed and exhibited countless times, but less well known are the cork, linoleum, glass, and materials that Wright designed for the buildings. Such materials were commonly used throughout the Art Deco period, but they are not often found in the workplace today.

Although they are still serving their original functions, the Johnson Wax buildings are well treated as the works of art that they are. Another Wright design in the Streamline

S.C. Johnson & Son Wax Company, 1525 Howe Street, Racine, Wisconsin. Architect: Frank Lloyd Wright, 1936 and 1944. Two National Historic Landmarks, the Johnson Wax Administration Building, left, and the later Research Tower, right, are proudly maintained to this day. According to historian Jonathan Lipman, Wright decided to design a streamlined building while he and Mr. Johnson were mutually admiring their Lincoln Zephyr automobiles. Tours of the unique facility are offered daily, by appointment.

S.C. Johnson & Son Wax Company, 1525 Howe Street, Racine, Wisconsin. Architect: Frank Lloyd Wright, 1936. The Johnson Wax building was an engineering triumph because of the controversial interior roof supports, the famous lotus-blossom dendriform tapered columns. Wright, America's master architect, supervised every detail, designing desks, chairs, shelving, and lamps. In place of windows he developed a system of Pyrex glass tubes that admit light but no distracting outside views. This upper-level passageway illustrates the effect he achieved. (Photograph by Michael D. Kinerk)

style is Wingspread, the home built by Mr. Johnson on the other side of Racine. Today it is maintained by the Johnson Foundation and is used for retreats and conferences related to the foundation's interest in social issues.

The Racine County Courthouse, 730 Wisconsin Avenue, is a 1929 Holabird & Root design with sculpture by Carl Milles, who worked with them in their Michigan Square Building in Chicago and the Ramsey County Courthouse in Saint Paul, Minnesota.

13

MINNEAPOLIS AND SAINT PAUL

WHERE ART DECO CAME OUT OF RETIREMENT

So we beat on, boats against the current,
borne back ceaselessly into the past.

—F. Scott Fitzgerald
Last line of *The Great Gatsby*

THE TWIN CITIES OF MINNEAPOLIS AND SAINT PAUL have very important connections to Art Deco. Both have fine examples of architecture from the period. But more important, it was here at the Minneapolis Institute of Arts in 1971 that Art Deco was brought out of retirement and given a starring role once again.

In 1969, museum curator David Ryan proposed an exhibition to explore the role that Art Deco had played in both Europe and the United States. The museum's board greeted the proposal with enthusiasm, and the planning began. Ryan contacted Bevis Hillier, whose book *Art Deco* had been published the previous year, and convinced him to write the catalog for the exhibition. The result was the comprehensive exhibition "The World of Art Deco," a display of nearly fifteen hundred objects borrowed from all over the world and selected to give an overview of the many forms taken by Art Deco throughout the 1920s and 1930s.

The twin cities were heavily settled by Scandinavian immigrants. A descendant of one of these immigrants is another of Minneapolis's connections to Art Deco. David Gebhard, the man who coined the term *Streamline Moderne*,

Rand Tower (Dain Bosworth Tower), 527 Marquette Avenue, Minneapolis. ARCHITECT: Holabird & Root; Sculptor: Oskar J.W. Hansen, 1928. Rufus Rand installed Hansen's ethereal sculpture Wings in the lobby of his office tower. The building's decoration celebrates flight and aviation. Hansen's starkly beautiful work floats over illuminated etched-glass clouds surrounded by polished black and Tosa-Grey Nelle marble. The tower won an award from the American Institute of Architects (AIA) in 1930. (Photograph courtesy the Minneapolis Star-Tribune)

Forum Cafeteria (Mick's at the Forum), 40 South 7th Street in City Center (original address: 36 South 7th Street), Minneapolis. ARCHITECT: George B. Franklin, 1929; Restoration architects: 1979, Herb Polachek, with John Woodbridge; 1992, Shea Architects. Rejoicing in Vitrolite colored-glass panels on all its walls, this cafeteria had clean, gleaming-glass surfaces everywhere, a perfect ambience for a restaurant. The decorative glass featured such regional images as Viking ships, Minnehaha Falls, icicles, snow drifts, mountains, lakes, and pine cones. The Forum was a national chain with restaurants in several cities, all designed by Franklin, a Kansas City architect. (Photograph by George Heinrich, courtesy Shea Architects)

Forum Cafeteria (Mick's at the Forum), 40 South 7th Street in City Center (original address: 36 South 7th Street), Minneapolis. ARCHITECT: George B. Franklin, 1929; Restoration architects: 1979, Herb Polachek, with John Woodbridge; 1992, Shea Architects. This unique downtown eating spot was dismantled and reassembled in a shopping mall/office tower on the original site. In 1929, this interior was created in the shell of the Strand, a 1911 moving picture theater. It was designated a local landmark in 1975. (Photograph by George Heinrich, courtesy Shea Architects)

comes from Scandinavian stock and had his first job in Minneapolis. He was an intern in the firm of McEnary & Krafft, where his aunt's husband was a partner.

McEnary & Krafft designed one of the premier Art Deco buildings in downtown Minneapolis, the Farmers & Mechanics Bank at 90 South Sixth Street. This 1941 building features Warren Mossman's sculptural representations of farmers and mechanics on each side of the door. As our tour-guide Jarrett Smith explained to us, all laborers and industrial workers were called "mechanics" at the turn of the century, when the bank was founded. The farmers grew the wheat that made Minneapolis the center of the flour industry. Pillsbury is headquartered here. Also notable in this building is the enormous piece of sculpted Corning Glass above the door. The only comparable glass sculpture is above the entrance to the RCA Building (now the GE building) in Rockefeller Center.

One industry employing mechanics was Minnesota's rock-quarrying companies. Minnesota's stone is used all over the country, and only the superb Bedford limestone quarried in Indiana was more widely used. (Bedford limestone was so popular in the 1930s that its boosters said that half of New York originated in Indiana.) Minnesota's Kasota-Mankota stone is a kind of limestone. Its colors range from cream to pink to blue-gray. The stone can be given a high polish to make it look like marble, which made it possible for architects to achieve an opulent effect on a limited budget. A good example of the use of Kasota stone is Minneapolis's 1930 Northwestern Bell Telephone Company, 224 South Fifth Street, by Rhodes Robertson for the firm of Hewitt & Brown. The setbacks on this twenty-six-story building are capped by local Kasota stone.

Across the street from the Farmers & Mechanics Bank at 527 Marquette Avenue is the Rand Tower, now called Dain Bosworth Tower. Designed in 1928 by Holabird & Root, it was recently restored by Dain Kalman Quail Inc. The relief panels above the doors are related to air travel, a theme that is continued in the lobby by Oskar Hansen's sculpture *Wings*.

One of the best known of the Art Deco towers downtown is the Foshay Tower, 821 Marquette Avenue, designed in 1926 by Leon Arnal for Magney & Tusler. Modeled on the Washington Monument, the walls of this tower slope inward

Foshay Tower, 821 Marquette Avenue, Minneapolis. ARCHITECT: Leon Arnal for Magney & Tusler, 1926. Celebrated as the first concrete skyscraper with sloping sides, this graceful tower was designed by French-born Leon Arnal, Art Deco specialist for this local firm. This National Register Landmark is faced with Indiana limestone, quarried and delivered sequentially in varying sizes because of the slope of the sides.

Foshay Tower, 821 Marquette Avenue, Minneapolis. ARCHITECT: Leon Arnal for Magney & Tusler, 1926. Arnal taught at the University of Pennsylvania during the period when it was an incubator of Art Deco inspiration under the influence of the great Paul Philippe Cret, who taught there from 1903 to 1937. This detail shows an image of the building in silhouette on each of the beautifully crafted elevator doors.

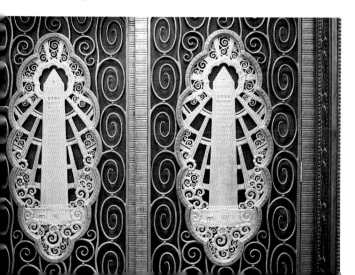

as it climbs thirty-two stories. A two-story building surrounds the tower on three sides and contains an arcade with terrazzo floors, elaborate bronze grillwork, and elevator doors depicting the building itself. The architect of Foshay Tower, Leon Arnal, also designed a two-block-long postal facility on the banks of the Mississippi River at 100 South First Street. The interior features the original brass stand-up writing desks and an enormous continuous-strip brass light fixture, said to be the longest in the world at 365 feet.

On the endangered list is P.C. Bettenburg's Streamline Moderne National Guard Armory, 500 South Sixth Street. A county court judge recently ruled that the county has the right to demolish the structure, which sits on a prime site near the Hubert H. Humphrey Metrodome. The city and state are appealing to the State Supreme Court, which ruled in January 1993 that the armory may not be demolished. Further appeals are likely.

Another of this city's many Art Deco assets is a huge and important collection owned by the big financial firm Norwest Corporation. The collection is under the direction of David Ryan. The Northwestern Bank had a long history in Minneapolis when it built a new headquarters in 1928. The building, designed by Chicago's Graham, Anderson, Probst & White, was a local landmark for years until it burned in 1982. Most of the interior was destroyed and the corporation, by then a holding company renamed Norwest, decided that the building was a total loss and would have to be demolished. Many of the original Art Deco elements were rescued before demolition. Norwest found an architect, Cesar Pelli and Associates, willing to incorporate the old artifacts into the new building in a sensitive manner. Standing at Sixth Street and Marquette Avenue, the Norwest building makes a major Art Deco statement and is one of the few non-Adrian Smith-designed buildings to reflect the true majesty of the old Art Deco with such authority. The massing is pure Hugh Ferris and is an homage to Rockefeller Center—the RCA building in particular. The mammoth lighting fixtures, railings, and grillwork salvaged from the 1928 building have been incorporated into the three-story lobby, which has been called "the front porch of Minneapolis." Also included in the lobby spaces is a series of vitrines that are used for rotating exhibits of the best pieces from the Norwest Collection.

As David Ryan explained to us, the Scandinavians in the city have always had a strong commitment to the arts. For them art is not a frill but one of the several essential elements necessary for a satisfactory lifestyle. This attitude also has been essential to the success of the Minneapolis Institute of Arts and has created a social climate that ensures that the Norwest Corporation will continue to value its collection as a prudent investment. Norwest created a program to collect and exhibit important examples of twentieth-century design and hired Mr. Ryan as the collection's founding director. Although not exclusively Art Deco, the collection contains many Art Deco pieces and many others that show where the style came from and how it developed. Exhibitions are mounted several times a year in the lobby vitrines and are accompanied by brochures that are so well designed they have become collectibles.

Minneapolis's downtown has the feel of a modern bustling city, but it is very much a combination of new and old. When preparing for one of the new towers, the city mandated that the interior of a building scheduled for demolition had to be saved and incorporated into the new tower. This foresight preserved one of the most unusual and beautiful Art Deco interiors in the country, the Forum Cafeteria. In the late 1920s, a Kansas City company hired architect George B. Franklin to build a series of Forum Cafeterias across the country. Franklin favored Vitrolite Structural Glass for his interiors because it gave the clean, modern, up-to-date look he wanted to establish for the chain. The Minneapolis cafeteria was built inside a former movie theater, giving Franklin a chance to design a dramatic dining area in a two-story-high open space with a mezzanine. Bands of Vitrolite in five different colors completely encircle the two stories from floor to ceiling. Franklin's designs were regionally inspired so that the customers would still feel at home in such a modern interior. This was done by sandblasting designs into the glass panels and fusing metallic colors into the designs. In Minneapolis, Franklin used Viking ships, Minnehaha falls, icicles, snow drifts, mountains, lakes, and pine cones to create an unforgettable space.

In 1979, restoration architect Herb Polachek worked with John Woodbridge to design a plan for removing the glass panels and original fittings from the Forum. A new skyscraper was constructed on the site containing an identical space within the new building. They painstakingly reinstalled the pieces, thus recreating the original restaurant. In 1992, a successful restaurant chain from Atlanta leased the space and contracted with Shea Architects to update the previous restoration and to make the regionalism a unified theme for their new restaurant, Mick's at the Forum. It is a dining spot that truly captures the spirit of the age.

If that weren't enough, Minneapolis has another Art Deco dining spot, Peter's Grill. In 1930, Monel Angelikis designed everything for Peter's including the signs, menus, and waitress uniforms. The family-owned operation recently lost its lease and has called in Shea Architects to move the entire restaurant to a new location.

The Minneapolis *Star Tribune*, 425 Portland Avenue, was built in 1947 and is an example of Delayed Deco. Its heroic exterior stone-relief panels by University of Minnesota professor Ivan Doseff depict industries of the area.

Sears, Roebuck & Company began in Minneapolis before moving to Chicago. The 1927 Sears store at East Lake Street and Elliot Avenue is an early example of the "Sears Tower" style developed for the company by Sears's favorite corporate architects, Nimmons, Carr & Wright.

The area also has quite a few theaters by Liebenberg & Kaplan, prolific local architects who designed over two hundred theaters throughout the Midwest. These have been much written about by Herbert Shriner, librarian at the University of Minnesota. The firm's best examples are the 1937 Uptown Theater, 2906 Hennepin Avenue, with its sixty-foot marquee, and the 1937 Varsity Theater, 255 Bedford Street Southeast, 1938.

Saint Paul, Minnesota

The big story in Saint Paul is the splendid city-county building designed in 1930 by the Midwest's leading Art Deco architectural firm, Holabird & Root. As with all their major work, the Ramsey County–Saint Paul government center, at 15 West Kellogg Boulevard, has its share of Art Deco artwork. Outside is Lee Lawrie's relief sculpture of *Justice* with its Egyptian revival details placed next to the industrial symbol, cog wheels. The stark grain-tower exterior stands in contrast to the ground floor interior, which has one of the country's most important sculptures, the three-story onyx *Indian God of Peace* by Carl Milles, who is best known in America for his work at Detroit's Cranbrook Academy. He also has work in the Racine County courthouse in Wisconsin, at the Department of State building in Washington, D.C., and at 1 Rockefeller Plaza, New York City.

Directly across from Saint Paul City Hall stands the former Women's City Club that was renovated in 1972 for use by the Minnesota Museum of Art. This Moderne building, 305 Saint Peter Street, houses a permanent collection that includes work of artists of the 1930s and the archive of the great sculptor, Paul Manship. It was designed in 1931 by a Norwegian architect, Magnus Jemme, with his wife Elsa doing the designs for the brass-inlaid terrazzo floors.

Not far away is Mickey's Diner at 36 West Ninth Street. The diner is now operated by the son of the original owner. It was manufactured by the Jerry O'Mahony Company in 1937.

Minneapolis/Saint Paul had an early Art Deco Society that has been inactive lately. It was founded (once again) by Barbara Capitman when she visited the home of the Minneapolis retailing executive Charles Senseman, whom she had

met first at Burdines in Miami, when the Florida department store chain was assembling its early and very significant "design collection" of fine Art Deco pieces. The only founding member of the Minneapolis society we found still active is Jarrett Smith, who made sure that we didn't miss anything.

Another of the Society's founding members was Thomas R. Blanck, AIA, who had restored the 1936 Art Deco bar at the Commodore Hotel in Saint Paul and offered it for meetings when Barbara visited in 1981. The Commodore, 79 Western Avenue North, built in 1920, had been frequented by F. Scott Fitzgerald and Sinclair Lewis. Designer Werner Wittkamp immigrated to New York from Berlin in the 1920s and went to work for the Ziegfeld Follies. He moved on to the Fox Studios in Hollywood, where he also designed a few Art Deco buildings. He was brought to Saint Paul by a businessman who loved his style and commissioned him to design the Cinderella Cosmetic Company in the Moderne style. Today the Commodore has become a condo, but its Art Deco bar is operated by the University Club of Saint Paul and is available for parties and receptions. The barroom looks like the set from a Fred and Ginger film, with the reflections of indirect lighting off the polished black marble floors, mirrored walls, and liquor-bottle shelving units giving the room a dramatic intensity and elegance that becomes even more so after a few drinks at the brass-railed bar.

As Marjorie Nugent has written in the University Club's newsletter, *The Lookout:* " . . . true to Saint Paul's wild reputation for the period, the Cinderella Cosmetic Company, rather than manufacturing cosmetics, actually housed an illicit liquor business." The Commodore's bar, however, opened after Prohibition in 1934 and was simply the cat's meow.

Ramsey County Courthouse/Saint Paul City Hall, 15 *West Kellogg Boulevard, Saint Paul.* ARCHITECT: *Holabird & Root, with Tom Ellerbe; Sculptor: Lee Lawrie, 1931. Four themes are expressed in this relief panel installed on the left side of the building's main entrance. The symbols for each are: a book for Education; Justice holding scales for Law and Order; a nail keg for Commerce; and cogwheels for Industry. The panoramic skyline carved in the background includes the courthouse itself.*

Ramsey County Courthouse/Saint Paul City Hall, 15 *West Kellogg Boulevard, Saint Paul.* ARCHITECT: *Holabird & Root, with Tom Ellerbe; Sculptor: Lee Lawrie, 1931. Ceres, Roman goddess of the harvest, is the central figure in this relief panel located on the right side of the main entrance. She represents the abundance of the surrounding grain fields in this area, long famous for cereal manufacturing. Transportation, a key to Saint Paul's growth, also is included in the panel. These and other regional motifs are found in the exterior carving and are repeated elsewhere in the building.*

Ramsey County Courthouse/Saint Paul City Hall, 15 *West Kellogg Boulevard, Saint Paul.* ARCHITECT: *Holabird & Root, with Tom Ellerbe; Sculptor: Carl Milles, 1931. Swedish sculptor Milles's dramatic fifty-five-ton, white-onyx Indian God of Peace is spectacularly lit and set on a slowly revolving base in the three-story Memorial Hall in the courthouse. The walls are Belgian marble and the ceiling comprises gold mirrors. Chicago's leading Deco architects, Holabird & Root, won this prestigious contract with Ellerbe, a local architect. The work was unveiled in 1936 when the building finally was dedicated.*

14

NEW YORK

CENTER OF THE ART DECO UNIVERSE
CITY OF SKYSCRAPERS

*"Of the 377 skyscrapers more than twenty sto-
ries high, which stand in the United States in
1929, 188 rise within the narrow limits of New
York City."*

—Hugh Ferriss in *The Metropolis of Tomorrow,* 1929

IN TERMS OF ART DECO, NEW YORK IS KING OF THE
world. The city has more Art Deco than anyplace else. We
are not talking about a couple of high schools, lodge halls, or
fire stations. We are talking about the Empire State Building,
the Chrysler Building, and Radio City Music Hall. This is New
York!

   Some authors have undertaken to search out Art Deco
all over the U.S.A., then got stuck on New York City and just
stayed there for the rest of their book. In our travels we cataloged 547 Art Deco buildings in New York City. This
includes all five boroughs, not just Manhattan. The total is so
far beyond any other city that the numbers speak for themselves.

   Although the most interesting buildings are great skyscrapers, they are not the bulk of New York's Art Deco
treasure. In every city apartment buildings rank first as the
most frequent type of Art Deco building. In New York we
surveyed a whopping 292 Art Deco apartments—and that
represents only the best of the best. There were twenty-five
office towers, twenty-one stores, seventeen bank buildings,
thirteen schools, thirteen theaters, twelve hotels, ten swimming pools, nine churches, seven phone-company buildings,
six hospitals—all Art Deco, and all worth seeing. In any other
city, we were satisfied to find just one building in each of
these categories. The quantity and quality here is over-

RCA Building (G.E. Building), 30 Rockefeller Plaza
between 49th and 50th Streets, New York City.
ARCHITECT: Raymond Hood for Associated Architects;
Sculptor: Lee Lawrie, 1931. One of Lawrie's most memorable works, this sculpture above the door to the tallest
of Rockefeller Center's towers reads: "Wisdom And
Knowledge Shall Be The Stability Of Thy Times." The
work is fifty-five feet high, with a carved limestone top,
and below the inscription, 240 blocks of sculpted
Corning glass weighing thirteen tons. In the 1980s,
Rockefeller Center committed $260 million for restora-
tion, improvement, and maintenance of the Center,
which prompted an award from the National Trust for
Historic Preservation. (Photograph by Michael D. Kinerk)

Barclay-Vesey Building, *New York Telephone, 140 West Street, New York City.* ARCHITECT: *Ralph Walker for McKenzie, Voorhees & Gmelin, 1923. The world's first Art Deco skyscraper, the Barclay-Vesey Building was the frontispiece of the English-language edition of Le Corbusier's important manifesto,* Towards a New Architecture. *While it predated the Paris Exposition by two years, the architect was well aware of emerging design movements in Germany, Austria, Holland, and France. He used relief sculpture, murals, and geometric figures, and generally introduced a toolbox of design elements that would prove enduring.*

Barclay-Vesey Building, *New York Telephone, 140 West Street, New York City.* ARCHITECT: *Ralph Walker for McKenzie, Voorhees & Gmelin, 1923. In this section of the lobby-ceiling mural, angels wire heaven for telephones. Artist Edgar Williams worked with color consultants Mack, Jenney & Tyler to add interest to the lobby, a space that gained importance as buildings grew taller. Ralph Walker joined the McKenzie firm in 1918 and was quickly given full partnership after the success of this critically acclaimed proto-Deco skyscraper. Walker continued to design many of the phone company's buildings, and won the AIA Gold Medal in 1957.*

Chanin Building, 122 East 42nd Street at Lexington Avenue, New York City. ARCHITECT: *Sloan & Robertson with Irwin S. Chanin and Jacques Delamarre; Sculptor: René Paul Chambellan, 1927. Topped by a splendid private office for developer Irwin S. Chanin, this tower set new standards in New York with its dizzying height and unexpected artistry. Space in this project was marketed using the slogan "City of Opportunity," a theme Chambellan developed in his lobby bronzework.*

Chanin Building, 122 East 42nd Street at Lexington Avenue, New York City. ARCHITECT: *Sloan & Robertson with Irwin S. Chanin and Jacques Delamarre; Sculptor: René Paul Chambellan, 1927. The remarkable fifty-six-story Chanin Building stands across the street from the later Chrysler Building. Chanin girded his building with outstanding bronze and terra-cotta friezes at the second and fourth floors. A 1977 cleaning restored luster to the Paris Exposition–style metal frieze in the section at the left.*

Chanin Building, 122 East 42nd Street at Lexington Avenue, New York City. ARCHITECT: *Sloan & Robertson; Gate design: René Paul Chambellan, with Irwin S. Chanin and Jacques Delamarre, 1927. These gates of wrought iron and bronze are among the many exquisite treasures created for Chanin's 52nd-floor private office. As symbols of industry, the gates were featured in the Brooklyn Museum's 1986 exhibition "The Machine Age in America." Chanin and his designers used stacks of coins as the foundation upon which the cogwheels of industry are built.*

Cheney Brothers Building (Belmont Madison Building), 181-183 Madison Avenue,
with a separate entrance around the corner at 40 East 34th Street, New York City.
ARCHITECT: Howard Greenley; Metalwork: Edgar Brandt, 1925. These bronze doors
originally led to the stylish Cheney fabric store, which occupied the first four floors.
Fitted inside and out with fifty tons of metalwork made entirely in Paris by the master metalsmith Edgar Brandt, the store provided the U.S.A. with its definitive version
of the "Frozen Fountain" (seen here) and other motifs made famous at the Paris
Exposition that same year.

whelming. It took three trips and many weeks to see even this moderate sampling. Our friend and confidant, Anthony Robins, chief of surveys for the New York Landmarks Commission, could only laugh when we told him about our plan to survey all of the Big Apple's Art Deco. Maybe it was foolish, but it was fun.

Although steel frames for skyscrapers went up first in Chicago, the frenzy to build ever-taller buildings really took hold in New York City. One who was responsible for some of the early popularity of these romantic symbols of strength and commerce was the famed 1920s architectural renderer Hugh Ferris. His studies of the complex possibilities allowed by New York City's 1916 zoning code were visionary. His work was so stylized, bold, and compelling that virtually no important building got built without being drawn by Ferris.

First among all other Art Deco towers is the Empire State Building—probably the most famous of them all—at 350 Fifth Avenue, designed in 1930 by William Lamb for Shreve, Lamb & Harmon. Tourists swarm over the lobby and ride to its observation decks day and night. Every language and dialect may be heard there, for the visitors come from all over the world. Oscar Bach executed for the main lobby a beautiful map of New York, the Empire State, with a superimposed model of the building, and with sunbeams radiating outward from it. He added a series of giant medallions on the lobby walls that highlight the trades and crafts necessary to build the tower. Interior decor was the responsibility of B. Altman. The Empire State was built on the site of the first Waldorf-Astoria Hotel, which was demolished in 1929. To make the building possible, a heavyweight Board of Directors was assembled including former New York Governor Al Smith, Robert C. Brown, Pierre S. Dupont, and Louis C. Kaufman. Rising 1,250 feet, their magnificent creation proudly was born "Tallest in the World."

From the 96th floor observation deck of the Empire State Building one can see another legendary Art Deco attraction: the more stylish, slightly older, and perhaps more romantic Chrysler Building. Designed in 1927 by William Van Alen, its sixty-eight floors and spire climb to 1,046 feet at the corner of 42nd Street and Lexington Avenue. It opened in 1930. It uses horizontal bands of dark-colored bricks to con-

Chrysler Building, 405 Lexington Avenue between East 42nd and 43rd Streets, New York City. ARCHITECT: William Van Alen, 1928. As the sun sets over Manhattan, the stainless steel top of the most beloved Art Deco skyscraper in the world glistens. At a height of 1,048 feet, it is a tribute to the tenacity, power, and wealth of Walter P. Chrysler, the automobile magnate. Beautifully designed and perfectly finished, this New York landmark was restored at a cost of $23 million in 1975–1979 by the Massachusetts Mutual Life Insurance Company. In 1980, Teleprompter-mogul and Washington Redskins–owner Jack Kent Cooke bought the building and invested another $30 million in restoration. Van Alen's original plans for the building called for zigzag outline lighting of the spire that was not added until the 1980 restoration. (Photograph by Carl Rosenstein, copyright © 1992. Used by permission.)

Chrysler Building, 405 Lexington Avenue between 42nd and 43rd Streets, New York City. ARCHITECT: William Van Alen, 1928. Each of the thirty-two superb wood-veneer-over-steel elevator doors is identical, but the cab interiors are slightly different. Among the exotic imported woods used are Japanese ash, English gray harewood, Oriental walnut, and satinwood. The building had been conceived by developer William H. Reynolds, but was taken over by Walter P. Chrysler before construction began. Chrysler and his automobile business had a profound impact on the final design.

trast with its strong vertical patterns. One of its best-known features is a triangular lobby in handsome red marble and featuring probably the most beautiful elevator doors ever designed. They incorporate many kinds of inlaid woods and stainless steel that form lotus blossoms and other fanciful Art Deco patterns. The doors were manufactured by the Tyler Corporation in a special process called Metyl-wood. Huge stainless-steel eagles and other gargoyles adorn the façade. The shapes of tires and hubcaps in the surface of the tower were integrated to please the original building owner and automobile magnate, Walter P. Chrysler. A recent addition was the jazzy nighttime halo of lights that illuminate the stainless-steel top of the tower. This was done after consulting Van Alen's designs. It was a dramatic move, causing many New Yorkers to renew their love affair with all the soaring Art Deco skyscrapers.

Even if New York didn't have the Empire State and Chrysler buildings, it would still rank at the top of the heap for another reason: Rockefeller Center, particularly the RCA (now GE) building that towers magnificently over all the other buildings in the Center. Believed by many architecture critics to be the most beautiful and successful urban development in history, it has no peers. Its majestic buildings have been copied but never equaled. Rockefeller Center contains enough art and sculpture to establish a museum. It also contains a world-famous landmark attraction, Radio City Music Hall, the cavernous cathedral of Art Deco, with its definitive interior by Donald Deskey. It was the second Art Deco city landmark to be registered, and it is also in the National Register.

In 1929, a team called Associated Architects was formed to design Rockefeller Center. It was composed of three firms: Reinhard & Hofmeister; Corbett, Harrison & MacMurray; and Hood & Fouilhoux. Prior to 1935, Raymond Hood was the team's most influential designer, postulating so many of the brilliant ideas that make Rockefeller Center what it is today. After Hood's death, Wallace K. Harrison

EMPIRE STATE BUILDING · NEW YORK CITY

split from Corbett and MacMurray to begin working solo on the project, filling the creative void left by Hood's death.

The massive Rockefeller project was subdivided into separate blocks. Among the many discrete buildings to be included in the center were two separate theaters. Edward Durrell Stone was the Assiocated Architects' chief designer for the theaters. The aggressive young Deskey won a competition to lead interior design for the Music Hall. Under the overall supervision of the great Samuel F. Rothafel ("Roxy"), the most glorious and magnificent of all Art Deco auditoriums would soon emerge.

The Rockefeller Center Management corporation was given the 1990 Honor Award of the National Trust for Historic Preservation for its outstanding program of restoration and capital enhancement at the center, costing more than $260 million.

Forty artists contributed original works to Rockefeller Center, keyed to the theme of New Frontiers. A few of these were Frank Brangwyn, René Paul Chambellan, Dean Cornwall, Barry Faulkner, Leo Friedlander, Alfred Janniot, Carl Paul Jennewein, Lee Lawrie, Paul Manship, Carl Milles, Isamu Noguchi, Attilio Piccirilli, Diego Rivera, and José Maria Sert.

Donald Deskey designed the innovative furniture in the Music Hall, and he commissioned many artists to provide "modern" art to enhance further the beauty of the interior. Among these were Louis Bouché, Stuart Davis, Robert Laurent, Witold Gordon, Yasuo Kuniyoshi, Hildreth Meiere, Ruth Reeves, Ezra Winter, and William Zorach. The great metalsmith Oscar Bach executed works to the design of a few of the artists, including the splendid entrance doors to the auditorium. Also under Roxy's watchful eye, another team created the nearby RKO Center Theater (now demolished), which opened as the RKO Roxy, but changed its name quickly when the original Roxy Theater sued.

Film Center Building, 630 Ninth Avenue, between West 44th and 45th Streets, New York City. ARCHITECT: Ely Jacques Kahn for Buchman & Kahn, 1928. Here is a most appealing ziggurat elevator lobby. Floor terrazzo patterns, brilliantly colored tiles and horizontal wall banding contribute to the Art Deco perfection of this New York City Landmark. The lobby has a sculptural finish, with a hint of Vienna and a hint of the Far East. Kahn's work is unmistakable.

Film Center Building, 630 Ninth Avenue, between West 44th and 45th Streets, New York City. ARCHITECT: Ely Jacques Kahn for Buchman & Kahn, 1928. Kahn made this lobby letterbox a work of art. He delighted in working with metals, typically investing them with intricate geometric patterns. However, this example is of simpler Constructivist origins.

The magnitude of this project still staggers the imagination. Every inch of it was done strictly first class. Perhaps that is why it remains one of the most popular tourist attractions in New York, and retains its white-glove tenants.

Among the most famous of the artworks at Rockefeller Center are Lee Lawrie's *Atlas*, 1937, in front of the International Building, and Paul Manship's *Prometheus*, 1934, presiding over the fountain at the base of the Channel Gardens.

In our Art Deco overview of New York, we were taken backstage at Radio City by Rockettes Executive Producer Bruce Michael, and we were sent to the dizzying heights of the Rainbow Room, across the street, for another private tour. One floor below the Rainbow Room in one of many private dining rooms is an entire wall of illuminated display cases filled with Art Deco radios in brightly colored early plastic cases. Here they find a fitting repose in the "City" named for them.

After the three great projects we have already mentioned, the next best buildings in Art Deco New York are the Cheney and Chanin buildings. The Cheney Building is at 34th Street and Madison Avenue. It was designed in 1925 by Howard Greenley, with original metalwork by the master of the Paris Exposition, Edgar Brandt. This building introduced the 1925 Paris Exposition style to the world of New York fashion. On the lower four floors was the famed Cheney Brothers Fabric store. Today the store is gone and the building is known as the Belmont Madison. But remaining on view

Fuller Building, 41 East 57th Street at Madison Avenue (northeast corner), New York City. ARCHITECT: A. Stewart Walker for Walker & Gillette; Sculptor: Elie Nadelman, 1928. This wonderful entrance features Nadelman's sculpture, black-and-white architectural patterns, and the company name. The figures are four floors above the sidewalk. A thin tower rises to eighteen stories above the wider six-floor base. Egyptian and Roman themes occur throughout the building, and the interior is a designated New York Landmark. The Fuller was one of the buildings featured in the legendary parade of architects costumed as their own buildings at the 1931 Beaux Arts Ball in New York's Astor Hotel.

Goelet Building (Swiss Center), 608 Fifth Avenue at 49th Street, New York City. ARCHITECT: E.H. Faile & Co. with Victor L.F. Hafner, 1932. The inner doors to this lobby introduce one to this very special Art Deco tower. Construction of this building on Rockefeller Center's southeast corner added a definite touch of French elegance to Manhattan. In his book A City Observed, *Paul Goldberger called it "New York's really early modern gem."*

Health Department (Health, Hospitals and Sanitation Department Building), 125 Worth Street at Centre Street, New York City. ARCHITECT: Charles B. Meyers; Sculptor: Oscar Bach, 1935. Another example of Oscar Bach's delightful metalwork is this group of figures supporting a massive lantern at the side entrance to the building on Centre Street. The main entrance (not shown) is decorated by a sculpted metal surround, surmounted by magnificent eagles. Bach was America's preeminent metal craftsman. His work appears in dozens of the finest Art Deco buildings across the country.

McGraw-Hill Building (GHI Building), 330 West 42nd Street, between Eighth and Ninth Avenues, New York City. ARCHITECT: Raymond Hood for Hood, Godley & Fouilhoux, 1930. James H. McGraw had so much confidence in Hood that he gave him complete freedom to create this landmark. Hood's alternating bands of windows and blue-green terra-cotta were shockingly modern. The architect demanded precise color uniformity and fanatically monitored color variations in the shipments of terra-cotta for this huge order produced by Federal Seaboard Company, Perth Amboy, New Jersey. (Photograph by Carl Rosenstein, copyright © 1992. Used by permission.)

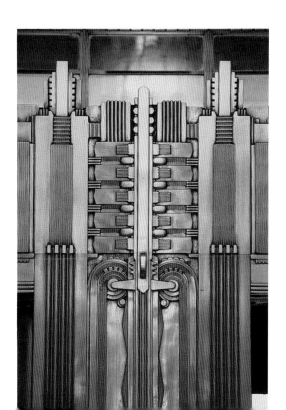

Office Tower, 2 Park Avenue, between 32nd and 33rd Streets, New York City. ARCHITECT: Ely Jacques Kahn for Buchman & Kahn, 1927. One of Park Avenue's most stunning Art Deco buildings, the detailing in the metalwork over the doors is typical of Kahn's wonderful work throughout the city. The building has excellent bronze work and ceiling murals.

are many of the elegant 1925 decorations, chief of which is the great entrance on Madison Avenue in black-painted wrought iron and with a fountain motif in gilded bronze.

The Chanin, at 42nd Street and Lexington Avenue, was a very personal project designed in 1927 by Irwin S. Chanin of the Chanin Construction Company. His architects were John Sloan and Markoe T. Robertson together with Chanin's architect, Jacques Delamarre. The façade of this building has an outstanding frieze of fish, birds, and plants encircling the upper portion of its four-story stone base. Rising above this is a fifty-six-story tower. The metalwork and carving throughout are exemplary. René Paul Chambellan did the models for the sculpture. And supervising every detail was Irwin S. Chanin, who decreed this building's motto should be: "City of Opportunity."

The must-see list also includes the extraordinary 1932 Irving Trust bank building, 1 Wall Street, by Ralph Walker of Voorhees, Gmelin & Walker; the New York phone company's 1923 Barclay-Vesey building, also by Walker; and row after row of Central Park high-rise apartments. Two of the best are the Majestic, 1930, and Century Apartments, 1931, on Central Park West. Both were by the same team that did the Chanin Building: Jacques Delamarre for Irwin S. Chanin.

During our visits in preparation for this book, almost half of these Art Deco apartments were enjoying a well-deserved refurbishing—a dusting and polishing, a repackaging and marketing of their handsome Art Deco embellishments, from Germanic patterns in brick to aluminum trim and banding. Sculpture and murals in the lobbies, along with exquisite inlaid-wood designs and montages, are the norm in these Manhattan dwellings. We found so many rehab projects it seemed as if the city were gussying itself up just to be ready for its starring role. It was obvious that the general public's rediscovering of Art Deco U.S.A. was already underway before the last decade of the twentieth century. But not a minute too soon!

Let us not fail to mention that New York still has many Art Deco subway stations and bridges. The Triborough bridge is a fine example of the latter. Now it is part of I-278, linking Manhattan, Queens, and the Bronx with four spans over nineteen miles of roadway crossing the East River and

Hell's Gate. It was built from 1929 to 1936, and its later stages were funded by the WPA. Overall, it cost $60 million. The designers were Aymar Embury II, Othmar H. Ammann, and Allston Dana.

There is one hotel in New York that reigns supreme over all others, and it is a classic of Art Deco style. Of course, it is the Waldorf-Astoria, 301 Park Avenue, designed by Schultze & Weaver. Broadway composer Cole Porter lived here for years, perhaps helping it become synonymous with class and elegance. It has been refurbished periodically, to good results, and remains one of the world's premier hotels. It has murals by Louis Rigal, and excellent carving and metalwork throughout.

Continuing New York's Art Deco honor roll, there are two monuments to publishing empires, past and present: First and foremost, the McGraw-Hill building, built in 1930. The McGraw-Hill corporation left the famous Raymond Hood building in 1972 to relocate in Rockefeller Center. However, the great building on West 42nd Street was renovated by the GHI Corporation, and remains an attractive address.

Another publishing empire was housed in a Raymond Hood masterpiece, the 1929 New York *Daily News* building, Third Avenue and 42nd Street. It has been cited for excellence by many authorities, including the New York Landmarks Commission. The *Daily News* has fallen on hard times in the last few years. In its prime, however, this was "The House That Tabloid Built." The thirty-six-story building went up when the paper had a three-million Sunday and 1.75 million daily circulation—twice that of any other paper in the country. The paper's great success paid for this superb structure. It should be noted that the *Daily News* building is just a block away from the Chrysler and Chanin buildings, at 42nd and Lexington, making this area the most outstanding hub of the Art Deco style in the world.

Hood's banding techniques, fenestration, and use of white brick in the *News* building is said to have influenced a generation of American architects. Hood's work here and at the McGraw-Hill building at the opposite end of 42nd Street set new standards for beautiful, modern urban towers in America.

RCA Victor Building (G.E. Building), 570 Lexington Avenue at East 51st Street, New York City. ARCHITECT: Cross & Cross, 1930. This "pyramid of power" rises over the elevator doors. The coffered trapezoidal ceiling, finished in silver leaf, is typical of the lavish use of metals and reflective surfaces found in this corporate headquarters. It was built for R.C.A., but General Sarnoff's troops had scarcely occupied it before they were redeployed to the undeniable power center of New York: the new Rockefeller Center. This building was then occupied by General Electric, and has been known ever since as the G.E. Building. Ironically, in the merger-mania of the 1980s, G.E. bought R.C.A. outright and once again replaced its name, this time on Rockefeller Center's tallest tower.

RCA Building (West 50th Street entrance), 30 Rockefeller Plaza at West 50th Street, New York City. ARCHITECT: Raymond Hood for Associated Architects; Sculptor: Leo Friedlander, 1931. Restoration architect (Rainbow Room): Hugh Hardy; Restoration designer (Rainbow Room): Milton Glaser; Restoration supervisor (Rainbow Room): Joe Baum, 1985. Just across from the Radio City Music Hall is the fabled entrance to the Rainbow Room and the massive NBC studios complex. The sleek, streamlined marquee and frosted-glass lighting strips portend the plush interior. On the sixty-fifth floor, 850 feet above, the two-story Rainbow Room, surrounded by windows, was the highest restaurant in the world when it opened October 3, 1934. It was and still is the epitome of elegance. After falling on hard times, it got a fabulous $20-million facelift in 1985 on orders from David Rockefeller himself. It reopened three years later.

Radio City Music Hall foyer, 1260 Avenue of the Americas at West 50th Street, New York City. ARCHITECT: Raymond Hood for Associated Architects; Interior: Donald Deskey; Muralist: Ezra Winter, 1931. The centerpiece of this magnificent foyer is Ezra Winter's sixty-by-forty-foot grand staircase mural, Author of Life, which is based upon Native American legends of the Fountain of Eternal Youth. The shiny banks of doors leading into the auditorium contain bronze panels by René Paul Chambellan representing theaters of twelve countries, as the original name for the building was to have been International Music Hall.

Radio City Music Hall auditorium (5,882 seats), 1260 Avenue of the Americas at West 50th Street, New York City. ARCHITECT: Raymond Hood for Associated Architects, Interior: Donald Deskey and Edward Durrell Stone, 1931. Hood's celebrated design for the auditorium of Radio City Music Hall is similar to the one designed by Joseph Urban at the New School in New York. An even earlier use of the concentric-arched proscenium was Lloyd Wright's first Hollywood Bowl of 1925. Deskey selected top artists and craftsmen of the day to complete the splendid showplace. The interior was designated a New York City Landmark in 1978. That same year plans to close and demolish the hall were announced. The idea was roundly condemned by the public, and the American Society of Interior Designers led a successful fight to save it. Its owners recently registered the famed name as a trademark. (Photograph by Michael D. Kinerk)

Radio City Music Hall, south façade, 1260 Avenue of the Americas at West 50th Street, New York City. ARCHITECT: Raymond Hood for Associated Architects; Sculpture designer: Hildreth Meiere; Metalwork: Oscar Bach, 1931. Dance, illustrated here, is one of three metal sculptures eighteen feet in diameter on the side wall of the great Music Hall, high above the street. The other two works are Drama and Song. These are good examples of Bach's mastery of metals. For color variety he uses brass, copper, aluminum, chrome, and nickel-steel, with additional colors applied in vitreous enamel. Meiere, the designer, is also known for her earlier work in the Nebraska State Capitol.

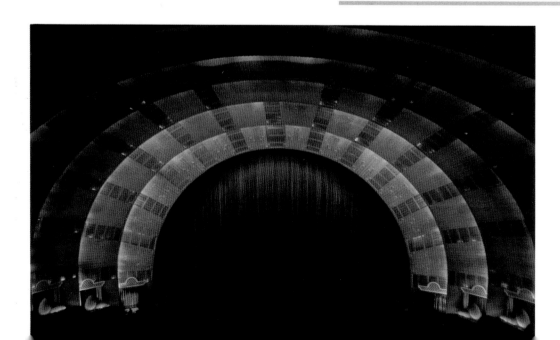

Hood, working with several different partners through the years, has four designated landmarks in New York City, making him the most honored architect in the history of the city. The first Art Deco building declared a landmark was the early American Radiator Building (now American Standard) at 40 West 40th Street. Hood did this design in 1924 when he was still practicing with André Fouilhoux. This building, and a twin in London, were built with black brick and have gilt tops.

One of the primary forces for exploring, cataloging, and celebrating these buildings and the others mentioned below has been The Art Deco Society of New York (ADSNY), founded October 1980 in Muriel Boverman's home in the famous Dakota apartment house. The meeting was called by designer Henrietta B. Nathan. Among the twelve present was Barbara Capitman, along with other visionaries like William T. Weber and Tom Cain of the National Endowment for the Arts. Although not present at the first gathering, noted artist Dennis Abbé soon was elected president.

After its establishment ADSNY grew rapidly to over four hundred members. Among its most notable achievements are the finest publications of any Art Deco Society under the guidance of long-time editor Glen Loney. They also have sponsored some of the finest lecture and walking-tour programs. The guiding light of their tour program has been charter member Anthony Robins of the New York Landmarks Commission, who was mentioned earlier. Dennis Abbé presided over the society in its formative years and always inspired the members to strive for excellence in all the society's endeavors. Perhaps it was his excellent managerial skills, or perhaps it was the fragments from the Ziegfeld Theater in his apartment, that inspired everyone. In 1981, he created a best-selling poster for the society, featuring a unicorn with a woman. She is crowned with laurel leaves, holding a globe aloft, and her hair flows out like rays of sunshine. One of the most notable early ADSNY activities was a soirée at the Chrysler Building's sixty-sixth-floor Cloud Club. Barbara Capitman flew to New York to be there. The club has memorable Vitrolite murals showing Chrysler automobiles being made, and also a painted mural by Edward Trumbull, in addition to rich inlaid-wood decoration and metalwork by Oscar Bach.

Several Art Deco Week and Weekend festivals, based on Miami Beach's trademark festival, have popularized the period. In 1984, Mayor Ed Koch declared "New York City Art Deco Week." One of the Society's most popular events has been its "Best of Broadway" awards. These were begun to honor the Broadway show that most effectively used the Art Deco style. The ceremony draws many of the Society's hundreds of members to mingle with winning designers and stars. ADSNY has arranged tours and sponsored events at some of the most elegant Art Deco locations in the world—the Waldorf-Astoria, the Rainbow Room, and Radio City Music Hall. Their lecture series has focused on all aspects of Art Deco—fashion, design, architecture, music, dance, and art. Many lectures are held at the New School for Social Research. The series is now in its seventeenth season.

Speaking of the New School, the location itself, 66 West 12th Street, warrants further mention. Here is an outstanding 1929 design by Joseph Urban, whose work is in a class by itself. The original school was filled with murals and an auditorium that itself is a landmark. Some of the murals, by José Clemente Orozco, are still in place, and a restoration and conservation was paid for by the Equitable Life Insurance Company. But there also were murals by Thomas Hart Benton, and these were moved into the Equitable's downtown high-rise headquarters, where they are well installed, under permanent conservatorship, and on display to the public daily. These are among Benton's most brilliant works, recounting the turmoil and color of life in the U.S.A. during its entire history.

One of the many highlights of our Art Deco trips to New York included our meeting with Jean-Claude Baker, owner of Chez Josephine restaurant on West 42nd Street. It is dedicated to the memory of his beloved adoptive mother, Josephine Baker. Ernest Hemingway called her "the most sensational woman anybody ever saw." We asked Jean-Claude about his mother's life as a world-famous star of the Art Deco era, and about her celebrated 1951 performances in Miami Beach's Copa City Club—the hottest club in that hot city—designed in 1940 by Norman Bel Geddes. Josephine had said she would not go on without the comfort of her friends and family in the audience. Since the city of Miami Beach had a "whites only" rule after dark, this was a daring and courageous demand. But she got it her way. Both police and club owners promised to "suspend" racial segregation for her performances. Jean-Claude said he was there, but the expected table full of African-American friends did not materialize. Small wonder, as it was extremely dangerous for them to venture into the area, with or without promises from local police. In any case, the superstar soon returned to her beloved France, leaving the U.S.A. to deal with its racial prejudice and hatred in its own way.

Before leaving Manhattan, it is appropriate for us to list the rest of our Top 40 Best Art Deco Sites in the city: *2 Park Avenue Building* (between 32nd and 33rd streets), said to be Ely Jacques Kahn's masterpiece, 1927; *Apartments*, 49 East 96th Street, rare nontheater building designed by famed Thomas Lamb, 1930; *Bankers Trust*, 16 Wall Street, Trowbridge & Livingston, 1931; *Barclay-Vesey*, 140 West Street, designed by Ralph Walker for McKenzie, Voorhees & Gmelin, 1923, for New York Telephone Company—

arguably the first Art Deco skyscraper in the world; *Beaux Arts Institute of Design*, 304 East 44th Street, Dennison & Hirons, 1928, with the Beaux Arts Apartment Hotel, 1930, and Beaux Arts Apartments, 1929, adjacent; *Beekman Hotel* (originally Panhellenic Hotel), 3 Mitchell Place, John Mead Howells, 1927; *Bloomingdale's*, 740 Lexington Avenue, Starrett & Van Vleck, 1930; *Cities Service Oil Company*, 70 Pine Street, Clinton & Russell, Holton & George, 1930; *The New York Times* architecture critic called this one "Jazz Gothic"; *Cliff Dweller Apartments*, 243 Riverside Drive, Herman Lee Meader, 1916, an acclaimed Pueblo Deco prototype; *Empire Diner*, West 22nd Street and Tenth Avenue, c. 1937; *Essex House Hotel*, 160 Central Park South, Frank Grad, recently refurbished and being marketed as an elegant Art Deco retreat, 1929; *Film Center*, 630 Ninth Avenue, Ely Jacques Kahn, 1928; *Fuller Building*, 41 East 57th Street, Walker & Gillette, 1928; *General Electric Building* (originally the *old* R.C.A. headquarters, near landmark Saint Bartholomew's Church), 750 Lexington Avenue, Cross & Cross, 1930; *General Electric Building* (formerly R.C.A. building), 30 Rockefeller Plaza, Raymond Hood of Associated Architects, et al, 1934; *Graybar Building*, 420 Lexington Avenue, Sloan & Robertson, 1927; *Hotel Carlyle*, 35 East 76th Street, Bien & Prince, 1929; *New York Criminal Courts & Prisons*, 100 Centre Street, Harvey Wiley Corbett and Charles B. Myers, 1939; *New York Telephone & Telegraph*, has buildings all over New York by the legendary Ralph Walker, first of McKenzie, Voorhees & Gmelin, then becoming full partner with Voorhees, Gmelin & Walker; some of the best are at Second Avenue and East 13th Street; West 17th Street at Seventh Avenue; 425 West 50th Street; and 32 Sixth Avenue; *Rialto Theater* (closed, renamed Cineplex Odeon Warner), 1481 Broadway, was once Oscar Hammerstein's Victoria Theater—first vaudeville theater in Times Square; then made over by legendary showman Roxy in 1915 in Viennese Expressionist style; then becoming the Rialto, the first movie palace on Times Square, which finally got an Art Deco makeover by Herbert J. Krapp in 1935 with a blue Vitrolite façade; *Ritz Tower*, 109 East 57th Street, Emery Roth with Carrère & Hastings, 1925; *Saks Fifth Avenue*, 611 Fifth Avenue, Starrett & Van Vleck, 1924; *Squibb Building*, 745 Fifth Avenue, Ely Jacques Kahn, 1929; *Temple Emanu-el*, 1 East 65th Street, R. D. Kohn, C. Butler, and C. Stein, 1929; *Western Union*, 60 Hudson Street, Ralph Walker for Voorhees, Gmelin & Walker, 1928.

Apartments, 1150 Grand Concourse, The Bronx, New York. ARCHITECT: *Jules Kabat for Horace Ginsbern, 1936. In the heart of the Bronx is a remarkable concentration of Art Deco apartments, most of them having lavish appointments, such as this exuberant terrazzo floor design in the "Fish" apartments, so-called because of a striking mosaic on the exterior. Other elegant features include recessed illumination and polished granite walls.*

Apartments, 1001 Jerome Avenue, The Bronx, New York. ARCHITECT: *Sugarman & Berger, 1937. This inner lobby mural of inlaid wood, installed over a streamlined fireplace, features athletes in a futuristic city much like the one the Bronx was trying to be in the 1930s. As in Miami Beach, a few local architectural firms created the vast majority of the Art Deco buildings in the Bronx in a single decade of explosive growth prior to World War II.*

Apartments, *888 Grand Concourse, The Bronx, New York.* ARCHITECT: *Emery Roth & Sons, 1937. Flowing curves, corner windows, and metal banding on the marquee make this apartment's corner entrance stand out. Most buildings along the broad Grand Concourse are a uniform six stories high, giving it an open, low-scale feeling. The Roths did several outstanding apartment buildings in both Manhattan and the Bronx. (Photograph by Michael D. Kinerk)*

Paul J. Rainey Memorial Gate, Bronx Zoo, East Fordham Road Entrance, The Bronx, New York. ARCHITECT: Charles A. Platt; Sculptor: Paul Manship, 1932. This turtle is but a small part of Paul Manship's monumental bronze gates in which animals are surrounded by archetypal Art Deco foliage. Other sculpted animals in the entrance include bears, birds, a stag, and a lion. Inscribed in the polished granite below the metalwork is a dedication of the gate to its namesake, Paul J. Rainey. Manship is best known for his masterpiece, the sculpture of Prometheus, in the fountain at Rockefeller Center. (Photograph by Michael D. Kinerk)

Apartments, 1035 Grand Concourse, The Bronx, New York. ARCHITECT: Jules Kabat for Horace Ginsbern, 1935. Cast stone is used in this inviting entrance to one of the hundreds of once-smart and modern-looking apartments found in the Bronx. Here the concentration of Art Deco architecture is second only to Miami Beach's eight hundred buildings. A combination of quitessentially Deco elements—metal doors, corner casement windows, horizontal banding, porthole patterns in threes—make this an outstanding example. A canopy has recently been added, making it difficult to recognize this gem.

Several of the firms responsible for much of the wonderful Art Deco in the Bronx also did stylish apartments on Manhattan's Upper West Side. Two of the best of these are by Emery Roth, who developed an unmistakable look of his own. They are the San Remo, 145 Central Park West, 1930; and the Normandy Apartments, 140 Riverside Drive, 1938.

The Bronx

Beyond Manhattan's Art Deco splendors lie many other amazing Art Deco treasures. Among them is the Bronx's incomparable Grand Concourse. With forty wonderful Art Deco apartment buildings and 260 others elsewhere throughout the borough, the Bronx is second only to Miami Beach in the sheer number of buildings, but actually surpasses Miami Beach in lavish interior appointments. Many of the best of these buildings were designed by Horace Ginsbern, Jules Kabat, Jacob M. Felson, and Emery Roth.

We talked about the Bronx Art Deco with First Lady Barbara Bush in the White House on April 16, 1991, when we presented her with an original oil painting of Miami Beach's Carlyle Hotel by our friend, the Chilean artist Gustavo Novoa. Mrs. Bush was well aware of the Art Deco style and knew that the Bronx had it. She had been there looking over the situation earlier in the year. Of course, she was appalled at the condition of many of the buildings there, and asked us if we could perform there some of our "Art Deco Magic," as we had done in Miami Beach.

The Bronx had its own magic in the 1930s. At that time developers vied to create more luxurious buildings than could be found in Manhattan. The Grand Concourse was one of the finest places in the country to live at that time, and it could be again some day. Nothing can diminish the glory of the hundreds of elegant Bronx Art Deco apartments. As in Miami Beach, there is a uniformity of scale—most buildings are only six stories no matter what their style.

There also is a fine Art Deco school in the Bronx, the Hermann Ridder Junior High, 1619 Boston Road. The school's façade is covered with fine relief sculpture in stone, and there are outstanding light fixtures as well.

Finally, there are the great bronze Rainey Memorial Gates that mark the entrance to the Bronx Zoo. The gates are filled with sculptures of assorted animals and birds executed in 1934 by Paul Manship. These gates are an easy exit off Fordham Road, and it is well worth a stop just to see them. The gates were entered on the National Register in 1972.

Brooklyn

The most celebrated Art Deco-styled ocean liner ever created was the French liner *Normandie*. It took refuge in New York harbor at the outbreak of World War II, and then mysteriously caught fire, finally capsizing and sinking in its berth when the fire department flooded it with water. Fortunately, the thousands of exquisite items designed for the liner by the greatest artisans of France already had been removed because the ship was slated to be outfitted as a troop carrier. Several of the glass panels from the dining hall are today at The Metropolitan Museum of Art, and two of the bronze doors from the *Normandie* found their way to Our Lady of Lebanon Church, Remsen at Henry Street in Brooklyn.

Also worth mention in Brooklyn is a satellite printing plant, 500 Pacific Street, designed in 1929 for *The New York Times* by Detroit's great industrial architect Albert Kahn. Today this plant has been annexed and pressed into service by the adjacent Sarah Hale High School.

One of the best surviving Sears, Roebuck & Company towers of the 1930s is standing at 2390 Bedford Street in Brooklyn. This one, while considerably more streamlined, is similar in design to the one threatened with demolition in Miami. These stores always had a central tower on the corner with the name spelled prominently in vertical strips on all sides. Sears, then "the world's largest store," had a full-time staff of architects cranking out the stores, so it is amazing so few of them survive.

The most prominent landmark in Brooklyn is the Art Deco Williamsburgh Savings Bank Tower at 1 Hanson Place on Flatbush Avenue. This 1929 landmark tower was designed by Halsey, McCormack & Helmer and features brilliant metalwork by the great Oscar Bach. It has classical Beaux Arts detailing, but its massive bulk is unmistakably Art Deco and so are the sculptural details and Bach's metal decorations.

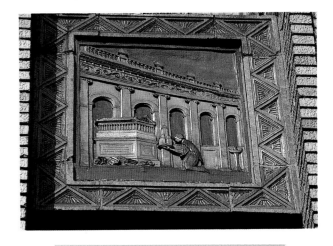

Park Plaza Apartments, 1005 Jerome Avenue, The Bronx, New York. ARCHITECT: Martin Fine for Horace Ginsbern, 1928. Highly unusual terra-cotta spandrel designs were used in the façade of the Park Plaza Apartments. Here a man (Paul Philippe Cret?) symbolically offers a skyscraper at an architectural altar topped by the Parthenon. Nowhere else has the bond between Art Deco and Greek Classicism been so graphically portrayed.

Astoria, Queens

Church of the Most Precious Blood, 32-30 37th Street, tucked away in the residential "Long Island City" section of Queens, is by far the most beautiful Art Deco landmark in the borough. It was designed in 1932 by Henry J. McGill, the same architect who created the beautiful Shrine of the Little Flower in suburban Detroit. This church is rather Pueblo, with a Spanish Mission look, embellished with WPA social-realist artwork, such as the sculptures of Saint Theresa and Saint Anthony by Hazel Clerc. It also has excellent stained-glass windows by Richard N. Spiers & Son. The Stages of the Cross murals are particularly noteworthy.

Hermann Ridder Junior High School, 1619 Boston Road at 173rd Street and Mumford, The Bronx, New York. ARCHITECT: Walter C. Martin, 1932. This school's styling is slightly Viennese, perhaps in tribute to its namesake, German-American newspaper publisher Hermann Ridder. He was the founder of Ridder Publications, which became part of the media conglomerate Knight-Ridder. The main building has a bold stepped-back, seven-story tower at its corner, embellished with urns, lyres, art glass, and outstanding light fixtures. Carved knights surmount the tower, in a visual pun: in German, Ridder means horseman or knight. Although still quite handsome, the school is in dire need of general repairs. (Photograph by Dennis W. Wilhelm)

KEY BUILDINGS OF THE NEW YORK WORLD'S FAIR OF 1939, AT NIGHT

PHOTO BY KEYSTONE

One of the scores of parks, playgrounds, and pools produced with WPA funding in New York in the mid-1930s is found here in the Astoria Play Center and Swimming Pool, designed in 1936 by J. M. Hatton.

Near Flushing Meadow lies what is now LaGuardia Airport. Originally, it was the North Beach Airport, and was built, in part, to service the 1939 New York World's Fair nearby. Pan American Airways established one of their fabled Clipper seaplane bases here. That is why, apart from the main airport, there is a building still known as the Marine Air Terminal located closer to the original shore, and deocrated with friezes of flying fish. This 1939 terminal was by Delano & Aldrich, the same firm that designed other Pan Am seaplane bases, including Miami's. Some of the original hangars nearby were WPA projects.

Flushing Meadow, Queens

On the former landfill here in Flushing Meadow, Queens, rose the most memorable of all the 1930s World's Fairs. The Trylon and Perisphere have never really been surpassed as signature icons for an event. Most of the great pavilions and attractions have long since been razed. One that remains is now the New York Marine Amphitheater designed by Sloan & Robertson. In 1939, this was the famous site of the Billy Rose Aquacade.

Although only the ghosts of the great 1939 fair remain today, it is worth noting all the talent that was assembled for that fair. Here is a selected list of those who were responsible for some of the fair buildings and attractions: Harrison & Fouilhoux; Voorhees, Walker, Foley, Smith; William Lescaze and J. Gordon Carr; Walter Dorwin Teague; Albert Kahn; Ely Jacques Kahn; Skidmore & Owings; Howard Cheney; Delano & Aldrich; Harvey Wiley Corbett, and Aymar Embury II (architect for the New York City Parks Department).

Staten Island

Here in New York's least-known enclave there is an ample share of Art Deco treasure. Most outstanding of all is the Ambassador Apartments, 30 Daniel Low Terrace, designed by Lucian Pisciatta in 1932. A resplendent terra-cotta entrance is the main attraction of the building.

An excellent example of the work of New York Parks Department master architect Aymar Embury II survives in the Joseph H. Lyons Pool and Bathhouse, designed in 1936. There also are two Art Deco hospitals to be found on the island: Halloran General and Bayley Seton. And to round things out, Staten Island has two Art Deco movie theaters; one, the 1938 Lane Theater by John Eberson, was named a city landmark in 1988. The second theater is the 1935 Paramount designed by brothers C. W. and George Rapp who, of course, did the rather more famous Times Square Paramount. But the Staten Island Paramount has one thing in its favor: it is still standing, while Times Square's is only a memory.

Theme Center Plaza (demolished), *New York World's Fair, Flushing Meadow, Queens, New York.* ARCHITECTS: *Wallace K. Harrison and J. André Fouilhoux, 1939. Here is a vintage post-card of the ubiquitous Trylon, Perisphere, and Helicline: Key Buildings of the New York World's Fair of 1939 at Night. These became the most enduring symbol of that famed fair, whose theme was "The World of Tomorrow." The only 1939 fair building still standing is the New York City Building, now the Queens Museum. The novelty and appeal of electric floodlight illumination in the 1930s is certified by the large proportion of postcards from the era that feature their subjects bathed in the glow of nighttime light.*

15

PHILADELPHIA

GRANDFATHER OF AMERICA'S BIG CITIES

There is so much pretentious writing by so many morticians, coffin-worms, statisticians, upstart propagandists and left-handed careerists that Modern Architecture as a theme is getting to be pretty dubious, I should say.

—Frank Lloyd Wright
Letter to Maxwell Levinson, editor of *T-Square Club Journal*, in discussions prior to Wright's article on Neutra
December 31, 1931

FITTINGLY, BARBARA CAPITMAN MET MAXWELL Levinson in 1951 in an elevator in the Empire State Building. Max was the architect for the showroom of Jansen Mills on the fifteenth floor. He got on the elevator and was looking at some publicity photos of the space that his client had just taken. Barbara introduced herself as the associate editor of *Lamps and Lighting* magazine and asked if she could take a look at the photos. Thus began a thirty-year friendship. Max had been the editor of the *T-Square Club Journal* during the 1930s and then publisher of *Shelter* magazine and *U.S.A. Tomorrow*. In 1983, Barbara persuaded Max to start the Art Deco Society of Philadelphia (ADSP). He became the founding president and was succeeded by architectural historian Gersil Kay, owner of Newmark Engineering. Gersil had previously founded the Preservation Coalition of Philadelphia, an umbrella group for thirteen of Philadelphia's preservation groups. The ADSP has been fairly inactive lately, their last big project having been the Art Deco symposium when the National Trust for Historic Preservation (NTHP) met in Philadelphia in 1989. Speakers included John Manship on his just completed book, *Paul Manship*, about his father. Barbara helped organize the symposium and took along Miami Beach

Navy YMCA (Metropolitan), 117 Arch at 15th Street, Philadelphia. ARCHITECT: Louis E. Jallade, 1928. A frieze at the entrance that featured the Constitution and Enterprise amid Paris Exposition and nautical motifs helped make this Barbara Capitman's favorite Philadelphia Art Deco building. Jallade was responsible for several other fine Art Deco buildings in Philadelphia. This structure was converted to commercial apartments in 1984.

PSFS (Philadelphia Savings Fund Society), 1234 Market Street at South 12th Street, Philadelphia. ARCHITECTS: George Howe and William Lescaze, 1930. After their first year as a partnership, Howe and Lescaze produced this extraordinary thirty-two-story tower to be the new home for the oldest savings-and-loan in the U.S.A. Its stark modernism was a startling contrast to mainline Philadelphia's Colonial tradition. The thrift's conservative and reluctant directors had to be bludgeoned into acquiescence before this masterpiece could be built. (Photograph courtesy Philadelphia Savings Fund Society)

preservation-development advocates Tony Goldman and Denis Russ. Because Levinson had published and edited several of the seminal architectural journals of the day, he had a vast archive of photographs, design drawings, and correspondence with all of the greats, including Frank Lloyd Wright, George Howe, Le Cobusier, and many more. Recently, the archive was acquired by Phyllis Lambert for her Canadian Centre for Architecture.

Innovative Program Inc. was a Philadelphia Historic preservation umbrella organization formed to "acquire" façades of buildings. By giving the façade as a gift to the corporation, the owner received a tax credit based upon the façade being valued at ten percent of the building's worth. In 1983, this corporation acquired twenty-four façades, valued at $5 million. The WCAU Radio façade (now the Art Institute of Philadelphia) was restored using this program in 1983. That unusual 1931 Germanic-style structure, at 1622 Chestnut Street, was designed by Harry Sternfeld and

Gabriel Roth. It was renovated to create the museum in 1983 by Kopple Sheward & Day. Elsewhere in Philadelphia is the Atwater Kent Museum, site of many ADSP meetings.

Philadelphia has several great Art Deco theaters, including the 1936 Mayfair Theater, 7300 Frankford Avenue, by David Supowitz. It is Philadelphia's first streamlined movie house. Philadelphia also has a great new Neo-Deco United Artists Riverview, a nine-plex cinema, at Washington Avenue and Dickinson Street off I-95.

Barbara wrote her own essay on Philadelphia and its role in the history of Art Deco when she first proposed that this book be written. Here is her view:

PHILADELPHIA

Cradle of Deco Expression

Compared to New York, Los Angeles, or Miami Beach, Philadelphia's Art Deco is not that great. Philadelphia is one of those places where you see Art Deco vestiges on every hand, in octagonal windows, topping fluted pilasters, in friezes . . . but the number of extant pure Art Deco buildings is very small and rather overwhelmed by the richness of preceding periods.

But Philadelphia belongs in any account of the Art Deco revival mainly because of the presence of its architects, who seem to have picked up and carried a line of cogent thought from the great architects of its past.

Through the literature of the Philadelphia architects the Art Deco revival has emerged with a written

Suburban Station (One Penn Center), Pennsylvania Railroad, 17th Street at John F. Kennedy Boulevard, Philadelphia. ARCHITECT: Graham, Anderson, Probst & White, 1929. This railroad station was part of a multibuilding contract awarded to Chicago's eminent architectural firm. It employed a startling mixture of classic Roman themes with ultramodern materials and colors and a distinctive use of aluminum. The larger 30th Street Station by the same firm is classical, with Art Deco lighting fixtures. In the Suburban Station, however, they used a more cohesive Art Deco design.

past and a futuristic style that has swept the American scene—Post-Modernism. More than any other firm, Venturi and Scott Brown have had an impact on the American scene far beyond the actual buildings they have designed. It's not only the look they have made popular—the devices such as the ocular window or arched portal, the historic look on the simple contemporary façade—but it's the way they have taught us to see a new beauty in vernacular, everyday buildings of the past.

Denise Scott Brown had first brought the Art Deco "enclave" of Miami Beach to the attention of planners and architects in Miami Beach in 1972, long before anyone else had realized such a source of architectural history existed. When she read about our rediscovery of Miami Beach's treasure in the *Saturday Review* in 1977, she phoned and our long friendship began. With her husband, Robert Venturi, she began a long series of visits to Miami Beach's Art Deco District, staying when it opened in 1979 at the Cardozo, always fiercely championing and instructive.

Early on we drove through the Art Deco District, Bob and Denise arguing about attribution—were we looking at Bauhaus or later Art Deco? It was Denise who persuaded famous critics such as Paul Goldberger of *The New York Times* and Vincent Scully at Yale that something important was happening in the South Beach area.

In 1978, Paul Rothman, a planner, explorer, and photographer, a young man of many talents who had become engrossed in the government effort to revitalize inner cities (of which, of course, Miami Beach with its slums and impoverished elderly was a prime example) joined me in a mission to Washington. We were going to seek funding for planning from the National Endowment for the Arts. It was a historic visit. We met for the first time with Robert Rettig, then chief of the National Register of Historic Places (now in Cambridge, a leader of the Massachusetts preservation movement), and his staff and discovered the importance of being listed on the Register, a fact that somehow, in our isolation in America's southernmost area, we had missed.

For their part, the National Register people were overwhelmed at the slides we brought with us—the late Andy Sweet's photographs of blue skies and colorful buildings, seen in their own city, which that day seemed a dour red-brick city with leaden skies.

We had phoned Denise in Philadelphia from Miami and she had invited us to come visit on the way. "I've been on the review committee," she said. "The

WCAU Radio Station (Art Institute of Philadelphia), 1622 Chestnut Street, Philadelphia. ARCHITECTS: Harry Sternfeld and Gabriel Roth, 1931; Renovation architect: Kopple Sheward & Day, 1983. The central glass expanse of this former radio station was said to glow like a radio tube when the station was on the air at night. This highly unusual German Expressionist-style structure had one studio large enough to accommodate the entire Philadelphia Orchestra for its regular live broadcasts. President Herbert Hoover inaugurated the studios, whose façade has ziggurat motifs extending through three dimensions, up, down, and sideways. Sternfeld was a student of Paul Philippe Cret at the University of Pennsylvania. Roth is credited with the interior.

whole thing is what you say in the first paragraph, the precis of what you intend to do and why it matters."

So there we were some days later, standing in a drafting room on the third floor of a Philadelphia row house—red brick with a white stoop—looking at the work on the tables, a Post-Modern (a term we didn't know at the time) residence. And out of the old small-paned, mullioned windows we saw old Philadelphia streets and roof tops. More than at any time before I had the sense of being on an adventure that had its roots in American tradition. One could feel the presence of Ben Franklin here in the offices of these very cosmopolitan futuristic twentieth-century architects. A job they had completed only a few years earlier (1973 to 1976) is illustrative of the Venturi new approach to history. It was the Ben Franklin Court on Market Street. Franklin had owned his own house and print shop in a courtyard behind a row of tenants' houses. The house had burned, and lacking sufficient evidence to reconstruct the house faithfully, the National Park Service commissioned the architects to design an interpretive complex. The result, a stark steel frame, shocked some traditionalists; but it has become an image few can forget, and the Philadelphia architecture handbook published by the Foundation for Architecture says: "The resulting project is one of the most imaginative historic restorations in the country."

While we were there for our first meeting we met Steven Izenour, perhaps one of the most influential architects writing about and studying the early twentieth century. Steven, one of the authors with Robert Venturi and Denise Scott Brown of *Learning From Las Vegas*, has explored vernacular architecture, including the influence of the chains, from Woolworth's to fast-food restaurants. His book, *The White Towers*, also published before we met, explored these Deco hamburger forerunners of fast-food chains. With the designs coming from a head office, the White Towers used the Art Deco styles and the new materials of enamel-coated metal, glass blocks, and aluminum to express corporate identity and cleanliness.

There in Philadelphia in the old historic house, Steve and I clashed on the company's position that even today's corporate symbolism, like proliferating gas-station signage in deserts and rural roadways, must be considered imagery of our times and respected as such. Still close to my own Madison Avenue marketing-research labors for giant corporations, I felt that Steven was falling into the hands of the enemy. Perhaps my own position was confirmed in 1988 with the successful battle against the shopping-mall interests which would have desecrated the rural and revered battlefield of the Civil War at Manassas. Ronald Fleming, the planner in Cambridge, presented aerial slides that showed how historic lands and views are vanishing all over the United States, giving way to "ticky-tacky" development housing and malls and shopping centers. Nevertheless, it is Steven Izenour who has become a leading exponent of the Art Deco Societies' point of view—expressed in our Miami Beach 1987 Art Deco Weekend Seminars—that it is the small, indigenous-neighborhood Art Deco stores, restaurants, and gas stations on the fringes of the great cities that can mean so much in the revitalization of depressed neighborhoods.

In *Learning From Las Vegas*, Essays in the "Ugly and the Ordinary," there is a section titled "The Philadelphia Crosstown Community" on a study done in 1968. Citizen action had stopped the State Highway Department and the Chamber of Commerce from destroying South Street to build a Crosstown Expressway. At that point the authors wrote: "For all its decay and for all the evidence of social and individual distress, South Street is a lively, lovely piece of the city."

I remember visiting Denise's house, working on the NEA grant, conversations with her about her struggle as a woman architect. We had a great time. It was good fortune to be her friend.

(Winter, 1989)

This is the end of Barbara's thoughts on why Philadelphia would be an important chapter in this book.

Barbara was lucky enough to have close associations as well with Maxwell Levinson. One of Levinson's heroes was architect George Howe, designer of some of the trend-setting buildings in New York. But probably more important for Max, Howe was architect of the Philadelphia Savings

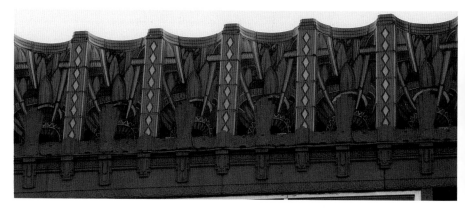

Fund Society (then known simply as PSFS), 1234 Market Street, designed by Howe & Lescaze in 1930, just one year after they formed a partnership. The thirty-two-story tower has an interior that still retains an Art Deco feel, with long shining escalators, smooth metal trim, and an elegant black and gray color scheme. Howe had done many branch offices for the PSFS, beginning in the early 1920s. Beaux-Arts trained, Howe designed some of these earlier offices in neo-Renaissance, but he made a jarring transition here, after teaming with the Swiss-born Lescaze. PSFS president James Wilcox had great faith in Howe, and insisted his board approve designs despite great opposition. (Lescaze also did the Magnolia Lounge at the 1936 Dallas Centennial Exhibition; see Dallas chapter.)

Terra-cotta detail, 7042-60 Terminal Square, Upper Darby, Pennsylvania. ARCHITECT: George Stavropoulos, 1929. This superb terra-cotta parapet, featuring classic French design elements and rich colors, is typical of several buildings in this western Philadelphia suburb. Most were built by McClatchy Development.

Levinson published articles about the bold colors used by these Art Deco architects, There was a strong relationship between these modernists who had belonged to the T-Square Club, to which Max was so central. No doubt these associates influenced such T-Square members as Joseph Urban and Palm Beach architect Belford Shoumate. Max and Barbara discussed colors, comparing them with those used by the Werkbund and by architects like Gerrit Rietveld, Le Corbusier—and, of course, like her friend, Miami Beach colorist/designer Leonard Horowitz.

Paul Philippe Cret, whom we already have heard so much about, taught at the University of Pennsylvania and lived in Philadelphia, where he no doubt absorbed and reapplied a good measure of Philadelphia's classic and distinctly non-Modern architectural beauty. Benjamin Latrobe came from London in 1798 with a set of handbooks on Greek and Roman orders of architecture. Philadelphia then helped usher in a Greek revival in the 1820s, thus setting the stage for Cret. Here in the Art Deco year 1925, Cret, along with frequent collaborators Zantinger, Borie, and Medary, designed the Fidelity Mutual Life Insurance building (now Reliance Standard Life), 2005 Pennsylvania Avenue, with typical outstanding sculpture by Lee Lawrie.

Another Philadelphia resident was Edward W. Bok, wealthy publisher of the *Ladies' Home Journal*, which was very influential throughout the country because it frequently published design plans from the Arts-and-Crafts movement. Bok, a Dutch immigrant, so loved his adopted country that he felt compelled to create a work of lasting beauty in it as a gift to his fellow citizens. He eventually chose Lake Wales, Florida (see illustration in U.S.A. chapter, under "monuments").

Philadelphia was fortunate to have two train stations by Chicago's preeminent Graham, Anderson, Probst & White, D. H. Burnham's successor. The firm did the well-known 30th Street railroad station (1929–1954). With its marble walls, coffered ceiling, columns, Greek *porte-cochere*, Art Deco sculpture, and great light fixtures there are very few stations in the U.S.A. today that can compare with it. The second was the 1929 Suburban Station on Seventeenth Street at John F. Kennedy Boulevard, by the same distinguished architects. It is even more Art Deco, and was renovated in 1986 through a façade-revitalization program of the Philadelphia Historic Preservation Commission.

In 1989, the year after she had made such a splash with the National Trust for Historic Preservation, (NTHP) at their Cincinnati convention, Barbara scored again. She was the main speaker on Art Deco, and invited Paul Manship's son to share the podium and talk about his great father. This was some show and was exhausting, so Barbara stayed home while Trust delegates went on a tour of Manayunk, an old industrial neighborhood; she had arranged for the tour to conclude in the office of her friends at Venturi Rauch Scott Brown. Barbara viewed Manayunk (a Native American word) as a case study for development in the Art Deco District. After the tour, Barbara and Robert and Denise went to a fancy dinner. The distinguished architects offered a toast to Barbara, and she was absolutely delighted. The next night, feeling more energetic than ever, they went to dinner again and she gratefully saluted them. "We seemingly had a profound effect upon each other," Barbara wrote.

Barbara's final exciting Art Deco find in Philadelphia during the NTHP convention was made while on a Sunday-morning walk near her hotel. She found at 117 Arch Street a former YMCA converted to an apartment building called the Metropolitan. It was completely finished in Art Deco geometric carving, but had unusual references to sailing and oceans. It turned out that in its day it was the YMCA for sailors and merchant marine, designed in 1930 by Louis E. Jallade. It was renovated in 1984.

Elsewhere
Upper Darby, Pennsylvania

Among Philadelphia's other Art Deco treasures, there is a collection of commercial buildings in suburban Upper Darby, built by developer John McClatchy, which have vibrant and wild Paris Exposition–style terra-cotta façades.

Bear Run, Pennsylvania

Frank Lloyd Wright's greatest residential design may be found at Bear Run. Fallingwater, the legendary residence of department store baron Edgar Kaufmann, Sr., was done in 1936 with the addition of a guest house in 1939. Finishes and materials have a strong Art Deco feel—cork, floors highly waxed even though they are made of stone from the river bed, corner windows and beautiful custom hardware.

Pittsburgh, Pennsylvania

A great example of Gothic–Art Deco is the Cathedral of Learning at the University of Pittsburgh, designed in 1924 by Charles Zeller Klauder. Although the detailing is Gothic, the massing is Art Deco. This four-hundred-foot tower was the first skyscraper university.

16

SAN FRANCISCO

PACIFIC UNITY REIGNS

Serene, indifferent of fate
Thou sittest at the Golden Gate.

—Bret Harte, 1836–1902
Inscription at Golden Gate Park, 1937

A PHOENIX, SYMBOL OF SAN FRANCISCO, IS FOUND above the door of the Art Deco landmark, Coit Tower. This city is a survivor and as such has always welcomed other survivors. As the indomitable port city blossomed in the late nineteenth century, it became the greatest in the West, welcoming all newcomers to its Golden Gates. Art Deco was a newcomer, and predictably took hold in the West right here in San Francisco.

In 1924—a year before the Paris Exposition—the city's most influential Art Deco architect, Timothy Pflueger, designed a new headquarters building for the Pacific Telephone and Telegraph Company. Ralph Walker's Barclay-Vesey Building in New York preceded it by only a year. Both were commissioned by the local phone companies, which were part of the giant parent corporation known as American Telephone & Telegraph. So we may observe that Art Deco was spread first by telephone, coast-to-coast.

Many of the country's great engineering projects were created in the West. After the Hoover Dam, the most massive—and probably San Francisco's best-loved asset after its cable cars—is the Golden Gate Bridge, taking U.S. Highway 101 across the treacherous channel leading into one of the world's great natural harbors. It was designed in 1933 by Joseph Strauss, chief engineer, but architect Irving Morrow provided the Art Deco style. Morrow used telescoping setbacks on the bridge's twin towers allowing them to climb gracefully like a skyscraper. There were many doubters, but when the bridge finally opened it was proclaimed one of the

Berkeley High School and Auditorium, 2246 Milvia at Martin Luther King (formerly Grove Street), entrance via quadrangle courtyard, also near 1930 Allston Way, Berkeley. ARCHITECT: Gutterson & Corlett; Sculptor: Jacques Schnier, 1938. Schnier executed this odd scene over the school's entrance: at the bottom, a group of young Fur Eastern musicians, and above them a scene from the story of Saint George and the dragon, with the axiom: "You Shall Know the Truth and the Truth Shall Make You Free." His inspiration may have come from the Pacific Unity theme of the Golden Gate Exposition of 1939, where he was working at the same time.

Four Fifty Sutter Medical Building, 450 Sutter Street, San Francisco. ARCHITECT: Timothy Pflueger for Miller & Pflueger, 1928. This main-entrance vestibule is topped by a reverse-ziggurat, featuring exotic Mayan-temple glyph designs. The entry was fabricated by Michel & Pfeffer Iron Works in bronze and cast iron, burnished to a golden brown. Four Fifty Sutter was one of the first buildings to have corner bay windows.

Aquatic Park Casino (National Maritime Museum), *Golden Gate National Recreation Area, Beach Street (foot of Polk Street), San Francisco. ARCHITECT: William Mooser, Sr., and William Mooser, Jr.; Murals: Hilaire Hiler; Sculptor: Sargent Johnson, 1939. Easily mistaken for an oceanliner, this "vessel" is landlocked. Converted to a museum in 1951, the building is now filled with exhibitions on the city's maritime history and wonderful nautical murals. The main entrance is surrounded by a massive aquatic relief by Johnson, one of the most successful African-American artists of this period. (Photograph by Dennis W. Wilhelm)*

Aquatic Park Casino (National Maritime Museum), *Golden Gate National Recreation Area, Beach Street (foot of Polk Street), San Francisco. ARCHITECT: William Mooser, Sr., & William Mooser, Jr.; Murals: Hilaire Hiler, 1939. This Nautical Moderne mural by Hiler is one of the best features in this very popular Fisherman's Wharf–area attraction. Sargent Johnson did similar nautical mosaics on the outside rear terrace. This work blends Art Deco colors and geometry with a touch of surrealism. (Photograph by Michael D. Kinerk)*

Berkeley High School and Auditorium, *2246 Milvia at Martin Luther King (formerly Grove Street), Entrance via quadrangle courtyard, also near 1930 Allston Way, Berkeley. ARCHITECT: Gutterson & Corlett; Sculptor: Jacques Schnier, 1938. This beautiful façade is inscribed with names of the world's great inventors in panels over the third-floor windows. Examples of their inventions are displayed in relief over second-floor windows.*

Coit Tower, *Pioneer Park, Telegraph Hill Boulevard (top of Lombard Street), San Francisco.* ARCHITECT: *Henry Howard for Arthur Brown, Jr.; Muralist: John Langley Howard, 1933. In this detail from J.L. Howard's fresco* California Industrial Scenes, *measuring ten by twenty-four feet, social issues dominate. The twenty-seven interior murals and frescoes were done by twenty-five of San Francisco's most noted artists, who worked for the PWAP (Public Works of Art Project). The tower's artwork provoked so much political controversy that the public unveiling had to be delayed for a full year after completion.*

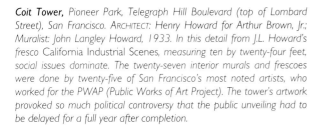

Coit Tower, *Pioneer Park, Telegraph Hill Boulevard (top of Lombard Street), San Francisco.* ARCHITECT: *Henry Howard for Arthur Brown, Jr., 1932. This vintage postcard toasted the opening of the Golden Gate city's best-known tower. To create this sleek monument honoring the city's fallen firemen, Lillie Hitchcock Coit provided $125,000. A five-year, $1.2-million restoration of the murals inside the tower was completed in 1989.*

Golden Gate Bridge, *U.S. Highway 101, San Francisco Bay.* ARCHITECT: *Irving Morrow; Joseph Strauss, chief engineer, 1933. The two support piers (746 feet high) for the bridge cable have setbacks and sculpted decoration just like their skyscraper cousins. The color is "International Orange." The bridge utilized a prize-winning new design idea: Put the roadbed on top of all girders and bracing to provide an unobstructed view of San Francisco Bay and its surrounding hills.*

divided and were in a state of disrepair and neglect. Just as was true in Miami Beach's Art Deco District, no one really paid attention to these *grande dames* until a few daring homeowners began to use bright—and many said outrageous—colors to draw attention to their rich decorative detailing. The book *Painted Ladies* (1978) brought this preservation movement to national attention, and as a result today these homes are widely known and loved.

Two important fairs were held in 1939: the New York World's Fair in Flushing Meadow, Queens, and the Golden Gate International Exposition (GGIE) on Treasure Island in San Francisco Bay. Their themes, "The World of Tomorrow" and "Pacific Unity," were expressions of optimism. The Depression was winding down and times were getting better. GGIE's Pacific Unity theme brilliantly foretold the city's present-day multiethnic key to success, for most recent California immigrants have come here from the Pacific Basin. At the fair, the main attraction was a long lighted courtyard filled with fountains and statues of peoples from all over the Pacific Basin. Presiding over all this was a giant statue of the goddess *Pacifica* by Ralph Stackpole. The sprawling Court of Pacifica was designed by architect Pflueger. Most striking of the buildings along the court was the Tower of the Sun by Arthur Brown, Jr. Another attraction was the Pacific House, which contained a series of painted maps entitled *Pacific and Its People* by Miguel Covarrubias. These are now installed at the San Francisco World Trade Center at the Embarcadero. The Pacific Basin fountain inside the Pacific House was a giant ceramic relief map of the ocean weighing thirty tons. It was designed by Antonio Sotomayor and made by the Gladding, McBean Company.

Of all the fair's splendid majesty, less than a dozen of the cast-concrete sculptures survive along with the disassembled sections of the ceramic basin. Anne Schnoebelen

wonders of the world. If it were a building, the Golden Gate would be sixty-two stories high. Clearly, it is San Francisco's signature landmark. Crews have kept its "International Orange" paint fresh since the day it opened, painting year-round without stop. The bright orange bridge with its soaring steel cables gracefully spanning the mouth of San Francisco Bay is so powerful an image that few ever examine it closely. Most motorists, anxious merely to cross the bay, fail to notice its outstanding matching support structures: streamlined toll booths, street lamps, ramps, and railings. Some of these have been carefully maintained and updated, but lately, some have been disrespectfully altered. When we mentioned that the Golden Gate was to be in our book it took every one of our San Francisco friends by surprise. How could a bridge be Art Deco? Just look at it to recognize why it is.

Most San Franciscans have overlooked other wonderful examples of Art Deco in their city. The city's many elaborate Victorian homes had also been thoroughly neglected at one time. Now the rehabilitation of the Victorians is San Francisco's biggest preservation success story. Built on a grand scale when San Francisco was enjoying its wealth before the turn of the century, by 1960 most had been sub-

Stock Exchange, remodeled original building, 301 Pine Street, San Francisco. ARCHITECT: Timothy Pflueger for Miller & Pflueger; Sculptor: Ralph Stackpole, 1929. To create the Stock Exchange the architect remodeled the 1915 subtreasury building and added a larger new building with a main entrance at 155 Sansome Street. Here is Earth's Fruitfulness, one of a pair of sculptures placed at the entrance to the original building during Pflueger's remodeling. Stackpole carved the pieces in 1930 from granite slabs that were twenty-one feet high and weighed seventy-five tons each.

Exchange Club (City Club), Stock Exchange Building, 155 Sansome Street, San Francisco. ARCHITECT: Timothy Pflueger for Miller & Pflueger; Club designer: Michael Goodman, 1929. A sumptuous gold-leaf ceiling crowns the club lounge. Carved above the handsome stone Pueblo-Deco fireplace is a Native American warrior with bow. The dining area begins at the left.

Exchange Club (City Club), Stock Exchange Building, 155 Sansome Street, San Francisco. ARCHITECT: Timothy Pflueger for Miller & Pflueger; Club designer: Michael Goodman; Muralist: Diego Rivera, 1929. Occupying the tenth and eleventh floors of the 1929 addition to the Stock Exchange is a private club where Rivera's giant mural dominates the stairwell. The central figure personifies California's energy and beauty. Around her are references to California's resources: agriculture, labor, and industry. Designer Goodman urged Rivera to continue the mural onto the ceiling to maximize its heroic effect.

GOLDEN GATE INTERNATIONAL EXPOSITION ON SAN FRANCISCO BAY

Golden Gate International Exposition (demolished), Treasure Island, San Francisco Bay. ARCHITECT: Arthur Brown, Jr., 1939. This vintage postcard extolls the now-lost splendors of this exposition: the Sunken Garden, the 400-foot Tower of the Sun, and other pavilions and palaces. The theme, Pacific Unity, was intended to promote the bond between all Pacific-basin cultures. This resulted in unusual and exotic variations of Art Deco architecture.

founded Golden Gate International Exposition Associates (GGIE Associates) to preserve these remaining exposition artifacts stored near the original fair site on Treasure Island, now a U.S. Naval base. Schnoebelen has acted as a one-woman task force to convince the public and the Navy to reassemble the Pacific Basin fountain and encircle it with the remaining Pacific Unity sculptures from the former Fountain of Western Waters. She proposes to place these artifacts in front of the original Pan Am Airways administration building, now the Navy War Museum, the one edifice still standing from the fair. The museum currently has a small exhibition dealing with this great fair. Normally it is open to the public, but due to the military nature of the island, it is best to call first.

The theme of unity and friendship also was expressed by Diego Rivera in his 1939 series of ten panel frescoes called *Marriage of the Artistic Expression of the North and South of this Continent* (also known as *Pan-American Unity*) now at City College on Phelan Avenue.

Timothy Pflueger designed many major buildings in San Francisco. He had no local architectural rivals; he was the best. He designed the first Art Deco skyscraper on the West Coast (Pacific Telephone), the first truly modern glass-curtain-wall skyscraper (Four Fifty Sutter), and the earliest, biggest, and best Moderne movie palace, the Oakland Paramount. He designed the Stock Exchange and the I. Magnin store.

In the 1924 Pacific Telephone building, 140 New Montgomery Street, Pflueger pioneered the concept of working with the best local artists and sculptors. (Through the years he worked with Diego Rivera, Ralph Stackpole,

Gerald Fitzgerald, Robert Howard, and Michael Goodman.) The building had Gladding, McBean eagles at the top, which were restored in 1989 by Manuel Palos of the original manufacturer. The telephone company hired Garcia Wagner Restoration Architects to stabilize other structural problems. This was another of the Art Deco towers that had a weather-forecast lighted beacon on top.

Pflueger's second major contribution, the Four Fifty Sutter Medical-Dental Building, 1928, was years ahead of its time in the use of what is now called glass-curtain wall, and also in use of rounded-corner bay windows giving the offices lots of light, a commanding view, and, of course, fetching the landlord higher rents. Pflueger excelled in his use of Mayan designs in the entrance and lobby.

Next was his San Francisco Stock Exchange, 1929. Originally a Classical-style federal bank, with entrance on 301 Pine Street, it was remodeled by Pflueger to become Art Deco. He connected it to a new tower of his own design around the corner on Sansome Street. The new lobby has a ceiling like the later Oakland Paramount, a lattice of aluminum in fanciful patterns, lit indirectly from above. This became a very attractive Pflueger trademark. Pflueger commissioned Ralph Stackpole to create sculpture to unite the buildings, with large pylons in front of the Pine Street façade, and with medallions and a relief over the Sansome entrance. The Exchange Club on the two top floors of the new building is one of the most elegant Art Deco settings anywhere.

What is probably Pflueger's masterpiece, the 1930 Paramount

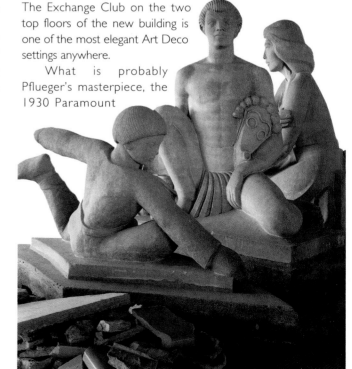

Golden Gate International Exposition (Treasure Island Museum), U.S. Naval Station, Treasure Island, off I-80, Buena Vista exit, San Francisco Bay, 1939. Twenty cast-concrete figures once circled the spectacular (now-demolished) Fountain of Western Waters. They helped express the exposition's theme by representing nationalities of the Pacific Rim. Pictured here are Alaskan Boy Spear Fishing by Ruth Cravath; Polynesian Adolescent by Brents Carlton; and American Indian Woman by Carl George. These larger-than-life statues are among sixteen surviving at the U.S. Navy's Treasure Island Museum now on the exposition site.

Theater, is across the bay in Oakland, at 2025 Broadway. The façade is undoubtedly the most monumental and most artistic of all Art Deco theaters. Pflueger moved beyond the French Zigzag style still prevalent at the time by commissioning Gerald Fitzgerald to design a mosaic that would be a major statement on the theater's façade. Fitzgerald created two 100-foot-tall stylized puppeteers that control more than forty figures on strings. These represent the world of film and the arts. The Gladding, McBean Company executed the design in over seventy colors of tile and each panel was installed on the side of a soaring stainless-steel, three-color neon sign displaying the name of the theater. The interior is an integrated work of decorative art. It underwent major restoration and conversion to a performing arts center in 1972 under the direction of Jack Bethards and Peter Botto. As is also true of New York's Radio City Music Hall, an entire book has been devoted to the Paramount, so all we will say here is: Don't miss it.

Pflueger also designed two of the premier night spots of the day, the Top of the Mark and Patent Leather Lounge, both being in the venerable Mark Hopkins Hotel on Nob Hill. San Francisco is blessed to have a master of music of the Art Deco period, Peter Minton, holding forth at the Top of the Mark today. Listening to his piano stylings, one can easily drift back to this grand age of elegance. Another very special treat in the city is a visit to the Redwood Room at the Clift Four Seasons Hotel. Art Deco detailing abounds and the soaring wood paneling frames large-scale reproductions of Gustav Klimt works.

Important roadway projects were built here in the 1930s, establishing the city as a major Art Deco engineering capital. Largest of these is the 1933 Oakland Bay Bridge, the only twin-span suspension bridge ever built. A very long Art Deco tunnel is part of this project. Timothy Pflueger, as design consultant, wanted to give the bridge a "clean" functional look with no adornments other than structural cross-bracing. He eliminated proposed heroic figures for the central anchorage piers to have been done by his favorite sculptor Ralph Stackpole.

The 1937 Broadway Low-Level Tunnels (Caldecott Tunnels) connecting Berkeley and Orinda were designed by Henry H. Meyers. Most interesting here are monumental 1925 Paris Exposition–style entrance piers. The General MacArthur tunnel at the entrance to the Presidio is also of the period.

The city's popular residential Sunset District, developed by Henry Doegler, and the northside Marina District both were built in the mid-1930s. Most of these buildings are the same height and scale, though of varying styles, but Art Deco is well represented. The Marina District's collection of apartments is somewhat like the Bronx's Grand Concourse, only more dispersed and on a smaller scale. Several of the best apartments in the District are by Herman C. Baumann.

Here are some of San Francisco's other noteworthy Art Deco buildings. Coit Tower, at Pioneer Park on Telegraph Hill Boulevard, at the top of Lombard Street, was designed in 1932 by Henry Howard, under the patronage of Lillie Hitchcock Coit, who left funds at her death in 1929 for beautification of the city. Her estate decided to build this unusual memorial to firefighters, the people so critical to the survival of the city after the last major earthquake and fire in 1906. Many famous artists contributed to this project, including John Langley Howard, Victor Arnautoff, Clifford Wright, Ralph Stackpole, Lucien Labaudt, Frederick Olmstead, Jr., and Otis Oldfield. A $1.2 million restoration of the murals done between 1984 and 1989 was funded by the National Endowment for the Arts, San Francisco Parks and Recreation Department, and California Office of Historic Preservation. The Coit Tower murals were the first relief project for artists under PWAP. Edward Bruce had barely pushed the project through the Treasury Department (he was a painter as well as a banker), when San Francisco applied for funds for Coit Tower. The mural themes became the basis for what was called the "American Scene" or Social Realism. It became the prototype for other New Deal programs. It took nine months to do the frescoes covering over 3,500 square feet inside the tower. So biting was the social commentary in the murals that the city, in a very controversial move resulting in protest and picketing, refused to allow the interior of the monument to be opened to the public for almost a year. Coit Tower finally opened in October 1934. The phoenix over the door was sculpted by Robert Howard.

San Francisco was a magnet for talented artists in the 1920s and 1930s. Many came here to attend the California School of Fine Arts, where most of the GGIE artists taught or studied. In 1936, Alfred Dupont created outstanding façade panels on the famed J. S. Malloch Apartments, 1360 Montgomery at Filbert, by Irving Goldstine and J. S. Malloch.

More murals were done at the 1939 Aquatic Park Casino (now the National Maritime Museum) in Golden Gate National Recreation Area on Beach Street, at the foot of Polk Street. The architects were William Mooser, Sr., and William Mooser, Jr. The Nautical Moderne undersea painted murals are by Hilaire Hiler, with additional sculpture by Sargent Johnson.

Gilbert Stanley Underwood in 1940 designed the Rincon Annex to the U.S. Post Office (now Rincon Center) at 99 Mission Street, restored by Jay Turnbull. It features nautical images and reliefs of dolphins.

On a bluff overlooking the Pacific and the Golden Gate Bridge twenty-one similar buildings were created as a veterans' hospital, at 4150 Clement Street. Designed 1932–1933, it was built in 1934, with design and construction supervised by the Treasury Department, which at that time had administration control over veterans' affairs. The designs were adapted from earlier Treasury Department prototypes. An independent Veterans Administration was formed in 1930. In researching this hospital we were in touch with the staff preservation officer for the Veterans Department, who assures us that this is the only Art Deco veterans' hospital.

Art Deco Society of California

The San Francisco–based Art Deco Society of California has its offices in George Kelham's twenty-nine-story 1929 Shell Oil Building, 100 Bush Street. To help establish his client's corporate identity, Kelham used shells on the building's façade and over the door. The building was restored in 1990 by Heller & Leake. When the Shell Corporation was here, it occupied the first seventeen floors of this landmark, which was the tallest building in the city when it was built.

The Art Deco Society of California (ADSC) was founded in 1981, and was "dedicated to the appreciation and preservation of California's unique art and architecture of the Art Deco period." Today it has 750 members throughout California, the majority being in the Bay Area and Northern California. The Society has several annual events: the Gatsby Summer Afternoon Picnic, Art Deco Preservation Ball, and Art Deco Weekend by the Bay. They have events such as the Victory Canteen with a 1940s wartime Art Deco theme and the Captain's Gala with a nautical theme. Annual awards are given for best preservation projects in the state. A dedicated group also worked for years to make an inventory of the archives of architect Timothy Pflueger, only to see much of it sold at auction several years ago.

Current president Jeffrey Tucker is the Society's expert on music of the period, especially jazz. He has written many articles in the ADSC's quarterly, *The Sophisticate*. Founding president Michael Crowe and education director Lori Leigh Gieleghem are resident experts on architecture and fashion, respectively.

One endangered building that the ADSC is working to save and convert to another use is the 1941 U.S.O. Hospitality House at 100 Larkin Street next to the library. It is streamlined, with blue-glass windows.

Elsewhere

Oakland, California

In 1931, the Downtown Property Owners' Association of Oakland adopted a pivotal façade modernization program. This resulted in many downtown buildings receiving an Art Deco exterior. Several of the best Art Deco buildings in Oakland are I. Magnin, 2001 Broadway, Weeks & Day, 1931; Oakland Floral Depot, 1900 Telegraph, Albert J. Evers, 1931; and Lake Merritt Hotel, 1800 Madison, William Weeks for Weeks & Day, 1927. Oakland's Paramount Theater (1930) has already been discussed.

Berkeley, California

Secluded in a handsome wooded campus is Berkeley High School and Auditorium, a very Deco enclave on 2246 Milvia at Martin Luther King (formerly Grove) Street. Entrance is via the inner quadrangle courtyard, near 1930 Allston Way. Architect was Gutterson & Corlett, with great sculpture by Jacques Schnier, 1938.

Oakland Floral Depot, 1900–1932 Telegraph Avenue, with entrance at 468–498 19th Street, Oakland. ARCHITECT: Albert J. Evers, 1931. An explosion of splendid black-and-silver glazed terra-cotta richly ornaments this very small blip of a building. Just after it was built a 1932 Downtown Property Owners' Association street-improvement program "modernized" many of Oakland's older buildings with Art Deco façades.

Paramount Theater (3,434 seats), 2025 Broadway, Oakland. ARCHITECT: *Timothy Pflueger for Miller & Pflueger; Mosaic designer: Gerald Fitzgerald, 1929. Restoration supervisors: Jack Bethards and Peter Botto, 1972. Colossal puppeteers dominate the exterior tile mosaic by Fitzgerald, executed in seventy colors by Gladding, McBean, of Lincoln, California. As symbols of the drama, these thirty-six marionettes are hard to top. In 1992, city officials were considering turning over the showplace to private interests. The new operator proposed reverting to movie exhibition by knocking holes in the lobby walls to connect new minitheaters to the original complex. Many citizens protested, feeling betrayed after a public campaign had restored it as a performing-arts center. Final decision is pending.*

Paramount Theater, 2025 Broadway, Oakland. ARCHITECT: *Timothy Pflueger for Miller & Pflueger, 1929. Restoration supervisors: Jack Bethards and Peter Botto, 1972. Oakland's Paramount is the only rival to New York's Radio City Music Hall. As seen through a peek-a-boo oval window high in an upper-lobby vestibule, the stunning etched-glass sculpture, Fountain of Light, towers fifty feet high. Backlit galvanized-metal strips in the ceiling grille have been sculpted into exotic foliage.*

Paramount Theater, 2025 Broadway, Oakland. ARCHITECT: *Timothy Pflueger for Miller & Pflueger, 1929. Restoration supervisors: Jack Bethards and Peter Botto, 1972. Exotic Egypto-Deco dancing girls fill the mezzanine-level sidewalls. Interior design was a collaboration between Pflueger and artists Anthony Heinsbergen, Gerald Fitzgerald, and sculptor Robert B. Howard. During restoration, under direction of Bethards and Botto, Pflueger's brother, Milton, worked with Skidmore, Owings & Merrill on the project. (Photograph by Michael D. Kinerk)*

Seattle Art Museum, *Volunteer Park, Seattle. ARCHITECT: Charles Bebb & Carl Gould, 1932. Seattle was fortunate to enjoy the beneficence of collector Dr. Richard Fuller, who not only donated his extensive and valuable art collection, but also provided this splendid building. The main façade has fine French-style metal grillwork in three central bays.*

17

SEATTLE

Less is more.

—Mies van der Rohe

Less is a bore.

—Robert Venturi

AS HEADQUARTERS FOR THE BOEING AIRCRAFT Company, Seattle is more a product of the Space Age than the Machine Age. But in the 1920s and 1930s it was a different kind of transportation that ruled the great Northwest. This was a seaport city, dominated by industries tied to its natural resources, and Seattle has an abundance of those. In fact, with Mount Rainier and the Cascade Mountains on the east and Puget Sound and the Olympic Mountains to the west, this is a city where nature can't be overlooked. Business has been booming here for a long time, and there are some tall towers to prove it.

Historic preservation wasn't much of a concern in Seattle until a wave of urban renewal hit the city in the 1970s. Many visitors who came to see the famous Space Needle at the 1962 World's Fair fell in love with the city's natural beauty and lack of congestion. The resulting surge of immigrants created development pressures that the city had never experienced in the past. When plans were unveiled to raze the city's produce hub, the Pike Street Market, in favor of new development, protest led to its being declared a historic district in 1972. Investors were encouraged to use tax incentives available to restore buildings whose lavish details never could be duplicated. Several other districts soon followed, as the enlightened residents equated preservation not only with keeping a link to their past but also with maintining their quality of life.

Allied Arts of Seattle was founded as an Urban Design Advocacy Group during this period, and one of the mem-

Seattle Art Museum, *Volunteer Park, Seattle.* ARCHITECT: *Charles Bebb & Carl Gould, 1932. The beautiful metal grill-work in the front entrance seen in this detail photograph is imbued with French influences. In 1992, many of the collections were moved to a new building designed by Robert Venturi, who, along with his wife, Denise Scott Brown, were Barbara Capitman's earliest Art Deco preservation allies. This original building has been designated to house the museum's Asian art collection.*

United Shopping Tower (Olympic Tower), 217 Pine at 3rd Avenue, Seattle. ARCHITECT: *Harold Adams, chief designer for Henry Bittman, 1929. Beautiful metal spandrels accentuate the gleaming white terra-cotta façade, making it one of Seattle's Art Deco highlights. "Three-band-Bittman" was a nickname for the architect, known for his pervasive use of the Art Deco "Rule of Threes."*

bers, Larry Kreisman, urged the group to include Seattle's Art Deco buildings in its preservation studies and strategies. The group immediately nominated him to lead a task force to make an inventory of the buildings and research the history of each. The result was *Art Deco Seattle,* which was published by the group in 1979 with text by Kreisman and accompanying photos by Victor Gardaya. Allied Arts also staged an exhibition by the same name and hosted a series of walking tours to showcase the city's Art Deco. By drawing attention to the often opulent details to be found in Seattle's Art Deco buildings and by highlighting the elements unique to the Pacific Northwest region they hoped to motivate the public and gain further support.

these are favorite themes in the decoration of the buildings, in the carving and murals. This regional imagery is more noticeable here than in other cities.

Here is what can be found in Art Deco Seattle.

Northern Life Tower (Seattle Tower), 1928, by Joseph W. Wilson for Albertson, Wilson and Richardson is a twenty-seven-story tower with a reverse ziggurat stepped-back lobby ceiling. Three setbacks banding the top give this tower a square wedding-cake look. The brick becomes gradually lighter as it climbs the twenty-seven stories, reemphasizing the verticality of the window bandings. The lobbies suggest forests and mountains of the Northwest, with additional decorations combining Native American and Mayan design elements. Marble, bronze, and gold leaf are used throughout. Most unusual are the use of Chinese designs that are rarely found in Art Deco in the United States, and a lobby map showing trade routes important to Seattle's past and future development.

The 1929 Exchange Building, at 821 Second Avenue, is by John Graham, Sr. This is a twenty-three-story tower with symmetrical setbacks, a massive look with busy French-Deco flowers on the exterior. A dramatic black marble, gold-leafed chevron motif repeats in the main lobby ceiling.

The Coleman Building (Ranier Bank), 811 First Avenue, by Arthur Loveless, has exceptional bronze panels added during a 1930 renovation. Sculptor Dudley Pratt depicts local industries in eight panels. Among them is Seattle's signature aeronautical theme, the city's bond to machines that fly. The logging industry also is shown in the panels.

U.S. Marine Hospital (Public Health Service Hospital), 1131 Fourteenth Avenue South, by Charles Bebb, Carl Gould, and John Graham, Sr., has a campus similar to the one at San Francisco's V.A. Hospital, but this one is not in Zigzag style. It is smoother—what Vincent Scully has called "Jukebox-Deco." The main building is sixteen stories with flanking thirteen- and seven-story wings, all in Streamline style with rounded-corner windows on several buildings and square-corner windows on smaller outlying buildings. The central section of the main building has a strong vertical emphasis between two symmetrical side sections with contrasting horizontal alternating bands of brick and windows.

The 1932 Seattle Art Museum, also by Charles Bebb and Carl Gould, is a serene presence in Volunteer Park. The museum often has been overlooked due to its location off the beaten path in a park atop Capitol Hill. To increase the museum's visibility and to accommodate major new donations, the city recently commissioned Robert Venturi to design a large new modern facility in the heart of the city not far from the famous Pike Street Market. The new building has already attracted national attention. Meanwhile, the original Art Deco building is being renovated for display of the museum's large holdings of Asian art. It will reopen in 1993 and will be publicized not only for its unique collections but also for being a gem of Art Deco architecture.

Seattle has suffered some preservation losses: the J.C.

As Kreisman put it:

Seattle has often been credited with taking a lead in the preservation of its oldest extant districts. The continued rehabilitation and occupancy of its high-quality Art Deco buildings is another way in which Seattle respects its built heritage at the same time as it constructs a new skyline to meet its continuing growth.

Images from the mountains, forests, rivers, lakes of the Northwest, Native American designs, airplane manufacturing, logging, lumbering, construction, shipping, international trade, the beautiful Puget Sound and the great Pacific Ocean—

Penney store is gone, but its decorative elements were saved and warehoused by Allied Arts for future use. The Pacific National Bank was demolished for a full-block development.

Kreisman has served the past twelve years as a tour guide for the Seattle Architectural Foundation. These Seattle Architectural Tours are given in conjunction with the Seattle AIA, and include some of the Art Deco buildings mentioned here.

Elsewhere
Mount Hood, Oregon

Timberline Lodge, designed by Gilbert Stanley Underwood, has small traces of urban Art Deco and plenty of geometric craftsmanship in the ruggedly designed furniture. This lodge provides a great example of Rustic Deco, with original interiors and decorative details.

Fox Theater (2,251 seats), 1005 West Sprague Street at 1st Avenue & Monroe Street, Spokane. ARCHITECT: R.C. Reamer, 1930. The unusual terra-cotta butterfly relief includes flower details in the style of Edgar Brandt. The theater's lobby is one block wide, the same width as the auditorium. Floral murals, uncommon aluminum work, and etched glass decorate the interior.

Kala Kala Motor Ferry, Seattle-Bremerton, 1935. This original souvenir postcard bills the Kala Kala, a Nautical Deco treasure, as the world's first streamlined ferry. Holding 2,000 passengers, she first saw service as the Peralta in San Francisco Bay. When damaged by a 1933 fire, the ship was purchased and rebuilt by Puget Sound Navigation Company for service between Seattle and Bremerton, Washington.

121 MOTOR FERRY "KALAKALA", WORLD'S FIRST STREAMLINED VESSEL

IN SERVICE BETWEEN SEATTLE AND BREMERTON, WASH. ON PUGET SOUND   5A-H1519

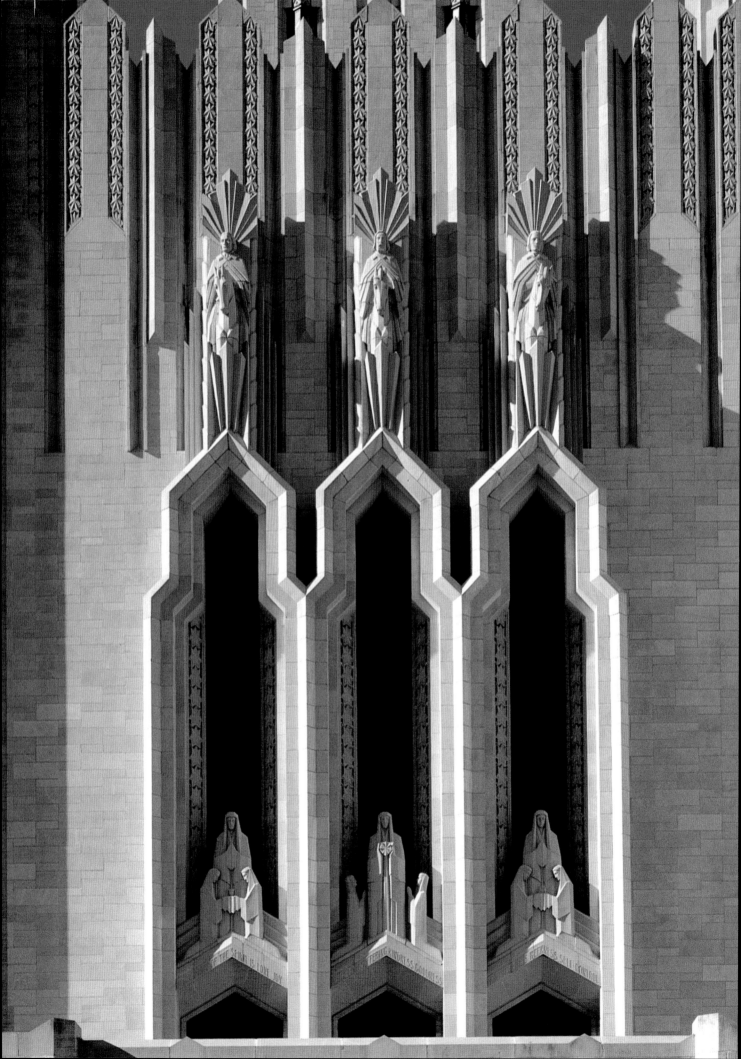

18

TULSA

THE CITY THAT OIL BUILT

Some of us were not so sure that we liked Art Deco architecture when we began work on this project, but we have all gained an appreciation and an affection for it and our understanding of it has enriched our understanding of the city.

—Susan Petersmeyer Henneke
Introduction to *Tulsa Art Deco,* 1980

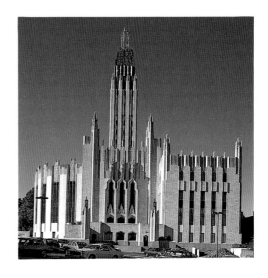

ART DECO AND MODERNE ARE *NOT* WORDS THAT spring to mind when thinking of Tulsa, Oklahoma. Flat, dry, brown, red, sandy, tumbleweeds, oil derricks, windmills—these are what come to mind. But as we found, most of these words do not accurately describe Tulsa. They do apply to other parts of the state, even Oklahoma City, but not to Tulsa, a city surrounded by man-made lakes and rolling green hills. No dust bowl or tumbleweeds blowing here.

The term Art Deco, however, can be used over and over to describe the more than twenty buildings that were built in the city's center during the oil boom of the late 1920s and early 1930s. Prior to that Tulsa was just a small town. In fact, just before the turn of the century, it was only a trading post with a few hundred people. Then came oil. Oil brought wealth and prosperity and created a reason to build a great city where none had stood before.

Oil money built the city, but the desire to match its symbols of wealth, class, and sophistication with cities possessing richer histories motivated the men with the money. They wanted to be *au courant*, as sophisticated as their counterparts in Chicago or New York.

The fresh modern style now called Art Deco was the means by which these tycoons could accomplish their goals.

Boston Avenue Methodist Episcopal Church (Boston Avenue Methodist), 1301 South Boston Avenue, Tulsa. ARCHITECT: Ada M. Robinson, with Bruce Goff for Rush, Endacott & Rush, 1929. This church, with its graceful and striking tower, which is 255 feet high, and pseudo-Gothic pinnacles, is sited on a wooded, slightly hilly lot with large parking areas behind. This view from the rear reveals the harmony and utility of the design. While not symmetrical, it is well-balanced with opposite wings—one rounded, the other angular—thus differentiating between its dual functions of worship and social fellowship.

Boston Avenue Methodist Episcopal Church (Boston Avenue Methodist), 1301 South Boston Avenue, Tulsa. ARCHITECT: Ada M. Robinson, with Bruce Goff for Rush, Endacott & Rush; Sculptor: Robert Garrison, 1929. This gleaming-white, Bedford-limestone entrance has Gothic-Deco triple portals, each topped by Garrison's terra-cotta Wesleyan circuit riders on horseback. Often cited as the best Art Deco church in the U.S.A., it received rave reviews from Sheldon Cheney in his influential 1930 work, The New World Architecture, who called it "Daringly new . . . fresh and vital."

Art Deco's stylized flowers, foliage, ziggurats, and chevrons were like hieroglyphs of the ancient Egyptians. The learned few could read these images on sight and the translation was: Wealth, Power, Savvy, Sophistication, Brains.

The end of World War II saw a new architectural language take hold around the country. Art Deco was out. In Tulsa, as elsewhere, the symbols of Art Deco soon became arcane. The buildings remained, but they were only aging places undeserving of a second glance. No one cared about them, or understood them. They were just buildings beginning to show their age badly.

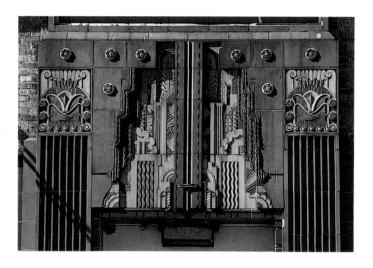

In 1977, this attitude changed. That was the year that the women in Tulsa's Junior League decided they were going to relearn this lost architectural language. They believed that the buildings had a story to tell and knew it would be an interesting one if only they could understand the language.

The city fathers propelled them into action when they pronounced there was no past worth preserving in Tulsa's downtown area. New construction was what was needed! Committees were formed and the detective work which would last several years began. The initial survey showed that the majority of the downtown buildings went up in the 1920s and 1930s. Someone noticed that the decorations on many of the buildings had similar elements. Someone eventually wondered if it might be "Art Deco"? Solving this mystery became the *raison d'être* for the women of the League. The rest is history.

Hours were spent combing libraries and city record rooms. Lists of architects, sculptors, artisans, and builders were compiled and calls were made to find family members who might shed light on the period. Experts in the building techniques of the day were consulted and architectural historian David Gebhard, the Dean of Deco, was pulled into the project by the unbridled enthusiasm of the large group of volunteers. The fruit of their labors was a book, *Tulsa Art Deco, An Architectural Era 1925–1942*, published in 1980.

Overnight, Tulsa achieved a prime place on the Art Deco map of the U.S.A. We in the budding Art Deco District in Miami Beach were in awe of the depth of their research. They not only documented fifty-five buildings, they analyzed the stages that Art Deco went through and categorized the buildings accordingly. And if that weren't enough, the book delved into the background, careers, and lives of the forty-eight architects who created the buildings, giving them the recognition they deserved.

Tulsa Art Deco has been out of print for many years. In order to keep interest alive, Christine Kallenberger, director of Tulsa's Philbrook Art Museum, and Robert Powers, of the Tulsa County Historical Society, jointly updated the materials and produced a self-guided map to the area, available from either organization. They say the greatest loss since the publication of the book was the Union Bus Depot, demolished by a Baptist church to gain a parking lot.

We were lucky enough to be guided on our tour by Christine and Robert. Their knowledge and understanding of both the architects and the buildings was invaluable. Highlights of their Art Deco Tulsa tour include the following.

Farmers' Market, 925 South Elgin Avenue, features the brightest colors and most interesting patterns in its glazed terra-cotta. The deep rich colors used here are similar to the palette used by Winold Reiss in his early 1915–1919 New

Farmers' Market (Warehouse Market), 925 South Elgin Avenue, Tulsa. ARCHITECT: B. Gaylord Noftsger, 1929. With the most colorful and lively terra-cotta designs in Art Deco Tulsa, this versatile little building has served as a grocery, liquor store, and nightclub. Its symbols of Oklahoma's rich economic and agricultural heritage, including this one of Mercury holding an oil derrick and a steam engine, convey the message of swift economic success through technology and machinery.

Farmers' Market (Warehouse Market), 925 South Elgin Avenue, Tulsa. ARCHITECT: B. Gaylord Noftsger, 1929. Above the brilliant blue-and-orange terra-cotta at the entrance is this gold, green, and fuchsia tablet containing a rich panoply of Paris Exposition motifs, both geometric and floral. The terra-cotta is attributed to Northwestern Terra Cotta Company of Chicago. A wonderful tower rises above this, giving the façade a final burst of spectacle. The building is currently vacant and has been approved by the city for destruction.

York projects. Other outstanding examples are the State Fair Pavilion, Seventeenth Street and New Haven Avenue, with its sculpted parapet borders and corners incorporating cows, bulls, sheep, and other livestock. Also outstanding are details in the hallways and auditorium of the well-maintained 1938 Will Rogers High School, 3903 East Fifth Place, designed by Arthur M. Atkinson, Leon B. Senter, and Joseph Koberling, Jr.

Many of Tulsa's buildings either were built by the petrochemical industry or have allusions to it in the decorative elements. The Philcade Building, 511 South Boston, is a major example. It was designed by Leon B. Senter for Waite Phillips of Phillips Petroleum and features a lavish arcade for those wishing to avoid the hot summer sun.

The relief panel on the Tulsa Fire Alarm Company at 1010 East Eighth Street is an example of decorative detailing serving as an advertising medium for the firm within. Anyone seeing the fire-breathing dragons would feel compelled to take advantage of the service offered by this firm.

Christ the King Church, 1539 South Rockford Avenue, and Boston Avenue Methodist Church, 1301 South Boston Avenue, are two of the best examples of Art Deco churches anywhere in the U.S.A. Much has been written about each, but the research done in the history of the Methodist religion by designer Ada Robinson adds so much to the design that the Boston Avenue church is in a class by itself.

Although the Alfonso Iannelli fountain that originally graced the entrance to the Riverside Studio, 1381 Riverside Drive, is no longer in place, it is easy to see why this is one of architect Bruce Goff's seminal works. Few buildings like this were being built anywhere in this country in 1929. Perhaps only Andrew Rebori in Chicago was as inventive.

Thanks to our guides, Christine and Robert, we were able to spend time in a private residence designed by Frank

Lloyd Wright. Westhope, now the home of Dwight and Sandra Holden, is much more personal in scale than either Fallingwater or Wingspread. Perhaps for that reason it states Art Deco more emphatically. The scale allows the symmetry to be observed at close range. Especially memorable are the reverse-ziggurat glass atriums turned on end, sideways, running floor to ceiling. Designed as aviaries or greenhouses, they have copper-lined planters (with water pipes) along the baseboards. These glass constructions are the sunniest and most interesting spots in the home, which originally was built

for Wright's cousin, Richard Lloyd Jones, founder of the *Tulsa Tribune.*

Barbara Capitman had traveled to Tulsa several times and was even declared an honorary citizen when the Union Station's adaptive reuse was commemorated in 1984. She always spoke admiringly of the city, calling it one of the Art Deco capitals.

Elsewhere
Oklahoma City, Oklahoma

The state of Oklahoma has more treasures in its capital city. On our tour, we took a detour to see Oklahoma City's 1936 Civic Center and a few other gems. The sixteen-story Municipal Building, 200 North Walker Street, faces the Civic Center Music Hall across a plaza. Both were built in 1936 and are Stripped Classic with Art Deco grilles, light fixtures, and carving in the limestone. An inscription reads "Dedicated to the People for the Perpetuation of Good Government."

Then, spotting a thirty- or forty-story skyscraper, we diverted further into the city's heart to discover the First National Bank (now First Interstate Bank) at Park and Robinson Streets, with a magnificent lobby that could easily be at home in New York City.

Appropriately, just as we were departing, we got a taste, both literally and figuratively, of what it was like to be in Oklahoma in those legendary times chronicled by John Steinbeck and others in the fiction of the Art Deco era: We got a firsthand taste of an Oklahoma dust storm!

Tulsa Union Depot, 3 South Boston Avenue; New entrance: 111 East 1st Street, Tulsa. ARCHITECT: R.C. Stephens, 1931. This medium-size railway depot on the edge of downtown is a Stripped Classic beauty, with Native American and other regional motifs carved into the Indiana limestone façade. Saved and "re-created," with some original interior fixtures sadly removed, it continues as an office complex. Barbara Capitman was made an honorary Tulsan at its reopening in May 1983.

19

WASHINGTON, D.C.

OUR NATION'S CAPITAL

I pledge you, I pledge myself, to a New Deal
for the American People.

—Franklin Delano Roosevelt
Democratic Party Convention Acceptance Speech
July, 1932

IF ALL ROADS LEAD TO ROME IN ITALY, THEN HERE
in the U.S.A. all roads lead to Washington, D.C. This is the
American city that looks most European, where the Art
Deco is most classical, and the city is criss-crossed by WPA-
era parkways and mile after mile of elegant Art Deco apartment buildings. The beautiful Art Deco parkways were
created in 1929 by the Rock Creek & Potomac Parkway
Commission, which enlisted the aid of landscape designer
Frederick Law Olmstead, Jr.

This also is a city of outstanding Art Deco sculpture and
monuments. James M. Goode's book, *The Outdoor Sculpture
of Washington, D.C.*, reports on many of these. A 1933 sculptural panel entitled *Heating Plant Machinery*, by the amazingly
versatile Paul Philippe Cret, may be found at the Central
Heating and Refrigeration Plant, Thirteenth Street between
C and B Streets, S.W. One of the few monuments to
African-Americans in Washington is the 1934 PWAP commission by Maurice Glickman entitled *Negro Mother and Child*
in the inner courtyard of the Department of the Interior, at
C Street between Eighteenth and Nineteenth Streets, N.W.
There are even Delayed Deco sculptures and monuments,
such as the 1951 equestrian sculpture *The Arts of War*, by
Leo Friedlander, at the entrance to Arlington Memorial
Bridge. Many more sculptures can be found in the suburbs,
such as a 1928 memorial by Carl Milles in the National
Memorial Park, Falls Church, Virginia, entitled *Sunsinger*.

After Franklin Delano Roosevelt became president in
1933, the new government programs began hatching like

Hecht Company Warehouse, 1401 *New York Avenue,*
N.E., Washington, D.C. ARCHITECT: *Gilbert V. Steele for*
Abbott, Merkt & Company, 1937. The New York engi-
neering firm that designed this large department-store
warehouse won the Pittsburgh Glass Institute award of
1937, and it remains the preeminent glass-block edifice
in the U.S.A. Due to the 1991 efforts of the Art Deco
Society of Washington, the new owner, the May
Company, was persuaded to restore this gem. The
restoration was complicated by the fact that the original
glass blocks were no longer manufactured. However,
they commissioned Pittsburgh Corning Glass to re-create
matching replacements.

baby ducks. WPA, PWA, PWAP, TVA, and NRA—these agencies suddenly were responsible for thousands of projects. Their influence touched the most remote parts of the land. By the thousands, these relief agencies built airports, firehouses, post offices, armories, bridges, dams, auditoriums, high schools . . . the list is very lengthy. All this construction employed hundreds of thousands of mostly out-of-work laborers and artisans. And most of these projects were Art Deco in style. The surge in construction easily may be seen in our statistics. In 1932, President Hoover's last year in office, the construction cycle had plummeted. Construction hit a desperate low in 1934. But by 1936 there was a resur-

gence that surpassed even the boom years of 1929 and 1930. Clearly this helped lift the country out of the Great Depression. And for Art Deco lovers, the New Deal was a Great Deal.

New Deal programs generally were supervised by the Treasury Department's James A. Wetmore and Louis A. Simon. One or the other was supervising architect for thousands of projects, and they got their names on so many plaques in so many WPA lobbies across America that any observer would assume they were the busiest architects alive in their time.

In Washington there are hundreds of privately built Art Deco apartments as well. At the top of the list is the 1931 Kennedy Warren, 3133 Connecticut Avenue, N.W., designed by Joseph Younger. It has huge lobbies, its original ballroom, and holds a commanding place in Washington's Art Deco hierarchy. Outside the District of Columbia, in Maryland and Virginia, there are thousands of garden apartments in Art Deco–era suburbs, which were always much in demand for housing the well-paid federal bureaucrats. As in Miami Beach and the Bronx, here a handful of architects specialized in these buildings and created many of the largest and grandest of them: George T. Santmyers (19 buildings), Alvin Aubinoe (10), and Mihran Mesrobian (4).

In Washington a monument was built to the supreme English dramatist, William Shakespeare. It was funded by the Folger family, and, of course, is called the Folger Shakespeare Library, 201 East Capitol Street, S.E. Designed in 1929, it is a splendid example of Paul Philippe Cret's beloved "Modern Classic" style, combining the best of Moderne influence with the essentials of classic Greek and Roman temples. Barbara Capitman had a well-rehearsed lecture on the importance of Greek and Roman buildings to the Art Deco style that many Modernists found ludicrous. Yet, when one examines some Art Deco master-

Greyhound Bus Terminal and Tower, 1100 New York Avenue, N.W., Washington, D.C. ARCHITECT: W.S. Arrasmith for Wischmeyer, Arrasmith & Elswick, 1939. Restoration architect: Hyman Myers for Vitetta Group/Studio Four; New tower architect: Keyes Condon Florance Eichbaum Esocoff King; New building developer: Manulife Real Estate, Toronto, Canada, 1991. A Louisville architectural firm was responsible for this streamlined treasure and seventeen other Greyhound stations built nationwide. The Art Deco Society of Washington fought a successful battle to save this building in its entirety, preventing an undesirable "façadectomy." Eventually, the terminal was left intact as a grand lobby for a compatible, but much larger, stepped-back tower that opened in 1991. (Rendering courtesy Keyes Condon Florance Eichbaum Esocoff King Architects)

Federal Trade Commission, 600 Constitution Avenue, N.W., Washington, D.C. ARCHITECT: Bennett, Parsons & Frost; Supervising architect: Louis A. Simon; Sculptor: William McVey, 1937. Critical to the flow of international trade, and symbolic of the mission of the FTC, was this streamlined oceanliner. This aluminum panel is one of six decorating each of the four original entrances to the building. The panels illustrate the history of commercial shipping from Columbus's fleet, to clippers, to the great liners. This was the first exterior project in Washington, D.C., of the Federal Section of Painting and Sculpture, a lesser-known agency that commissioned art for federal buildings.

pieces all over the U.S.A., it is soon obvious that she was right again. The elements of classicism are readily apparent in many of the handsomest Art Deco buildings.

The Folger Shakespeare Library, one of the few buildings Cret designed himself, and not just as a consultant, features sculpture by John Gregory depicting scenes from many of the Bard's plays. There is also a fountain with a statue by Brenda Putnam of the eternal prankster, Puck, from *A Midsummer Night's Dream*. Cret, a great teacher, scholar, and architect, had a profound influence throughout the country. He acted as an intermediary between the recidivist classicists who would have had all Washington looking like the Acropolis, and the harsh modernists, who would have had it looking like Brasilia. Cret's "Modern Classic" style, which we call Stripped Classic, is a carefully measured mix of Bauhaus, Greek, and Roman. In 1969, Cret's Folger Shakespeare Library became the first Art Deco building listed in the National Register of Historic Places. His tremendous contribution to architecture was recognized in 1938 when he was awarded the prestigious Gold Medal of the American Institute of Architects (AIA). He was among an elite few. The other AIA Gold Medalist architects who created Art Deco landmarks in the U.S.A. include Bertram Goodhue (1925), Milton Medary (1929), Eliel Saarinen (1947), Frank Lloyd Wright (1949), William Delano (1953), Louis Skidmore (1957), Ralph Walker (1957: AIA Centennial Medal of Honor), and John Wellborn Root (1958).

Many Modernist architects in other parts of the country jumped at commissions in Washington, if only for the prestige. But they often found themselves slipping into an unexpected classic idiom, so overwhelming was the city's historical persona. Cret showed the way so these architects could provide compatible and suitable governmental offices that had porticoes, pilasters, and architraves, and yet still could be called Modern.

Among the many notable out-of-town firms doing work in Washington were Abbot, Merkt & Company and John Eberson (New York), John Zink (Baltimore), Paul Philippe

Cret and the firm Zantzinger, Borie & Medary (Philadelphia). Here too, Voorhees, Gmelin & Walker, favorite architectural firm of the New York Telephone Company, won a commission from Chesapeake & Potomac Telephone in 1928 to do the first major Art Deco building in town.

Professor Richard Striner was co-author of an early, significant book detailing the capital city's rich Art Deco legacy, with Hans Wirz. Published in 1984 by the Smithsonian Institution, *Washington Deco* surveyed over 400 buildings. It has been out of print for years, but a revised edition is in the works.

Many of the best landmarks in Washington have been saved, thanks to the tireless and unrelenting efforts of Striner and his Art Deco Society of Washington (ADSW). Their most celebrated victory to date was saving the 1939 W. S. Arrasmith Greyhound Bus Terminal at 1100 New York Avenue, N.W. After a battle lasting from 1983 until 1988, it was decided to use the original Streamline bus building to serve as a front entrance and grand lobby for a compatible two-step high rise behind it. The entire 1991 Streamline project therefore rises in three graceful setbacks, neatly fol-

Greenbelt Center School and Civic Center (Greenbelt Elementary School), 15 Crescent Road, Greenbelt, Maryland. ARCHITECT: *Douglas Ellington & Reginald D. Wadsworth; Sculptor: Lenore Thomas, 1936. The Greenbelt school building is still standing—thanks to Richard Striner, who twice led the Art Deco Society of Washington (ADSW) to preservation victories here in 1983 and 1990. Built as part of an experiment in suburban planning, the building includes Federal Art Project sculptures illustrating themes from the U.S. Constitution. A Stripped Classic work of startling modernity, it sits on a beautiful campus. Parents wanted a newer, "modern" school, but ADSW convinced them the building was a masterpiece and could be updated to provide continuing utility and enjoyment for the community. (Photograph by Herbert Striner)*

lowing Art Deco's "Rule of Threes." This project received national recognition when completed, and was cited by the National Trust for Historic Preservation (NTHP), *Newsweek*, and other publications when it reopened in October 1991.

The Washington group also has labored mightily to save the original 1936 Greenbelt School & Civic Center project, now known simply as Greenbelt Elementary School. Philadelphia architect and publisher Max Levinson's indispensable design magazine, *Shelter*, reported in 1938 that Greenbelt was the first of three experimental suburban modern communities. The project was initiated by Roosevelt's Resettlement Administration and completed by the Farm Security Administration. The project had three goals: 1) to provide useful employment, 2) to demonstrate a new type of community, and 3) to demonstrate a better utilization of land in suburban areas. By 1960 most schools were built along these lines, but they generally used cheaper materials and omitted the great artwork. School architecture never again quite had the style and beauty after this era. The other two schools in this project were: Greenhills, Ohio, near Cincinnati, done in a Colonial theme, and Greendale, Wisconsin.

By 1983, Greenbelt residents wanted only a new school, but Striner and his associates convinced the town to keep the old Art Deco school and update it sensitively. Reportedly, it is once again the architectural centerpiece of the community. One of the Greenbelt School's architects, Douglas Ellington, also designed two very early Art Deco buildings of note in Asheville, North Carolina: the City Building and the Baptist Church.

Among Washington's other Art Deco treasures are some prime examples of Stripped Classic, such as the 1935 Library of Congress Annex by Pierson & Wilson, Second Street at Independence Avenue, S.E. It features sculpture by Lee Lawrie. Another prime example of this style is Bennett, Parsons & Frost's 1937 Federal Trade Commission, with sculpture by William McVey, among others.

The foremost example of the use of glass block in the country is probably Abbot, Merkt & Company's 1937 Hecht Company warehouse at 1401 New York Avenue, N.E. This too was saved from demolition through the work of the Art Deco Society of Washington.

One not-so-rosy ADSW project has been the bitter campaign to save the Silver Spring Shopping Center and Silver Theater by John Eberson. Washington, D.C., was the site of several early streamlined shopping centers; most are now gone. The ADSW continues to try to convince the Silver Spring developer to incorporate the original buildings into a massive new project. So far the pleas have fallen on deaf ears, but the site is not yet cleared, so there is hope.

The Art Deco Society of Washington was founded in 1982 in Annie Groer's living room. Richard Striner was a founding member, and Barbara Capitman and Leonard Horowitz were present. After serving long and well, Striner stepped aside and the current ADSW president is Lauren Adkins, a staff member at the NTHP. The society sponsors a lavish ball every fall, often in the Kennedy Warren Apartment Building. There are lectures, films, an Art Deco Expo each summer, and the society publishes a fine quarterly

Kennedy Warren Apartments, 3133 Connecticut Avenue, N.W., Washington, D.C. ARCHITECT: Joseph Younger, 1931. Highly stylized federal eagles, carved in the limestone exterior, perch atop the two windows flanking the entrance. The District of Columbia has abundant Art Deco apartment buildings, and this one is at the top of the list, with its ballroom and period restaurant off the lobby. It has been the site of several gala events for the Art Deco Society of Washington.

Library of Congress Annex, 2nd Street at Independence Avenue, S.E., Washington, D.C. ARCHITECT: Pierson & Wilson; Sculptor: Lee Lawrie, 1935. Massive metal entrance doors incorporate Lawrie's exotic panels with figures from world civilizations. Illustrated here is an Assyrian priest performing an ancient rite. The annex opened in 1939 after a long construction period. The metalwork is by Flour City Ornamental Iron of Minneapolis.

newsletter, *Trans-Lux*, named to commemorate their worst demolition loss, the beautiful 1936 Thomas Lamb Trans-Lux Theater. The Washington area has lost several other splendid Moderne movie theaters, including the Senator and Apex (both by John Zink), and the Penn Theater by John Eberson.

Members of this society probably have fought the most battles, have spent the most time testifying before commissions and panels, and have saved more buildings than any other Art Deco Society except the Miami Design Preservation League.

Elsewhere
Baltimore, Maryland

There is a Baltimore Art Deco Society, presided over by interior designer Sheryl Cucchiella. Sheryl specializes in Art Deco, and began researching Baltimore Art Deco in 1982 to fulfill degree requirements in Interior Design from the Maryland Institute. Through assistance from the National Endowment for the Arts, she was able to publish her work as *Baltimore Deco* in 1984. Though she worked very hard from 1982 to 1988 to establish and run the Baltimore Art Deco Society, she never found an enthusiastic public response in this historic old port city. They have had several meetings and conducted walking and bus tours. Donna Beth Shapiro is now president, but no activities are scheduled.

Richmond, Virginia

The most notable Art Deco building in Richmond is a high-rise downtown bank building designed in 1929 by John Eberson, who is much better known for designing theaters. In fact, he seems to have gotten this commission right after his successful atmospheric-style Italianate Loew's Theater here. At this point, however, Eberson, perhaps urged by his son and partner Drew, began switching over his firm's output to Art Deco projects.

Also of note in Richmond is the second surviving 1939 New York World's Fair building (the first is now the Queens Museum on the fairground). The nomadic building has an odd history indeed: The Belgian Pavilion was designed by Victor Bourgeois and Leo Stijen under supervision of famed architect Henry van der Velde. At the fair's close in 1940 the pavilion was disassembled and prepared for shipment to

Belgium, but the outbreak of World War II interfered with these plans, so the Belgian government gave the building to the Virginia Union University in Richmond, where it stands today. Barbara visited it and always mentioned it when speaking of Richmond.

Penland, North Carolina

Barbara Capitman also visited a special project in North Carolina to house the poor while providing work in the home. She went there to speak to the project administrator, who happened to be the father of her daughter-in-law, Valerie Batts. This project encouraged cottage industry to provide jobs for the low-income residents. They could remain home, tend to their households, and work in industries like sewing, needlepoint, and similar crafts. Upon her return to Miami Beach, Barbara tried for several years, along with her friend Edith Irma Siegel, to launch similar crafts projects for the poor elderly population of the Art Deco District. To her regret, the "Teachery," as she called it, never took off. She was no doubt hindered by the ongoing gentrification in the Historic District. (In 1992, there were almost no elderly left in the Miami Beach District.)

Folger Shakespeare Library, 201 East Capitol Street, S.E., Washington, D.C. ARCHITECT: Paul Philippe Cret; Sculptor: Brenda Putnam, 1929. The architecture of scores of buildings was influenced by Paul Philippe Cret, the dean of Stripped Classic design. Finally, here is a building he designed himself: the library and performance center dedicated to the works of Shakespeare that opened in 1932. The building also features reliefs by John Gregory illustrating nine of Shakespeare's plays. The marble fountain features Puck from A Midsummer Night's Dream, exclaiming "Lord, What Fools These Mortals Be!"

GLOSSARY

adobe: sun-dried brick, often plastered over with mud and whitewashed. Often used in 1920s, especially California, for Spanish Pueblo Deco works

bas relief: from the French: low relief. Sculpted figures that do not stand far out from the surface. Shallow three-dimensional decorative images applied as architectural decorative ornament.

bay: vertical division on building exterior, marked by windows, columns, pilasters, finials, other horizontal elements.

capital: decorative top of a column, most common in Greek and Roman architecture, where columns had a structural role. Most Stripped Classic Art Deco buildings use columns and pilasters freely taken from Greek sources.

casement window: freely opening (in or out) windows with a horizontal axis, commonly used in Art Deco structures in the 1920s and 1930s.

chevron: molding which contains zigzag patterns, with strong angular repeated motif, sometimes modified into arrowhead patterns in Pueblo Deco. Present in almost all early Art Deco buildings.

coffer: ceiling decoration involving recessed, repeated patterns set off by special colors or decoration, usually extending upward beyond the ceiling plane.

cornice: projecting molding on top of wall or arch.

façade: front or exterior of a building, sometimes only the front.

FAP: Federal Art Project (1935–1943), successor to the PWAP, administered under discrete state agencies of the WPA to employ artists. Generally referred to as the WPA/FAP, it was responsible for art in federal buildings. The so-called WPA Art is noted for "social realism" and cubist influences. One of many New Deal programs begun under President Franklin Delano Roosevelt, it employed over 5,000 artists at its peak, and commissioned hundreds of thousands of works, not including 2 million posters produced for the government. When World War II began this program merged into the War Services Division and continued in a propaganda role. This program paid for $35 million worth of artwork, much of which still exists in public buildings.

FERA: Federal Emergency Relief Agency (1933–1935), earliest of the job-creating agencies set up as part of President Franklin Delano Roosevelt's New Deal.

loggia: a breezeway or outside passageway with an overhead trellis supported by a colonnade.

mosaic: surface decoration, floors, steps or ceiling arches, faced in small colored ceramic or glass tiles forming a discernible pattern, design, or even picture.

parapet: low upward-extending wall along top of a roof.

pediment: triangular upright front end of a pitched roof, often decorated with bas relief or frieze. Usually found in Art Deco Stripped Classic (classic Roman-inspired Art Deco).

pilaster: flat vertical decoration applied to a wall to suggest a classic column. Projects slightly from surface of exterior wall, built to resemble a real structural column. Often done in marble or plaster, with standard capitals at top. Breaks a wall into distinct bays.

PWA: Public Works Administration (1933–1935) of the U.S. government, begun under presidency of Franklin Delano Roosevelt. This program built roads, bridges, post offices and other buildings. In its buildings it used art created by the PWAP and later the WPA/FAP, predecessor to the WPA.

PWAP: Public Works of Art Project (1933–1934), initial pilot project begun by the U.S. government to employ artists as part of the New Deal under presidency of Franklin Delano Roosevelt.

the "section": Section of Painting and Sculpture, later called Section of Fine Arts (1934–1943), established to commission murals and sculpture for U.S. government buildings. This was not a relief program, and was intended to glorify federal buildings with the best available art. Artists were selected via juried competition.

spandrel: any panel, usually decorated in some fashion, joining two parts of a façade, such as the decorative panels between windows, or between two piers on a bridge pylon or over a door.

TVA: Tennessee Valley Authority (1933–present), builder of hundreds of dams and support buildings in the Tennessee River Valley and elsewhere in the Midwest. Only Roosevelt New Deal program to survive to present day, largely because it was self-sustaining from hydroelectric power generation revenue.

WPA: Works Progress Administration (1935–1943) of the U.S. government, begun under presidency of Franklin Delano Roosevelt. The program was the successor to the PWA and included four specific arts divisions: art, music, theater, and writers. It used federal tax funds administered at the state level, and was redefined continually by various acts of Congress. In 1939 renamed the Works *Projects* Administration. Best-known of all the New Deal initial-ID programs.

BIBLIOGRAPHY

BOOKS

Allen, Geoffrey Freeman. *Luxury Trains of the World.* New York: Everest House, 1979.

Allied Arts of Seattle, introduction by Robert Venturi. *Impressions of Imagination: Terra-Cotta Seattle.* Seattle: Allied Arts of Seattle, 1986.

Anger, Kenneth. *Hollywood Babylon II.* New York: E. P. Dutton, 1984.

Arceneaux, Marc. *Streamline, Art and Design of the Forties.* San Francisco: Troubador Press, 1975.

Arend, Geoffrey. *Great Airports: Miami, A Picture History.* New York: Air Cargo News, 1986.

Baigell, Matthew. *Thomas Hart Benton.* New York: Harry N. Abrams, 1975.

Balfour, Alan. *Rockefeller Center, Architecture as Theatre.* New York: McGraw-Hill, 1978.

Ball, Rick A., et al. *Indianapolis Architecture.* Indiana Architectural Foundation. Indianapolis: Hilltop Press, 1975.

Banham, Reyner. *Buffalo Architecture: A Guide.* Cambridge: MIT Press, 1981.

Bartlett, John. *Bartlett's Familiar Quotations* (14th ed.). Boston: Little, Brown, 1968.

Battersby, Martin. *The Decorative Thirties.* New York: Collier Books Division, Macmillan, 1969.

Battersby, Martin. *The Decorative Twenties.* New York: Collier Books Division, Macmillan, 1969.

Bayer, Patricia. *Art Deco Interiors, Decoration and Design Classics of the 1920s and 1930s.* Boston: Bulfinch Press Division, Little, Brown, 1990.

Bayley, Stephen, editor. *The Conran Directory of Design.* The Conran Foundation. New York: Villard Books Division, Random House, 1985.

Beardsley, Charles. *Hollywood's Master Showman, The Legendary Sid Grauman.* New York: Cornwall Books, 1983.

Bel Geddes, Norman. *Horizons.* New York: Little, Brown, 1932. New edition, New York: Dover, 1977.

Bishir, Catherine W., photography by Tim Buchman. *North Carolina Architecture.* Published for the Historic Preservation Foundation of North Carolina. Chapel Hill: University of North Carolina Press, 1990.

Bradley, Bill. *The Last of the Great Stations, 50 Years of the Los Angeles Union Passenger Terminal, Interurbans Special 72* (rev. ed.). Glendale, Calif.: Interurban Press, 1989.

Breeze, Carla. *Pueblo Deco.* New York: Rizzoli International, 1990.

Breeze, Carla. *L.A. Deco.* New York: Rizzoli International, 1991.

Brunhammer, Yvonne. *1925.* Paris: Les Presses de la Connaissance, 1976.

Brunhammer, Yvonne. *Le Style 1925.* Paris: Baschet, undated, c. 1977.

Bush, Donald J. *The Streamlined Decade.* New York: George Braziller, 1975.

Capitman, Barbara, with photographs by Steven Brooke. *Deco Delights.* New York: E.P. Dutton, 1988.

Cerwinske, Laura. *Tropical Deco, The Architecture and Design of Old Miami Beach.* New York: Rizzoli, 1981.

Cheney, Sheldon. *The New World Architecture.* New York: Longmans, Green, 1930.

Cheney, Sheldon and Martha Cheney. *Art and the Machine.* New York: Whittlesey House Division, McGraw-Hill, 1936.

Christ-Janer, Albert. *Eliel Saarinen.* Chicago: University of Chicago Press, 1948.

Cohen, Judith Singer, foreword by David Gebhard. *Cowtown Moderne, Art Deco Architecture of Fort Worth, Texas.* College Station: Texas A & M University Press, with Fort Worth chapter, American Institute of Architects, 1988.

Cole, Doris. *From Tipi to Skyscraper, A history of Women in Architecture.* Boston: Little i Press, 1973.

Cole, Doris. *Eleanor Raymond, Architect.* Philadelphia: Art Alliance Press, 1981.

Cucchiella, Sharon. *Baltimore Deco, An Architectural Survey of Art Deco in Baltimore.* Baltimore: Maclay & Associates, 1984.

Danziger, James. *Beaton.* First published by Viking Books, 1980. New York: Henry Holt, 1986.

Davis, Ben, and Helen Davis. *Atlanta's Urban Trails, Vol. 1. City Tours.* Atlanta: Susan Hunter, 1988.

Delehanty, Randolph, drawings by William Walters, with views by John Tomlinson. *The Ultimate Guide to San Francisco.* San Francisco: Chronicle Books, 1989.

Dorsey, Robert W. *Architecture and Construction in Cincinnati, A Guide to Buildings, Designers and Builders*. Cincinnati: Architectural Foundation of Cincinnati, 1987.

Duncan, Alastair, architectural photography by Randy Juster. *American Art Deco*. Renwick Museum, Smithsonian Institution. New York: Harry N. Abrams, 1986.

Duncan, Alastair. *Art Deco*. New York: Thames & Hudson, 1988.

Dunster, David. *Key Buildings of the 20th Century, Houses 1900–1944*. New York: Rizzoli, 1985.

Ehrlich, George. *Kansas City, Missouri, An Architectural History 1826–1976*. Kansas City, Mo.: Historic Kansas City Foundation with Lowell Press, 1979.

Etter, Don D. *Denver Going Modern*. Denver: Graphic Impressions, 1977.

Federal Writers' Project, Works Progress Administration. *The WPA Guide to Florida*, 1939. Republished as *Florida, A Guide to the Southernmost State*. New York: Oxford University Press, 1946.

Federal Writers' Project, Works Progress Administration, introduction by Frederick Manfred. *The WPA Guide to Minnesota*. Saint. Paul: Minnesota Historical Society Press, 1985.

Ferris, Hugh. *The Metropolis of Tomorrow*. New York: Ives Washburn, 1929.

Ferris, Hugh. *Power in Buildings, An Artist's View of Contemporary Architecture*. New York: Columbia University Press, 1953.

Ferry, W. Hawkins. *The Buildings of Detroit, A History* (rev. ed.). Detroit: Wayne State University Press, 1980.

Ford, James, and Katherine M. Ford. *Classic Modern Homes of the Thirties*. Original publisher, New York: Architectural Book Publishing, 1940. Reprint, New York: Dover, 1989.

Francisco, Charles. *The Radio City Music Hall, An Affectionate History of the World's Greatest Theater*. New York: E. P. Dutton, 1979.

Frankl, Paul T. *New Dimensions, The Decorative Arts of Today in Words and Pictures*. New York: Payson & Clarke, 1928.

Frankl, Paul T. *Form and Re-Form, A Practical Handbook of Modern Interiors*. New York: Harper, 1930.

Garber, Randy, editor. *Built in Milwaukee*. City Development Department, Milwaukee, with the State Historical Society of Wisconsin, Historic Preservation Division. Madison: University of Wisconsin Press, 1983.

Gebhard, David, and Robert Winter. *Architecture in Los Angeles, A Compleat Guide*. Salt Lake City: Peregrine Smith, 1985.

Gebhard, David, Robert Winter, et al. *The Guide to Architecture in San Francisco and Northern California*. Salt Lake City: Peregrine Smith, 1985.

Gebhard, David, and Harriette Von Breton. *L.A. in the Thirties 1931–1941*. Salt Lake City: Peregrine Smith, 1975.

Giglierano, Geoffrey J., and Deborah A. Overmyer. *The Bicentennial Guide to Greater Cincinnatti: A Portrait of Two Hundred Years*, Vols. 1 and 2. Cincinnati: Cincinnati Historical Society, 1988.

Gill, Brendan, edited by Robert Kimball. *Cole, A Biographical Essay*. Complete lyrics of all published Cole Porter songs, by special arrangement with Cole Porter Musical and Literary Property Trust. Includes copyrighted Cole Porter biography from *New Yorker Magazine*, 1971. New York: Holt, Rinehart & Winston, 1971.

Goldberger, Paul, photography by David W. Dunlap. *The City Observed: New York, A Guide to the Architecture of Manhattan*. New York: Vintage Books Division, Random House, 1979.

Goldberger, Paul. *The Skyscraper, The City Observed*. New York: Borzoi Book Division, Knopf, 1981.

Goode, James M. *The Outdoor Sculpture of Washington, D.C., A Comprehensive Historical Guide*. Washington, D.C.: Smithsonian Institution Press, 1974.

Greif, Martin. *Depression Modern, The Thirties Style in America*. New York: Universe Books, 1975.

Greif, Martin. *The Airport Book, From Landing Field to Modern Terminal*. New York: Main Street Press, with Mayflower Books, 1979.

Griffin, Rachel, and Sarah Munro, editors. *Timberline Lodge*. Portland, Ore.: Friends of Timberline, 1979.

Gutman, Richard J. S., and Elliott Kaufman, in collaboration with David Slovic. *American Diner*. New York: Harper & Row, 1979.

Hall, Ben M. *The Best Remaining Seats, The Golden Age of the Movie Palace*. New York: Bramhall House Division, Clarkson N. Potter, 1961.

Halpern, John. *New York/New York, An Architectural Portfolio*. New York: E. P. Dutton, 1978.

Hanks, David. *The Decorative Designs of Frank Lloyd Wright*. New York: E. P. Dutton, 1979.

Hanks, David. *Donald Deskey*. New York: E. P. Dutton, 1987.

Hansen, Oskar J. W. F., III. *Beyond The Cherubim*. New York: Vantage Press, 1964.

Harris, Cyril M. *Dictionary of Architecture and Construction*. New York: McGraw-Hill, 1975.

Haslam, Malcolm. *Art Deco, Collector's Style Guide*. New York: Ballantine Books, 1987.

Hatton, Hap. *Tropical Splendor, An Architectural History of Florida*. New York: Knopf, 1987.

Heide, Robert, and John Gilman. *Dime-Store Dream Parade, Popular Culture 1925–1955*. New York: E. P. Dutton, 1979.

Heskett, John. *Industrial Design*. London: Thames & Hudson, 1980.

Hillier, Bevis. *Art Deco of the 20s and 30s*. First published, London: Herbert Press, 1968. New York: Schocken Books, 1985.

Hirshorn, Paul, and Steven Izenour. *White Towers*. Cambridge: MIT Press, 1979.

Hitchcock, Henry-Russell, and William Seale. *Temples of Democracy, The State Capitols of the U.S.A.* New York: Harcourt Brace Jovanovich, 1976.

Horsham, Michael. *'20s & '30s Style*. Secaucus, N.J.: Chartwell Books, 1989.

Huxtable, Ada Louise. *Goodbye History, Hello Hamburger, An Anthology of Architectural Delights and Disasters*. Washington, D.C.: Preservation Press, 1986.

Ingle, Marjorie. *Mayan Revival Style, Art Deco Mayan Fantasy*. Salt Lake City: Peregrine Smith, 1984.

Jacoby, Stephen M. *Architectural Sculpture in New York City*. New York: Dover, 1975.

Jennings, Jan, editor. *Roadside America, The Automobile in Design and Culture*. Ames: Iowa State University Press, 1990.

Jervis, Simon. *The Facts on File Dictionary of Design and Designers*. New York: Facts on File, 1984.

Jewett, Masha Zakheim, color photography by Don Beatty. *Coit Tower, San Francisco, Its History and Art*, San Francisco: Volcano Press, 1983.

Johnson, Carol Newton, introduction by David Gebhard, photography by David Halpern. *Tulsa Art Deco: An Architectural Era, 1925–1941.* Tulsa: Junior League, 1980.

Jolly, Ellen Roy, and James Calhoun. *The Louisiana Capitol.* Gretna, La.: Pelican, 1980.

Jordey, William H. *The Impact of European Modernism in the Mid-Twentieth Century, American Buildings and Their Architects,* Vol. 5. New York: Doubleday, 1972; Oxford University Press, 1986.

Kahn, Ely Jacques. *Contemporary American Architects: Ely Jacques Kahn.* New York: Whittlesey House Division, McGraw-Hill, 1931.

Kaplan, Sam Hall, principal photography by Julius Shulman. *L.A. Lost and Found, An Architectural History of Los Angeles.* New York: Crown, 1987.

Kilham, Walter H., Jr. *Raymond Hood, Architect, Form Through Function in the American Skyscraper.* New York: Architectural Book Publishing, 1973.

Klein, Dan, photography by Angelo Hornak. *All Color Book of Art Deco.* London: Octopus Books, 1974. Reprinted, New York: Crescent Books Division, Crown, 1974.

Klein, Dan, Nancy A. McClelland and Malcolm Haslam. *In the Deco Style.* New York: Rizzoli, 1986.

Krinsky, Carol Herselle. *Rockefeller Center.* New York: Oxford University Press, 1978.

Kubly, Vincent F., foreword by Solis Seiferth (capitol architect). *The Louisiana Capitol, Its Art and Architecture.* Gretna, La.: Pelican, 1977.

Kurtz, Gary F. *Architectural Terra Cotta of Gladding, McBean.* Sausalito, Calif.: Windgate Press, undated.

Lebovich, William L. *America's City Halls, Historic American Buildings Survey.* Washington, D.C.: Preservation Press, 1984.

Le Corbusier. *Towards a New Architecture.* New York: Payson & Clark, 1930.

Lesieutre, Alain. *The Spirit and Splendor of Art Deco.* New York: Paddington Press, 1974.

Loewy, Raymond. *Industrial Design.* Woodstock, N.Y.: Overlook Press, 1979.

Lowe, David. *Lost Chicago.* Boston: Houghton Mifflin, 1978.

Lucie-Smith, Edward. *Cultural Calendar of the 20th Century.* New York: E. P. Dutton, 1979.

Lyndon, Donlyn. *The City Observed: Boston.* New York: Vintage Books, 1982.

MacCann, Richard Dyer. *The First Tycoons.* Metuchen, N.J.: Scarecrow Press, 1987.

MacIntosh, Craig, and Ilga Eglitis. *Minneapolis Cityscape, An Artist's View.* Wayzata, Minn.: Macilo, 1986.

Mackertich, Tony, and Peter Mackertich. *Facade, A Decade of British and American Commercial Architecture.* New York: Stonehill, 1976.

Maddex, Diane, editor. *Master Builders, A Guide to Famous American Architects.* National Trust for Historic Preservation. Washington, D.C.: Preservation Press, 1985.

Mandelbaum, Howard, and Eric Myers. *Screen Deco, A Celebration of High Style in Hollywood.* New York: St. Martin's Press, 1985.

Manship, John. *Paul Manship.* New York: Abbeville Press, 1989.

Macrus, Leonard S. *The American Store Window.* New York: Whitney Library of Design, imprint of Watson-Guptill, 1978.

Margolies, John, and Emily Gwathmey. *Ticket to Paradise, American Movie Theaters and How We Had Fun.* Boston: Bulfinch Press Division, Little, Brown, 1991.

Massey, Anne. *Interior Design of the 20th Century.* New York: Thames & Hudson, 1990.

McCausland, Elizabeth, photographs by Berenice Abbott. *New York in the Thirties.* First published as *Changing New York,* Guilds' Committee for Federal Writers' Publications, New York: E. P. Dutton, 1939. Reprinted, New York: Dover, 1973.

McClinton, Katharine Morrison. *Art Deco, A Guide for Collectors.* New York: Clarkson N. Potter, 1972.

McCoy, Esther. *Five California Architects* (Irving Gill, R. M. Schindler, et al.). New York: Praeger Publishers Division, Holt Rinehart & Winston, 1975.

McMeekin, Dorothy. *Diego Rivera, Science and Creativity in the Detroit Murals,* translated from the Spanish by Maria E. K. Moon. Detroit: Michigan State University Press, 1985.

Meikle, Jeffrey L. *Twentieth Century Limited, Industrial Design in America, 1925–1939.* Philadelphia: Temple University Press, 1979.

Menten, Theodore. *The Art Deco Style.* New York: Dover, 1972.

Messler, Norbert. *The Art Deco Skyscraper in New York.* New York: Peter Lang, 1986.

Meyer, Katharine Mattingly, editor. *Detroit Architecture AIA Guide,* rev. by Martin C. P. McElroy. Detroit: Wayne State University Press, 1971, 1986.

Modden, Ethan. *The Hollywood Studios, House Style in the Golden Age of the Movies.* New York: Knopf, 1988.

Moore, Patricia Anne. *The Casino, Avalon, Santa Catalina Island, California.* Avalon, Calif.: Catalina Island Museum Society, Philip K. Wrigley Fund, 1979.

Morley, Sylvanus G. *The Ancient Maya.* Stanford, Calif.: Stanford University Press, 1946.

National Trust for Historic Preservation. *Deco America,* 1982 calendar. New York: Universe, 1981.

Naylor, David, edited by Diana Maddex and Janet Walker. *Great American Movie Theaters, A National Trust Guide.* Washington, D.C.: Preservation Press, 1987.

Naylor, David. *American Picture Palaces, The Architecture of Fantasy.* New York: Van Nostrand Reinhold, 1981.

Neuhaus, Eugen. *The Art of Treasure Island, First Hand Impressions of the Architecture, Sculpture, Landscape Design, Color Effects, Mural Decoration, Illumination and Other Artistic Aspects of the Golden Gate International Exposition of 1939.* Berkeley: University of California Press, 1939.

New York, the Wonder City. New York: Manhattan Post Card Publishing Co., c. 1935.

Peel, Lucy, with Polly Powell and Alexander Garrett. *An Introduction to 20th-Century Architecture.* London: Quintet, 1989.

Peterson, Geraldine, and Dan Peterson (AIA), photography by Don Silverek. *Santa Rosa's Architectural Heritage.* Santa Rosa: Sonoma County (California) Historical Society, 1982.

Pildas, Ave. *Art Deco Los Angeles.* New York: Harper & Row, 1977.

Pildas, Ave, text by Lucinda Smith. *Movie Palaces, Survivors of an Elegant Era.* New York: Clarkson N. Potter, 1980.

Queen Mary, Long Beach, California. Emeryville, Calif.: Mike Roberts Color Productions, 1979.

Queens Museum. *Dawn of a New Day, The New York World's Fair, 1939–1940.* New York: National Endowment for the Humanities, copublished by Queens Museum and New York University Press, 1980.

Queens Museum, introduction by Robert Rosenblum, essays by Rosemarie Haag Bletter et al. *Remembering the Future, The New York World's Fair from 1939 to 1964.* New York: Rizzoli, 1989.

Reinhardt, Richard. *Treasure Island 1939–1940.* San Francisco: Squarebooks, 1978.

Robinson, Cervin, and Rosemarie Haag Bletter. *Skyscraper Style, Art Deco New York.* New York: Oxford University Press, 1975.

Rodriguez, Ivan A. *From Wilderness to Metropolis, The History and Architecture of Dade County, Florida 1825–1940.* Metropolitan Dade County, Office of Community and Economic Development, Historic Preservation Division. Miami: National Endowment for the Arts and State of Florida, 1982.

Rolfes, Herbert. *The 1939 New York World's Fair in Postcards.* Pittstown, N.J.: Main Street Press, 1988.

Rolfes, Herbert. *The 1939 San Francisco World's Fair in Postcards.* Pittstown, N.J.: Main Street Press, 1988.

Rooney, William A. *Architectural Ornamentation in Chicago.* Chicago: Chicago Review Press, 1984.

Roos, Frank J., Jr. *An Illustrated Handbook of Art History.* New York: Macmillan, 1937.

Root, Keith. *Miami Beach Art Deco Guide.* Miami Beach: Miami Design Preservation League, 1987.

San Francisco Civic Art Collection, A Guided Tour to Publicly Owned Art of the City and County of San Francisco. San Francisco: San Francisco Arts Commission, 1989.

Scarlett, Frank, and Marjorie Townley. *Arts Décoratifs 1925, A Personal Recollection of the Paris Exhibition.* New York: St. Martin's Press, 1975.

Schatz, Thomas. *The Genius of the System, Hollywood Film Making in the Studio Era.* New York: Pantheon Press, 1988.

Schessler, Ken. *This Is Hollywood, An Unusual Movieland Guide.* La Verne, Calif.: Schessler Productions, 1978.

Sexton, R. W., and B. F. Betts. *American Theatres of Today.* New York: Architectural Book Publishing, 1927. Reprinted, Vestal, N.Y.: Vestal Press, 1977.

Short, Charles Wilkins, and R. Stanley-Brown, new edition introduction by Richard Guy Wilson. *Public Buildings, Architecture Under the Public Works Administration, 1933–1939,* Vol 1. Reprint of 1939 U.S. G.P.O. document: "Projects Constructed by Federal and Other Governmental Bodies, Between the years 1933 and 1939, with the Assistance of the Public Works Administration". New York: Da Capo Press, 1986.

Smith, Edward Lucie. *Cultural Calendar of the 20th Century.* Oxford, England: Phaidon Press, 1979.

Stern, Robert A. M. *George Howe: Toward a Modern American Architecture.* New Haven: Yale University Press, 1975.

Stone, Susannah Harris, photography by Roger Minick. *The Oakland Paramount.* Berkeley, Calif.: Lancaster-Miller, 1981.

Storrer, William Allin. *The Architecture of Frank Lloyd Wright, A Complete Catalog.* Cambridge: MIT Press, 1979.

Striner, Richard, edited by Diane Maddex and Janet Walker. *Mostly Moderne, 24 Authentic Old Postcards—Ready to Mail.* National Trust for Historic Preservation. Washington, D.C.: Preservation Press, 1989.

Summerson, John. *Heavenly Mansions and Other Essays on Architecture.* New York: W. W. Norton, 1963.

Tavernor, Robert. *Palladio and Palladianism.* New York: Thames & Hudson, 1991.

Thollander, Earl. *Earl Thollander's San Francisco, 30 Walking Tours from the Embarcadero to the Golden Gate.* New York: Clarkson N. Potter, 1987.

Thomas, Tony, with Jim Terry, and Busby Berkeley, foreword by Ruby Keeler. *The Busby Berkeley Book.* Greenwich, Conn.: New York Graphics Society, 1973.

Van Hoogstraten, Nicholas. *Lost Broadway. Theatres.* New York: Princeton Architectural Press, 1991.

Venturi, Robert, Denise Scott Brown, and Steven Izenour. *Learning from Las Vegas, The Forgotten Symbolism of Architectural Form* (rev. ed.). Cambridge: MIT Press, 1977.

Vieyra, Daniel I. *"Fill 'er Up," An Architectural History of America's Gas Stations.* New York: Collier Books Division, Macmillan, 1979.

Vlack, Don. *Art Deco Architecture in New York, 1920–1940.* New York: Harper & Row, 1974.

Wasmuth, Ernst. *Frank Lloyd Wright, Ausgeführte Bauten (Built Works).* Berlin: 1911. Translated into English and reprinted as *The Early Works of Frank Lloyd Wright.* New York: Dover, 1983.

Weber, Eva. *Art Deco in America.* New York: Exeter Books, 1985.

Weber, Eva. *Art Deco.* New York: Gallery Books Division, W. H. Smith, 1989.

Whiffen, Marcus, with Carla Breeze. *Pueblo Deco, The Art Deco Architecture of the Southwest.* Albuquerque: University of New Mexico Press, 1984.

Widen, Larry, and Judi Anderson. *Milwaukee Movie Palaces.* Milwaukee: Milwaukee Technical College Alumni Association, Milwaukee County Historical Society, 1986.

Wier, Albert E. *Thesaurus of the Arts.* New York: G. P. Putnam's Sons, 1943.

Willensky, Elliot, and Norval White. *AIA Guide to New York City* (3rd ed.), New York: American Institute of Architects, New York Chapter, and Harcourt Brace Jovanovich, 1988.

Williamson, Roxanne Kuter. *American Architects and the Mechanics of Fame.* Austin: University of Texas Press, 1991.

Wirz, Hans, and Richard Striner. *Washington Deco, Art Deco Design in the Nation's Capitol.* Washington, D.C.: Smithsonian Institution Press, 1984.

Woodbridge, Sally B. *California Architecture, Historic American Buildings Survey.* San Francisco: Chronicle Books, 1988.

Wrenn, Tony P., and Elizabeth D. Mulloy. *America's Forgotten Architecture.* New York: National Trust for Historic Preservation with Pantheon Books Division, Random House, 1976.

Wurts, Richard, et al. *The New York World's Fair 1939/1940,* in 155 photographs, text by Stanley Appelbaum. New York: Dover, 1977.

Zim, Larry, with Mel Lerner and Herbert Rolfes. *The World of Tomorrow, The 1939 New York World's Fair.* New York: Main Street Press, with Harper & Row, 1988.

CATALOGS, EXHIBITIONS AND COMMEMORA-TIVE PROGRAMS

Adlmann, Jan Ernst, guest curator. *Vienna Modern: 1898–1918, "An Early Encounter Between Taste and Utility,"* exposition catalog, Sarah Campbell Blaffer Gallery, University of Houston, Texas, with support of Cooper-Hewitt Museum, Smithsonian Institution, New York, and Austrian Ministry for Science and Research. Houston: University of Houston, 1978.

Anderson, Virginia. *The Auditorium at Indiana University,* Fiftieth Anniversary. Bloomington: Indiana University Press, 1991.

Boston Avenue Methodist Church. *Promise to Keep, In Celebration of Fifty Years in This Building.* Tulsa: Boston Avenue Church, 1979.

Brown, Mark M. *The Cathedral of Learning: Concept, Design, Construction.* Exhibition at University Art Gallery, Henry Clay Frick Fine Arts Building, University of Pittsburgh, March 19–May 17, 1987. Pittsburgh: University of Pittsburgh Press, 1987.

Brunhammer, Yvonne, introduction by François Mathey. *Les Années "25", Art Deco/Bauhaus/Stijl/Esprit Nouveau.* Retrospective show on Paris 1925 exhibition, March 3–May 16, 1966. Exhibit catalog, Part 1, in French, objects loaned for exhibition. Paris: Musée des Arts Décoratifs, 1966.

Brunhammer, Yvonne. *Les Années "25", Collections du Musée des Art Décoratifs.* Retrospective on Paris 1925 exhibition, March 3–May 16, 1966. Exhibit catalog, Part 2, in French, objects from permanent collection. Paris: Musée des Arts Décoratifs, 1966.

Butterfield & Butterfield. *The John Pflueger Collection of Architectural Renderings, Maquettes, Photographs and Paintings, Parts I and II.* Exhibition and auction of objects from firm of Timothy Pflueger, Dec. 5, 1989, and March 22, 1990. Butterfield & Butterfield, 1989–1990.

Carew Tower, building statistics brochure. Cincinnati: Privately published by Emery Realty, building rental agent, 1970.

Century of Progress International Exposition. *A Century of Progress, 1833–1933: Chicago World's Fair Souvenir* program, Burnham Park. Chicago: Arena Publishing, 1933.

The Cincinnati Union Terminal. Pictorial history, Cincinnati Union Terminal, 1933.

Curtis, Nancy. *Gropius House.* Boston: Society for the Preservation of New England Antiquities, undated.

Duci Bella, Joe. *The Paradise Theatre.* Chicago: Theatre Historical Society, Annual 4, 1977.

Ewing, William A., exhibition director. *Eye for Elegance: George Hoyningen-Huene,* traveling exhibition, Sept. 25, 1980–Nov. 28, 1982. International Center of Photography. New York: Congreve Publishing, 1980.

Garren, William I. *Four Fifty Sutter Medical Building and the San Francisco Stock Exchange.* Monograph published at buildings' openings. San Francisco: Mercury Press, 1929.

Gebhard, David, and Harriette Von Breton. *Kem Weber, The Moderne in Southern California 1920 through 1941.* Exhibition Feb. 11–March 23, 1969, at The Art Galleries, University of California, Santa Barbara. Santa Barbara: University of California Regents, 1969, revised 1976.

Glibota, Ante, curator. *A Guide to 150 Years of Chicago Architecture.* Museum of Science and Industry. Chicago: Chicago Review Press, 1986.

The Greater Penobscot Building. Building dedication monograph. Detroit: Privately published by building rental agent, 1928.

Greif, Martin. *The New Industrial Landscape, The Story of the Austin Co.* Printed privately by Austin Co. Clinton, N.J.: Main Street Press, undated.

Hambley, John, with Roy Strong and Patrick Downing. Foreword by Orson Welles. *The Art of Hollywood, Fifty Years of Art Direction.* An exhibition mounted at Victoria and Albert Museum, London, in connection with Thames Television's thirteen-hour documentary series. London: Macdermott & Chant, 1979.

Hansen, Oskar J. W. *Sculptures at Hoover Dam.* Report by sculptor. Washington, D.C.: U.S. Department of the Interior, Bureau of Reclamation, 1978.

Hayes, Loeb, & Company. *The Field Building.* Building dedication monograph. Chicago: Privately published by building rental agent, 1931.

Hillier, Bevis. *The World of Art Deco.* Exhibition catalog, Minneapolis Institute of Arts, July–Sept. 1971. New York: E. P. Dutton, 1971.

Hunter-Stiebel, Penelope. *20th Century Decorative Arts.* Objects in the permanent collection of the Metropolitan Museum of Art. New York: Metropolitan Museum of Art, 1979.

Kashey, Elisabeth, and Robert Kashey, curators. *Winold Reiss 1886–1953 Centennial Exhibition, Works on Paper: Architectural Designs, Fantasies and Portraits.* Shepherd Gallery, Nov. 19, 1986–Jan. 3, 1987. New York: Privately published, 1986.

Kittleson, Gloria. *Paul Manship, Changing Taste in America.* Exhibition catalog, Minnesota Museum of Art, May 19–Aug. 18, 1985. St. Paul: West Publishing, 1985.

Lipman, Jonathan. *Frank Lloyd Wright and the Johnson Wax Buildings: Creating a Corporate Cathedral.* Traveling exhibition organized by the Herbert F. Johnson Museum of Art, Cornell University, April 26, 1986–June 19, 1988. Ithaca, N.Y.: Cornell University, 1986.

LOF (Libbey-Owen-Ford) Glass Co. *Vitrolite in Architecture and Decoration.* Contains construction details and specifications. Toledo, Ohio, c. 1933.

McMillian, Elizabeth. *Bullocks Wilshire, 1929–1979, A Legend Still.* Fiftieth anniversary monograph. Los Angeles: Privately published, 1977.

National Park Service. *National Register of Historic Places 1966–1988.* Nashville: American Association for State and Local History, 1989.

Northwestern Terra Cotta Company. *Architectural Ornament,* Vol. 1: *Modern.* Chicago: Northwestern Terra Cotta Company, c. 1931.

Posters of Alfonso Iannelli. Exhibition brochure, Chicago School of Architecture Foundation, 1965.

Preddy, Jane. *Glamour, Glitz and Sparkle: The Deco Theatres of John Eberson.* Chicago: Theatre Historical Society, Annual 16, 1989.

Preddy, Jane. *Palaces of Dreams, The Movie Theatres of John Eberson, Architect: Working Drawings and Photographs.* Exhibition Sept. 16, 1989–Feb. 15, 1990, at McNay Art Museum, San Antonio, Texas. Sponsored by Robert L. B. Tobin. New York: Abrams Gleber Warhover, 1989.

Proske, Beatrice Gilman. *Brookgreen Gardens Sculpture.* Catalog of objects in largest sculpture garden in United States. Published by order of the Trustees, Brookgreen Gardens, S.C., 1968.

215

Robsjohn-Gibbings, T. H. *Neo-Classical Art Moderne Furniture, Parts 1 and 2.* New York: Sotheby Parke-Bernet, 1980–1981.

Rueppel, Merrill C., Director. *1930's Expositions.* Presented in New Dimensions Pavilion, State Fair of Texas, Oct. 7–Nov. 5, 1972, Dallas Museum of Fine Arts, 1972.

Ryan, David. *Modernism at Norwest Minneapolis.* Opening exhibition of the Norwest Corporation Collection, Jan. 1989. Minneapolis: Norwest Corporation.

Schnoebelen, Anne. *Treasures, Splendid Survivors of the Golden Gate International Exposition.* Berkeley: GGIE Research Associates, 1991.

Sullivan, Donald G., and Brian J. Danforth. *Bronx Art Deco Architecture, An Exposition.* Hunter College Graduate Program in Urban Planning. New York: Publishing Center for Cultural Resources, 1976.

The Vitrolite Company. *Table, Counter and Furniture Tops of Vitrolite.* Sales catalog and list of installations (before purchase by LOF). Chicago, 1928.

Webb, Michael. *Hollywood Legend and Reality.* Smithsonian Institution Traveling Exhibition Service, Apr. 1986–Feb. 1987. Boston: Little, Brown, 1986.

Weisberg, Gabriel P., et al. *Art Deco and the Cincinnati Union Terminal.* Catalog for exhibition, Cincinnati Contemporary Arts Center, Jan.–Feb. 1973.

Western Pennsylvania Conservancy. *Frank Lloyd Wright's Falling Water.* Mill Run, Pa., 1988.

Wilson, Richard Guy, with Dianne H. Pilgrim, and Dickran Tashjian. *The Machine Age in America 1918–1941.* Catalog from traveling exhibition, Brooklyn Museum. New York: Harry N. Abrams, 1986.

HISTORICAL SOCIETY PUBLICATIONS AND GUIDES

Abbie, Lynn, editor. *Chicago Art Deco Society Newsletter.* Various issues: Autumn 1987, Winter, 1988–1989, Spring 1990.

Abbie, Lynn. *Deco Info, The Independent Art Deco Publication.* Oak Park, Ill., Spring 1992.

Allen, Francie, et al. *Downtown Fort Worth,* walking tour. Downtown Fort Worth Inc., undated.

Boston Landmarks Commission. *Building Information Forms: Various Art Deco Buildings,* 1979–1980.

Brown, Marvin, et al. *Palaces of Finance,* walking tour. Los Angeles Conservancy, 1983.

Calder, J. Kent. "The House of the Interpreter, Origins of the Lilly House Mural," *Traces, Indiana and Midwestern History.* Indiana Historical Society (Summer 1990) 2:3, 34.

Cirgenski, Chuck, editor. *The Modern,* Detroit Area Art Deco Society, (Spring 1988) 2:4.

Commission on Chicago Historical and Architectural Landmarks. *Chicago Board of Trade Building* (Aug. 1975).

Dudley, Mimi, and Norman Dudley. *Terra Cotta: "A Visual Feast,"* walking tour. Los Angeles Conservancy, undated.

Fader, Stephen. *Seventh Street: Mecca For Merchants,* walking tour. Los Angeles Conservancy, 1986.

Foster, Kathleen A. "Thomas Hart Benton's Indiana Murals," *Traces, Indiana and Midwestern History.* Indiana Historical Society (Winter 1990) 3:1, 16–26.

Gallery, John Andrew, editor. *Philadelphia Architecture, A Guide to the City.* Prepared for Foundation for Architecture, by Group for Environmental Education. Cambridge: MIT Press, 1984.

Gebhard, David. *Streamline Los Angeles,* walking tour. Los Angeles Conservancy, 1984.

"A Guide to the Week's Events June 9–17, 1984," *Art Deco Week,* Art Deco Society of New York, 1984.

Halmay, Helen, and Michael Reams. *Art Deco Treasures of San Diego.* Art Deco Society of San Diego, 1989.

Hendry, Fay, researcher, with Keith Everett, Thomas Hensle, Thomas Kuck, et. al. *Beverly Shores/Century of Progress Architectural District, Porter County, Ind.* National Register designation nomination form, National Park Service, U.S. Department of the Interior, 1976. Updated, 1984.

Hlava, Diane Williams. *Wiltern, From Pastureland to Performing Arts Center.* Rededication monograph. Los Angeles Conservancy, 1985.

Hoye, Daniel P. *Art Deco Los Angeles.* Los Angeles Conservancy, 1988.

Hoye, Daniel P., and Brent R. Hurwitz. *Old San Pedro,* walking tour. Los Angeles Conservancy, 1988.

Irwin, Mark, with John Miller and Susan Richey. *Broadway Historic Theater District,* walking tour. Los Angeles Conservancy, 1986.

Johnson, Christy, and Paul Gleye. *Hollywood Boulevard,* walking tour. Los Angeles Conservancy and the Hollywood Revitalization Committee, 1978.

June, Glory. *Art Deco in Indianapolis.* Indiana Arts Commission and National Endowment for the Arts. Indianapolis: Indiana Architectural Foundation, 1980.

Junior League of Miami. *Historic Downtown Miami,* self-guided tour. Junior League of Miami, Fla., 1985.

Junior League of Miami. *Historic Coral Gables, self-guided tour.* Junior League of Miami, Fla., 1986.

Junior League of Miami. *Historic Coconut Grove,* self-guided tour. Junior League of Miami, Fla., 1987.

Kalleen, James. "Contemporary Roots, Art Deco," *Indianapolis Home and Garden* (Feb. 1979), 38–40.

Kehr, Dave. "Six Screen Esquire: No Room for Grandeur," *Marquee,* Theatre Historical Society, reprint from *Chicago Tribune,* (fourth quarter 1989) 21:4, 12–13.

Klein, Barbara, editor, et al. *The Sophisticate,* Art Deco Society of California. Various issues: Summer 1985, Summer 1986, Fall–Winter 1986.

Kreisman, Lawrence, photography by Victor Gardaya. *Art Deco Seattle.* Seattle: Art Deco Project for Citizens of Northwest, with Allied Arts of Seattle, 1979.

Levin, Steven, editor. *Oakland Paramount, Historic American Building Survey* (1976), edited and augmented reprint. Chicago: Theatre Historical Society of America, Annual 18, 1991.

Loney, Glenn, editor. *Art Deco Society of New York Newsletter.* Various issues: (Sept.–Oct. 1981) 1:1; (Nov.–Dec. 1981) 1:2; (Jan.–Feb. 1982) 2:1; (Winter 1982) 2:4; (Fall 1984) 4:3.

Loney, Glenn. *The Modernist* (quarterly). Art Deco Society of New York. Various issues: (Spring 1989) 8:1; (Summer 1990) 9:1; (Fall 1990) 9:2.

Loney, Glenn. "Rockefeller Center Rediscovered," *Art Deco Society of New York News, The Magazine of Modernism* (Spring 1986) 6:1.

Miller, Mark, editor. *Trans-Lux*, Art Deco Society of Washington. Various issues: (Spring 1986) 4:2, (Autumn 1988) 6:3; (Summer 1989) 7:2.

Mogul, Mitzi March. *Santa Monica's Art Deco Architecture*, walking tour. Art Deco Society of Los Angeles, 1988.

Olsen, Arlene R. *A Guide to the Architecture of Miami Beach*. Dade Heritage Trust, 1978.

Pickart, Margaret. *Designation Report for Barclay-Vesay Interior*. New York City Landmarks Preservation Committee, 1991.

Riddle, Peggy, photography by Molly Shelton Hussing. *A Guide to Fair Park*, with support from Atlantic Richfield and Dallas Morning News. Dallas Historical Society, 1983.

Riddle, Peggy, editor. *A Gathering of Symbols, Texas History in the Hall of State*, sesquicentennial project, Junior League of Dallas. Dallas: Dallas Historical Society, 1985.

Selm, Bill, *Circle Tower: Statement of Significance* for Indianapolis–Marion County Register of Historic Properties. Indianapolis Historic Preservation Commission, 1983.

Snyder, Lisa M. *Religious Architecture*, tour guide. Los Angeles: Los Angeles Conservancy, 1988.

Striner, Richard. *Greyhound Bus Terminal, Application for Historic Landmark Designation*, filed with Joint Committee on Landmarks of the National Capital, by Art Deco Society of Washington and Don't Tear It Down, Inc., Feb. 1984.

Striner, Richard. *Reflections on the Work of Historic Preservation in Washington, D.C.* Washington, D.C.: Art Deco Society of Washington, 1989.

Taussig, Meredith. *Staff Analysis of Landmark Criteria Applicable to the Carbide and Carbon Building*. Designation report, Commission on Chicago Landmarks, Apr. 5, 1989.

Taussig, Meredith. *Staff Analysis of Landmark Criteria Applicable to the Field Building*. Designation report, Commission on Chicago Landmarks, Oct. 1990.

Tucker, Jeffrey, editor. *The Sophisticate*, Art Deco Society of California. Various issues: Spring 1990, Winter 1990–1991, Fall 1991.

LETTERS & UNPUBLISHED DOCUMENTS

Crotty, Frances Kern. *The Cincinnati Union Terminal and the Art Deco Movement*. Unpublished thesis for M.A. degree, University of Cincinnati, Department of Art History, 1972.

Delaporte, Chris. Reflections upon learning of Barbara Capitman's death. Baltimore, April 24, 1990.

Gadsen, Renée Valjean. *Time of Transition: The Role of Art Deco Architecture in the History of the Bronx, 1927*. Unpublished honors thesis for the degree of bachelor of arts, Brown University, Providence, R.I. May 1985.

Gebhard, David. *The Richfield Building 1928–1968*. New York: Atlantic Richfield Co., 1968.

Hobbs-Halmay, Helen McCormick. "Development of Egyptian Revival Architecture in San Diego County," 1979. San Diego Historical Society Archives.

Lombardi, Joseph Bell. *The Chrysler Building Lobby*. Architect's report on current condition of lobby, its importance, feasibility of restoration, history of building, lobby alterations, etc. Prepared for Massachusetts Mutual Life Insurance company, owner, 1977.

Scott Brown, Denise. Letter to AIA chapter, outlining advantages of (and naming) a "Deco District" in Miami Beach. Philadelphia, 1972.

Wright, Frank Lloyd. Letter to Maxwell E. Levinson, Editor *T-Square Club Journal*, Philadelphia, accepting invitation to reply to critical article by Richard Neutra. Taliesin, Spring Green, Wis., Dec. 31, 1931.

MAGAZINE AND NEWSPAPER ARTICLES

Art and Decoration. Various issues; Nov. 1925–Apr. 1930, Vols. 24–31.

Brazell, Dawn. "Twenty-Three Skidoo: The Lingo of the '20s," *Charleston News and Courier* (Apr. 30, 1989), p. 1E.

Brown, Patricia Leigh. "Disney Deco," *New York Times Magazine* (Apr. 8, 1990), pp. 18–22.

Bruegmann, Robert. "Holabird & Roche and Holabird & Root: The First Two Generations," *Chicago History* (Fall 1980), pp. 130–165.

"Butler Mansion," *Historic Preservation* (Jan.–Feb. 1990), pp. 64–65.

Capitman, Barbara. "Travels with Barbara," *The Miami News*, various issues, 1981.

Capitman, Barbara, guest editor. *USA Tomorrow. Quarterly Review of Architecture and the Built Environment*, Art Deco America Issue (Jan. 1987).

Chandler, Arthur. "Where Deco Was Born, Paris 1925," *World's Fairs* (Jan.–March 1989), 9:1, 1–7.

Crotty, Francis Kern. "Cincinnati's Magnificent Mistake," *Cincinnati Horizons, Magazine of the University of Cincinnati* (Oct. 1972), 2:1, 6–10.

Dana-Sosnowski, Nazanin. "Art Deco Architecture in Philadelphia," *USA Tomorrow, Quarterly Review of Architecture and the Built Environment* (Sept. 1986), pp. 38–41.

Doyle, Deborah, editor. *The Chicago Architectural Journal*, issue on Andrew Rebori. Chicago Architectural Club (1984), Vol. 4.

Fortune Magazine, various editions (Jan. 1928–Jan. 1939), Vols. 1–11.

Gapp, Paul. "The Good Old Days of Deco," *Chicago Tribune Magazine* (June 11, 1978), pp. 18–20.

Gordon, Eleanor, and Jean Nerenberg. "Chicago's Colorful Terra Cotta Facades," *Chicago History*, 224–233.

Gordon, Eleanor, and Jean Nerenberg. "Deco in Chicago," *Chicago Tribune Magazine* (June 11, 1978), p. 21.

Haskell, Douglas. "The Empire State Building," *Creative Art* (Apr. 1931), 8:4, 243–244.

Hughes, Robert. "Tarted Up Till the Eye Cries Uncle: Reviving the Vulgarity of Thomas Hart Benton," *Time* (May 1, 1989), pp. 50–51.

Johnson, Alvin. "A Building of Adult Education, The New School," *USA Tomorrow, Quarterly Review of Architecture and the Built Environment* (Jan. 1987), pp. 19–22.

Johnson, Pamela, editor. "Yugoslavian Theme Issue," *Journal of Decorative and Propaganda Arts*, Wolfson Foundation (Fall 1990).

"Jones Beach State Park, Long Island," *Architecture* (July 1934), 70:1, 23–30.

Keister, George. "The Metal Playhouse, Earl Carroll Theatre," *Metalcraft* (Oct. 1931), pp. 130–135.

Klinkenborg, Verlyn. "Thomas Hart Benton Came from Missouri—And He Showed 'Em," *Smithsonian* (Apr. 1989), 20:1, 82–101.

Levinson, Maxwell, editor. "George Howe, Architect for Humane Living, Industrial Development Institute of America, 55th anniversary Commemorative Issue," *USA Tomorrow, Quarterly Review of Architecture and the Built Environment* (May 1986), pp. 24–32.

Lipman, Jonathan. "Designing the Johnson Wax Administration Building and Its Furniture," *The Prairie House Journal* (1987).

MacDougall, Allan Ross. "The Beauties of Modern French Wrought Iron," *Arts and Decoration* (Apr. 1927), p. 82.

Mack, Linda. "Deco Downtown," *Minneapolis Star Tribune* (Nov. 5, 1990), Section E, p. 1.

Nakamura, Toshio. "New York Art Deco Skyscrapers, 1924–1939," *Architecture and Urbanism*, text in Japanese and English, extra edition (Apr. 1987).

"Portfolio: Business Building Lobbies," *Architecture* (Oct. 1934), 70: 4, 225-240.

"Portfolio: Modern Lighting Fixtures," *Architecture* (Dec. 1934), 70: 6, 345-360.

Prognerm, Jean W. "Art Deco: Anatomy of a Revival," *Print* (Jan. 1970), pp. 27–36.

Rambusch, Catha Grace. "Rambusch Decorating Company: Ninety Years of Art Metal," *Journal of Decorative and Propaganda Arts*, metalwork theme issue, Wolfson Foundation (Summer 1988), 1:1, 6–43.

"Renovation of a Cathedral," *Energy People Quarterly* (Summer 1983), reprinted by Michigan Consolidated Gas Co.

Robins, Marjorie K., editor. "Art Deco's Enduring Exuberance," special *Newsday Home Magazine* (Apr. 23, 1989).

"Rockefeller Center, New York," Honor Roll column. *Historic Preservation*, National Trust for Historic Preservation (Nov.–Dec. 1990), 42:6, 49.

Saliga, Pauline A., editor. "The Sky's the Limit: High-Rise History in Chicago," *Inland Architect*, excerpted from book *The Sky's the Limit: A Century of Chicago Skyscrapers* (Jan.–Feb. 1990), 34:1, 60–63.

Scherer, Herbert. "Marquee on Main Street, Jack Liebenberg's Movie Theaters: 1928–1941," *Journal of Decorative and Propaganda Arts*, Wolfson Foundation (Spring 1986), 1:9, 62–75.

Scott Brown, Denise. "My Miami Beach," *Interview* (Aug. 1986).

Smith, Jane Webb. "Streamlining with Friction, An Exhibition Review," *Winterthur Portfolio*, University of Chicago (Spring 1990), 25:1, 55–66.

Stein, Shifra, photographs by Bob Barrett. "Boss Tom's Deco Empire," *Historic Preservation* (July–Aug. 1986), 38:4. 24–31.

Striner, Richard. "Art Deco, Polemics and Synthesis," *Winterthur Portfolio* (Spring 1990), 25:1, 21–34.

Tunick, Susan. "Architectural Terra Cotta: Its Impact on New York," *Sites* (4–37).

Vitek, Jack. "Grace Period: Art Deco Embraces Area Architecture with Futuristic Flamboyance," *Palm Beach Life* (Oct. 1990), 83:10, 40–43 and 50.

Vitrolite ad, *The American Architect*, listing Chicago head office, factory, Parkersburg, W. Va. (Sept. 20, 1926), p. 57.

Walker, John O., "Life in a Greenbelt Community," *Shelter* (Dec. 1938), pp. 16–23.

"Weather's Flicker Finger of Fate Foretold by Fixture on Sky Line," *Milwaukee Journal* (March 17, 1965).

Weisberg, Gabriel P. "A Terminal Case: Cincinnati's Fight to Save an Art Deco Landmark," *Art Journal* (Spring 1973), 32:4, 297–298.

Weisberg, Gabriel P. "A Terminal Case Revisited: The Preservation of Cincinnati's Union Terminal Concourse Mosaics," *Art Journal* (Spring 1974), 33:4, 328–330.

Whitehead, Russell F. (AIA). "Holabird and Root, Masters of Design," *Pencil Points* (Feb. 1938), pp. 67–90.

Wilson, Richard Guy. "Machine-Age Iconography in the American West: The Design of the Hoover Dam," *Pacific Historical Review* (Nov. 1985), 54:1, 463–493.

Wolner, Edward W. "Urban Icon: Norwest Center," *Inland Architect* (Jan.–Feb. 1990), 34:1, 44–48.

VIDEOS AND DOCUMENTARIES

Come to the Fairs, A Walk Through the 20th Century with Bill Moyers (editor). Documentary on world fairs: Mert Koplin, senior executive producer; Charles Grinker and Sanford H. Fisher, executive producers; Jane Roach, producer; Jamie L. Smith, associate producer; Corporation for Entertainment & Learning, with Bill Moyers, 1983.

Died Young, Cincinnati Union Terminal, 1933-1972. (Editor's note: Not demolished as implied by title.) Cincinnati Union Terminal Co.; Charles Vaughan, executive producer; Gene Walz, producer/director; Sue Schulkers, associate producer; Jack Gwyn, script; Cecil Hale, narrator; Gibson Yungblut, historic consultant, WCET Channel 48, Cincinnati, 1972.

The Once and Future Fair. Golden Gate International Exposition on Treasure Island, construction, 1938; opened to the public, 1939. *Pacifica* statue dominated esplanade, with fountains and light effects at night: Sandra Nichols, writer/producer; Linda Iacovetta, associate producer; Ron Johnson, editor; Sydney Walker, narrator; Chronicle Broadcasting, KRON, San Francisco, 1989.

Powell Crosley Jr. and the 20th Century. Documentary on the life and achievement of industrialist Powell Crosley, including WLW–The Nation's Station, most powerful radio station on earth for one year; Bill Nemo, host; Gene Walz, executive producer; Taylor Feltner and Sheri A. Lutz, producers; Taylor Filtner, director; Thomas Ashwell, writer/coproducer, with grant from Crosley Foundation, WCET Channel 48, Greater Cincinnati Educational Television Foundation, Cincinnati, 1988.

Pride of Place, Building the American Dream. Eight-part series on American architecture, written and narrated by Robert A. M. Stern, with Gwendolyn Wright, for PBS. Malone Gill, producer; Murray Grigor, director; Terry Hopkins, director of photography; Michael Gill, executive producer; produced with grant from Mobil Oil, 1986. Boston: Houghton Mifflin, 1986.

Relive the Magic. Documentary on Cincinnati's Coney Island; Glenn Ryle, narrator; Grace Hill, executive producer; Karyn Hecht-Heusser, producer/director; Steve Hill, writer/associate producer; WCET Channel 48, Crosley Telecommunications Center, Greater Cincinnati Educational Television Foundation, Cincinnati, 1984.

Texas Centennial Highlights. Jamieson Film Co.; Frank Morang, director; Jack Whitman, photography; Dick Byers, sound; Roy Cowan, narrator; Dallas, 1936.

Thomas Hart Benton. Ken Burns and Julie Dunfey, executive producers; Geoffrey C. Ward, writer; Donna Marino, editor; Jason Robards, narrator; Ken Burns and Buddy Squires, cinematography; Henry Adams, historical consultant; John Colby, music director. Based on the book *Thomas Hart Benton, An American Original*, by Nancy Adams. Florentine Films and WGBH, Boston, producers; partially funded by Equitable Financial Companies, Boston, 1988.

The World of Tomorrow. Lance Bird and Tom Johnson, producers; John Crowley, writer; Jason Robards, narrator; Kate Hirson, editor; Warren Susman, historical consultant; Gerald O'Grady, project director; New York Council for Humanities, Pew Memorial Trust, Independent Documentary Fund, Media Study, Buffalo, New York, 1984.

RESOURCE LIST–ART DECO SOCIETIES AND RELATED GROUPS

UNITED STATES
National Groups

Diner Hotline
72 McCormack Avenue
Medford, MA 02155
PH: 617 396-0634

Friends of Terra Cotta
771 West End Avenue, Apt. 10-E
New York, NY 10025
PH: 212 932-1750

League of American Theaters
1511 K Streets, N.W., Suite 923
Washington, DC 20005
PH: 202 783-6966

National Amusement Park Historical
Association
P.O. Box 83
Mount Prospect, IL 60056

National Coalition of Art Deco Societies
1 Murdock Terrace
Brighton, MA 02135
PH: 617 787-2637
FAX: 617 782-4430

Society for Commercial Archaeology
c/o Room 5010
National Museum of American History
Smithsonian Institution
Washington, DC 20506

Theatre Historical Society Archives
152 North York Road, Suite 200
Elmhurst, IL 60126

Tile Heritage Foundation
P.O. Box 1850
Healdsburg, CA 95448
PH: 707 431-8453

BALTIMORE
Baltimore Art Deco Society
7123 Pheasant Cross Road
Baltimore, MD 21209
PH: 301 653-1099

BATON ROUGE
Foundation for Historical Louisiana
900 North Boulevard
Baton Rouge, LA 70802
PH: 504 387-2464

BOSTON
Art Deco Society of Boston
1 Murdock Terrace
Brighton, MA 02135
PH: 617 787-2637
FAX: 617 782-4430

CHARLESTON, S.C.
Art Deco Society of South Carolina
Charleston Chapter
856-A Liriope Lane
Mount Pleasant, SC 29464
PH: 803 849-9289

CHICAGO
Chicago Art Deco Society
400 Skokie, #270
Northbrook, IL 60062
PH: 708 480-1211

Deco Info, The Independent Art Deco
Publication
Lynn Abbie, Editor
823 Lake Street
Oak Park, IL 60301

CINCINNATI
Cincinnati Historical Society
Museum Center
1301 Western Avenue
Cincinnati, OH 45203
PH: 513 421-5661

CLEVELAND
Art Deco Society of Northern Ohio
3439 West Brainard Road, Room 260
Woodmere, OH 44122
PH: 216 831-9110
FAX: 216 292-7529

DALLAS
Dr. Phillip Collins
Director of Public Outreach
Dallas Museum of Art
1717 North Harwood Street
Dallas, TX 75201
PH: 214 922-1330

Friends of Fair Park
P.O. Box 150248
Dallas, TX 75315
PH: 214 426-3400

DETROIT
Detroit Area Art Deco Society
P.O. Box 1393
Royal Oak, MI 48068
PH: 313 343-0636

LOS ANGELES
Art Deco Society of Los Angeles
P.O. Box 972
Hollywood, CA 90078
PH: 310 659-DECO

Los Angeles Conservancy
433 South Spring Street, Suite 124
Los Angeles, CA 90013
PH: 213 623-CITY

MIAMI
Miami Design Preservation League
P.O. Bin L
Miami Beach, FL 33119
PH: 305 672-2014
FAX: 305 672-4319

NEW YORK
Art Deco Society of New York
385 Fifth Avenue, Suite 501
New York, NY 10016
PH: 212 679-DECO

PALM BEACHES
Art Deco Society of the Palm Beaches
820 Lavers Circle, Room G-203
Delray Beach, FL 33444
PH: 407 276-9925

PHILADELPHIA
Art Deco Society of Philadelphia
1924 Arch Street
Philadelphia, PA 19103
PH: 215 567-0547

SACRAMENTO
Sacramento Art Deco Society
P.O. Box 162836
Sacramento, CA 95816
PH: 916 736-1929

SAN DIEGO
San Diego Art Deco Society
P.O. Box 33762
San Diego, CA 92103
PH: 619 296-3322

SAN FRANCISCO
Art Deco Society of California
100 Bush Street, Suite 511
San Francisco, CA 94104
PH: 415 982-DECO

GGIE [Golden Gate International
Exposition] Research Associates
1440 Kains Avenue
Berkeley, CA 94702
PH: 510 524-2015

SEATTLE
Allied Arts of Seattle
107 South Main Street
Seattle, WA 98104
Seattle Architectural Foundation
SAF/AIA tours: 206 448-0106

TULSA
The Philbrook Museum of Art
2727 South Rockford Road
P.O. Box 52510
Tulsa, OK 74152

WASHINGTON, D.C.
Art Deco Society of Washington
P.O. Box 11090
Washington, DC 20036
PH: 202 298-1100

International

AUSTRALIA

Melbourne
Art Deco Society of Victoria
P.O. Box 1324
Collingwood, Victoria 3066
Australia

Perth
Art Deco Society of Western Australia
182 Broome Street
Cottesloe 6011
Western Australia
PH: (61) 9 383-1627

Sydney
Art Deco Society of New South Wales
P.O. Box 752
Willoughby
New South Wales, 2068
Australia
PH: (61) 2 419-4259
FAX: (61) 2-690-1026

CANADA
Canadian Art Deco Society
101-1080 Barclay Street
Vancouver, B.C. V6E 1G7
PH: 604 662-7633
FAX: 604 662-7623

ENGLAND
The Twentieth Century Society
(formerly The Thirties Society)
58 Crescent Lane
London, SW4 9PV
England
PH: (44) 71 738-8480

NEW ZEALAND
Art Deco Trust, Inc.
P.O. Box 248
Napier, New Zealand
PH: (64) 04-835-9668
FAX: (64) 06-835-3984

INDEX

221